STEPHEN SONDHEIM

Stephen Sondheim

Art Isn't Easy

DANIEL OKRENT

Yale
UNIVERSITY
PRESS
New Haven and London

Published with assistance from the foundation established in memory of Amasa Stone Mather of the Class of 1907, Yale College.

Yale University Press books may be purchased in quantity for educational, business, or promotional use. For information, please e-mail sales.press@yale.edu (U.S. office) or sales@yaleup.co.uk (U.K. office).

Set in Janson type by Integrated Publishing Solutions.
Printed in the United States of America.

ISBN 978-0-300-27021-1 (hardcover)
Library of Congress Control Number: 2025944714
A catalogue record for this book is available from the British Library.

Authorized Representative in the EU: Easy Access System Europe, Mustamäe tee 50, 10621 Tallinn, Estonia, gpsr.requests@easproject.com

10 9 8 7 6 5 4 3 2 1

Frontispiece: Stephen Sondheim portrait, 1961
(Photograph by Richard Avedon, © The Richard Avedon Foundation)

ALSO BY DANIEL OKRENT

The Guarded Gate: Bigotry, Eugenics, and the Law That Kept Two Generations of Jews, Italians, and Other European Immigrants Out of America

Last Call: The Rise and Fall of Prohibition

Public Editor #1: The Collected Columns (with Reflections, Reconsiderations, and Even a Few Retractions) of the First Ombudsman of the New York Times

Great Fortune: The Epic of Rockefeller Center

The Way We Were: New England Then and Now

Nine Innings: The Anatomy of Baseball as Seen Through the Playing of a Single Game

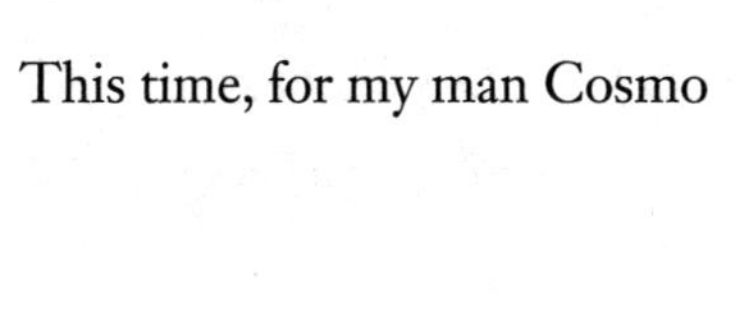

This time, for my man Cosmo

Only connect.

—E. M. Forster, *Howard's End*

CONTENTS

A PROLOGUE IN THE FORM OF AN AUTHOR'S NOTE

It was not long after Stephen Sondheim died in the late fall of 2021 that the chance to write this book presented itself. At the time, there was certainly no shortage of published material about this creative giant. As the cult of Sondheim fans expanded, so had the accompanying lore. Tales of his tortured entanglement with his despised mother, his life-changing tutelage at the knee of Oscar Hammerstein II, his electric relationship with producer-director Hal Prince, his curious obsession with games and puzzles, and endless other Sondheimiana would come to populate the musings and analyses of the Stephen Sondheim Society in England; *The Sondheim Review*, a quarterly publication in the United States; *The Sondheim Encyclopedia;* more than a score of books by journalists, scholars, collaborators, and fans; the websites everythingsondheim.org and sondheimguide.com; the subreddit r/Sondheim ("Your one-stop shop for all things Sondheim!"); the arresting Instagram accounts "sondheimletters" and "sondheimphotos"—even the 480-page *Oxford Handbook of Sondheim Studies.*

The most imposing entry on the Sondheim shelf was *Stephen Sondheim: A Biography,* by Meryle Secrest, published in 1998, when its subject was sixty-eight. Sondheim cooperated extensively with Secrest, sitting for fifty hours of interviews and providing introductions to his friends and associates. After his death, the tapes of those interviews, housed at Yale University in the Beinecke Rare Book and Manuscript Library (which Secrest generously made available to researchers), would necessarily stand as the most intimately detailed source material for anyone writing about Sondheim.

There was so much more. I proceeded to read millions of words about Sondheim and his work, chased down obscure leads in both Europe and the United States, and dug up interviews (both written and recorded) that few researchers had ever encountered. Most important, I interviewed more than thirty of his friends and colleagues (they're listed in the Acknowledgments). Some knew Sondheim for more than fifty years, and several of them worked with him intimately, notably his two most important collaborators in the last forty years of his life, James Lapine and John Weidman. I also plumbed nineteen different archives for letters to and from Sondheim—letters that, given the span of years, presented nearly every phase of his life as if in real time. At the time of this writing, his own papers had not yet been processed and opened to researchers, but after his death a remarkably detailed and intimate interview with Sondheim, conducted by the Columbia University Oral History Program in 1982, was made available for the first time.

It was in Secrest's book that I stumbled across one anecdote that grabbed me with particular force. It arose in her account of the creation of *Sweeney Todd* (1978), the gruesome, stunning, and operatic story of a deranged barber who slits the throats of his customers, and whose landlady bakes the chopped-up remains into meat pies. After listening to Sondheim sing the first few songs for her, Hal Prince's wife Judy—for much of his adult life, Sondheim's most intimate friend and his acknowledged muse—stopped him cold. He had told her that he saw *Sweeney* as an amusement, a form of Grand Guignol, but she heard something different. "It's nothing to do with Grand Guignol!," she exclaimed. "It's the story of your life!'"

I could not find any further elaboration in Secrest's book or in her interview tapes. Throughout her life Judy Prince has refused nearly all interview requests, including Secrest's. But Secrest did quote Sondheim's confirmation of her insight: "I was so shocked when Judy said that," he said. "But then the light clicked on and I thought 'But of course!'"

"It never occurred to me," he continued. "It's never been brought up in any article. Everybody always says, 'Oh, he's interested in murder.'"

Then he said, "They're missing the point entirely."

STEPHEN SONDHEIM

1

Before

Judging by the way he talked about them over his very long life, two distinct narratives framed Stephen Joshua Sondheim's childhood and reverberated for decades—one about Oscar Hammerstein II, and one about his mother.

The fact that he only rarely put the stories together is sort of odd, really. He might never have met Oscar (as he will be known here) without a connection forged by Foxy (likewise). After Etta Janet Fox Sondheim emerged from her wrenching divorce from Herbert Sondheim, when Stephen was ten, she bought a small farm near Doylestown, Pennsylvania, where she spent summers with her only child. Half a century later, he would variously characterize his mother as "vindictive," "graspingly materialistic," "a monster," "creepy," and a "celebrity fucker." She had picked the Doylestown area, he believed, because of its proximity to the Hammerstein family, and to other showbiz royalty.[1]

Foxy Sondheim, who had "the nerve to say exactly what she thought"

Oscar had earned his regal stature in 1927, when he collaborated with the composer Jerome Kern on *Showboat.* Its naturalistic setting and dramatic narrative signaled a revolution in Broadway musicals, which until then were a wobbly mix of largely plotless revues and overripe operettas. But Broadway did not heed the signal until, seventeen years later, Oscar and a new partner, Richard Rodgers, offered *Oklahoma!* to the world. It would be another twenty-six years until *Company*, with words and music by Stephen Sondheim, similarly jolted Broadway convention. But that's getting ahead of a story that would eventually be summed up after Sondheim's death by another Broadway revolutionary, Lin-Manuel Miranda. Sondheim's relationship with Oscar, he said, was "the most significant relationship in the history of our art form."[2]

Foxy didn't push her son into the relationship with Oscar so much as she simply pushed him away. She was a dress designer, a talented woman who, at twenty-six, married Herbert Sondheim and helped him become a major figure in "New York couture"—the segment of the city's garment industry that manufactured adaptations of Paris fashions for high-end U.S. retailers, among them Saks Fifth Avenue, Nieman Marcus, and Lord & Taylor. Herbert was as mild in demeanor as he was astute in the business world. One fashion writer said he was "so genial that even the deep furrows in his forehead are shaped like an intimate gathering of smiles."[3]

Foxy, less so. It wasn't that she was disagreeable; she had many friends, many of them prominent, most of them charmed (or entertained) by her forceful presence. The actress Barbara Billingsley remembered how Foxy helped her get modeling work when she was first starting out, and how she remained a valued mentor for years. A family friend who knew her as "Aunt Foxy" recalled her "husky voice, [her] ready laugh, the nerve to say exactly what she thought, which was plenty, and [her] boundless capacity for outrageous flirting." There was also a restless energy that made Foxy the life of every party she attended, and she attended more than most. But that energy exploded into something seemingly pathological after Herbert left her for another woman.[4]

Up to that point, her son—called Josh as a child, then Stevie, eventually Steve—had known only an artificial form of childhood. Born on March 22, 1930, he was raised, he often said, by governesses, nannies, and cooks, rather than by his two working parents. They were traveling parents as well: Attending the twice-yearly Paris shows was a necessary part of their professional lives. He was a prodigy at the Ethical Culture School, a private institution favored by liberal Manhattan families, especially secular Jews like the Sondheims. He bypassed kindergarten and, at five, found himself reading the *New York Times* aloud to his first-grade classmates. At school and at summer camp, he played well enough with others, but his obvious brilliance kept him somewhat apart. There was an emotional void at the center of his boyhood, but the surface was pleasant. Then came the divorce, which turned artifice into grotesquerie.

It left Stephen's early teenage years in ruins. Because of the divorce, Foxy relocated her principal residence from the family apartment in the San Remo on Central Park West to the Ritz Tower on Park Avenue, her design talents to the powerhouse Hattie Carnegie studios, and her heightened neuroses to her relationship with her son. In later life he said she behaved inappropriately, even provocatively with him when he was young, and at other moments vibrated between fury and self-pity. A family friend, a few years younger than Stephen, thought Foxy was wonderful and, he said many years later, "Stevie was a whining little shit." Perhaps. But her mercurial rages, alternating with overbearing efforts at intimacy, were more than he could handle. They fought often and ferociously. When they were not engaged in open war, remembered Oscar's son Jimmy, the relationship was expressed in "sarcasm and innuendo. He was just a kid, but he dished it out as well as she did." It was "something out of a play you didn't want to see."[5]

Sondheim's father had settled with his second wife, a Cuban-born fashion marketer named Alicia Babé, in an apartment on

Fifth Avenue facing the Metropolitan Museum of Art and a country house in Stamford, Connecticut. Stephen liked the amiable Alicia, and he and Herbert saw each other frequently. He loved his father and enjoyed his company, but he would instinctively withdraw when Herbert hugged him hello or goodbye. In 1995, he said "when you really get down to it the most damaging thing was, my father abandoned me and left me in the lion's den." Immediately after the divorce, he escaped to the New York Military Academy, a private boarding school in the Hudson River valley, just north of West Point. Presumably, it was Foxy's idea; she was the custodial parent. It suggests something about their relationship at this point that NYMA, which considered him sufficiently advanced to allow him to skip the seventh grade, dedicated itself to training teenage boys to "be obedient to proper authority, orderly, prompt, [and] courteous." And Stephen loved it. The strict rules and institutional regimentation of a military school provided him what was most missing at home: "Emotional order," as he would remember it. Or, he said, "What became a metaphor for order, anyway."[6]

As a little boy, Stephen would place his fingers atop his father's as Herbert, at the family piano, played show tunes for friends. At eight, he took piano lessons, more out of duty than passion, decades later describing himself as "the nice Jewish boy on the West Side [who] gives recitals at the piano teacher's house." But at nine, he was captivated by his first musical, *Very Warm for May* (by Kern and Hammerstein). And at ten, he discovered movie music, particularly the lush, emotionally powerful work of Bernard Herrmann and Max Steiner.[7]

He loved—would always love—horror films, partly because of the music that intensified their eerie enchantments. In Sondheim's mid-teens, one that particularly grabbed him was *Hangover Square*, a bleak, Jekyll-and-Hyde tale of a classical pianist whose periodic blackouts, according to the film's producers, turn him into "a fiendish slave of his own desire to kill." He often said that Herrmann's score so thrilled him that he saw the film a second time simply to memorize the first eight bars of music and later commit them to paper. "Concerto Macabre" begins with a dissonant, bone-chilling gesture Sondheim would call the "Herrmann Chord"—decades later, a foundational element of his own score for *Sweeney Todd*.[8]

Late in life, the mention of a B-movie from, say, the early '40s would prompt him to instantly name the director, the stars, and the composer. An equivalent fervor intensified boyhood interests that grew into similarly lifelong appetites. Sitting in front of his father's Capehart turntable—a '30s-era contraption that turned a record over after playing one side—he would find himself entranced less by the music on the shellac 78s than by the workings of the Capehart's intricate mechanics. In later life, he maintained a collection of cookbooks, even though he didn't cook, simply because he was addicted to understanding *process*. (In his eighties, he told an interviewer that he wanted to learn what he could about sheepshearing because "I want to know exactly how you take the wool off.") He had begun performing magic tricks as a ten-year-old, an early manifestation of his celebrated adult attraction to puzzles and games, and he even invented a board game that he tried to sell to the Milton Bradley Company, the prominent game publisher. More than a half-century later he was still convinced "they stole my fucking game," marketing it under another name. "If you listened to him tell you this, in his eighties," said his friend the playwright Jonathan Marc Sherman, "you would think he was still a pissed-off teenager."[9]

Sondheim was twelve years old when he found his way to Oscar Hammerstein's doorstep. The unhappiness induced by his parents' divorce was intensified by his discontent with life with Foxy. He was "full of rage and pain and anger" at the time,

Oscar Hammerstein II, circa 1948. He was, Sondheim said, the first of the teachers "who saved my life."

said Oscar's stepdaughter. But, she added, "Ockie"—as Hammerstein was known to intimates—"seemed able to bypass that and get to some other place in him," a place that might otherwise have been occupied by a present, loving, and emotionally stable parent.[10]

In numberless interviews, Sondheim would later claim that

if Oscar had been a geologist, he would have himself become a geologist. But Oscar worked in musical theater, so engagement with musical theater became both the expression of their bond and the object of Stephen's desire. His own father represented a distant world, his mother a terrifying one. In his relationships with Jimmy and the rest of the Hammerstein family, his inner wounds could become manifest in occasional expressions of nastiness and verbal cruelty. His severe teenage acne distressed him, and an unconscious competition with Jimmy discomfited him. But all the Hammersteins, especially Oscar, also knew his virtues: intellectual power, unflagging loyalty, and a creative urge desperate to be expressed.[11]

The world's impression of Oscar Hammerstein is based on the largely honeyed and sentimental shows he created with Rodgers, and on lyrics that, depending on one's taste, either soared or cloyed. Though Sondheim would always underscore Oscar's centrality in his life and in his work, and would always credit Oscar with teaching him the principles of writing lyrics and the essentials of dramatic form, he was no fan of his mentor's style. In a conversation with composer-lyricist Adam Guettel—Richard Rodgers's grandson—in 2009, Sondheim said he often found Oscar's lyrics "wet and embarrassing," built on "the kind of nature imagery that makes me cringe." Unlike nearly all Broadway songwriters, including Sondheim, Oscar wrote the libretto for his shows, creating characters who, Sondheim would say, "are always talking about willow trees and birds and rivers, and it gives them a sameness and a softness." Oscar also gave his rural or uneducated characters a speech habit that led other Broadway writers to say that he had invented a language called "Apostrophe": as Oscar told Irving Berlin when Berlin was struggling to shape the hillbilly/cowboy argot for *Annie Get Your Gun*, "All you have to do is to drop the final *G* from most of the verbs." He once told an interviewer, "I'm not very interested in urban irony."[12]

That approach, of course, couldn't be further from the urbane, witty, caustic, at times brutal lyrics that would color Sondheim's own shows. Oscar applied his imagined vocabularies to Oklahoma settlers, say, or New England fishermen, or nuns in an Austrian convent. Not one of the characters in those shows could have survived in the New York world that Sondheim would render in *Company*, or *Merrily We Roll Along*, much less the barbaric London of *Sweeney Todd*. In *Oklahoma!* Oscar perceived *a bright golden haze on the meadow;* in *Company*, Sondheim saw *the postered walls/With the crude remarks*. But it was Oscar who made Sondheim's lyric voice possible, by firmly dismissing some of his protégé's early efforts for being as sentimental as some of Oscar's own. Sondheim appreciated what he called Oscar's "hyper-critical" instruction—"that's the worst thing I've ever read," he'd said about a script Sondheim wrote at fifteen—but valued him all the more for that; he in fact had asked Oscar to comment on the script as he would have to a professional. In the rigorous instruction Oscar gave him—not just in lyric writing, but also in character development and pacing and other elements of writing for the theater—he found both inspiration and challenge. At one point Oscar told Stevie (as he continued to call him, well into his twenties), "You're writing like me, you're imitating me, you're talking about nature and things like that. You don't believe in those things. Is that right? What do you believe?"[13]

"And then he said something very telling," Sondheim recalled. "He said, 'write what you believe, and you'll be 99% ahead of the game.'" So he did, and so he would be.

By his own account, Sondheim was a late bloomer—not intellectually, but somewhat socially and definitely sexually. He was not alone in this assessment. Lois Benjamin Gould, whose mother, the fashion designer Jo Copeland, was possibly Foxy's closest friend, based a character on him in *Necessary Objects*, her novel published in 1972. Like Sondheim, fifteen-year-old Jason has divorced parents, plays the piano, goes to a military academy, writes a musical at boarding school, is beset by acne, and is completely indifferent to sex with Jill, Gould's teenage avatar. At one point Jill asks him, "Do you still hate your mother?" Jason replies, "Sure."[14]

Stephen Sondheim's first show—he composed twenty songs for it and collaborated on some of the lyrics—was a student production at the George School, a Quaker institution fifteen miles from Doylestown. Arriving in the ninth grade, he became both mascot and magnet: mascot because his bypassing of kindergarten and seventh grade left him two years younger than his classmates, and magnet because of his evident brilliance. He cruised through four years of Latin in two years. In his math classes, he developed a fascination with number theory. He also began to take his piano playing seriously. As at NYMA, he was a boarding student, which kept him at a remove from Foxy. When he was home for the summer, he would get on his bike daily and pedal over to the Hammersteins' hundred-year-old brick farmhouse. There he would lose himself in both the life of the family and in Oscar's lessons in writing for the theater.[15]

Lose himself, yes—but also find himself.

In his mid-to-late teens, Sondheim consciously began to extend his distance from Foxy. He spent more and more of his vacation time with Herbert and Alicia and his two very young half-brothers, Herbert Jr. and Walter. He taught the boys to swim and to play chess, and he confounded (and delighted) them with magic tricks. Foxy remained present in his life, yet to some degree he grew able to regard her as neither enemy nor tormentor, but simply as a fact. After he enrolled at Williams College, at sixteen, he even managed to enjoy her company now and then. When Foxy came to Massachusetts with Oscar's stepdaughter to see him play the lead—a deranged murderer—in a

Sondheim, at Williams College in 1948, as the psychopathic murderer in *Night Must Fall*, "the only part I ever wanted"

college production of the very dark Emlyn Williams play *Night Must Fall*, he reported that "it was fun having them up."[16]

Sondheim had done some acting in high school, but his life on the stage concluded with this performance. Except for one television appearance he undertook as a favor to a friend in 1974, his acting career was over. Having had to learn how to smoke to play the part, "I became a confirmed and addicted smoker," he told Meryle Secrest. "But it was worth it." It wasn't the only addiction he would wrestle with; it was merely the first one.[17]

Sondheim's Williams was overwhelmingly an enclave for New York and New England WASPs in those years. But even though he had spent his childhood in the comforting cocoon of assimilated, well-off New York Jews, his years at NYMA and the George School had widened his cultural experience. He barely considered himself Jewish, at times claimed to be a Quaker, and once asked his roommate, who was himself Jewish, "I'm told I'm Jewish. Is that true?" He'd had no religious training of any kind, and his time at NYMA meant he missed the seventh-grade frenzy of bar mitzvahs that could have dominated his Manhattan weekends. As he remembered it, he didn't even know what a bar mitzvah was, and didn't attend his first one until he was twenty-one.[18]

But in the eyes of at least some of his schoolmates, he was Jewish enough to be blackballed from the fraternity he wanted to join, which he had been attracted to partly because its social life had a strong musical component, and partly because it was, he said, made for "oddballs" and "individualists." The intervention of friends eventually overcame the blackball, and his college years were largely bright. He may have been, as the musicologist Steve Swayne has written, "a Jew to the goyim," but not to himself.[19]

Sondheim had determined by then that he was homosexual, and when a female friend suggested that psychotherapy might help him change, he said, "I don't know if I want to change." But if he was sexually active, it wasn't apparent to those around him. They knew him as a boon companion, witty and quick and caustic. He was opinionated about most things and unafraid to express what he thought; a classmate recalled, "he had one of the most effective sneers I've ever known, a marvelous curl of the lip that left its recipient red-faced and apologetic." Still in his teens, he was supremely confident in his judgment. He even found Shakespeare wanting; *Hamlet*, he said, was "terrible," and *Macbeth* even worse. He thought *Julius Caesar* was pretty good.[20]

Sondheim's classmates considered him eccentric in other ways as well. He was a self-described "slob" who sometimes "smelled a little ripe," said the future author and screenwriter Dominick Dunne. But Dunne, a Sondheim friend for the next half-century, also said, "We all knew we had a genius in our midst." Another friend introduced Dunne, Sondheim, and a few other oddball individualists to a toast, adapted from Robert Burns, that would resonate with Sondheim for decades: "Here's to us! Who's like us? Damn few."[21]

Night Must Fall may have satisfied, and thereby concluded, any performing ambitions Sondheim had retained, but his studies at Williams confirmed him as a songwriter—more accurately, as a composer. He had intended to major in math, attracted both to the subject's precision and to the puzzle-solving search for solutions it required. ("When I pick up a mathematical problem," he said more than thirty years later, "I can feel the excitement in the groin.") But a course he took with the music professor Robert Barrow led directly to the core of his life's work. Barrow's influence as a teacher was so potent it led Sondheim to equate him with Oscar, even if only unconsciously: in an interview in the 1970s, he applied to Barrow the same line he used over and over to memorialize his relationship with Oscar: "Robert Barrow was so sensational that if he had taught geology I would probably have become a geologist."[22]

"Sensational" was an odd descriptor for a man whom Sondheim also remembered as "very dry" and "totally unimaginative, totally unloose." A fellow music major dismissed Barrow as "doctrinaire, organized, conservative, and bitter." Except for the bitterness, this was what Sondheim was looking for—the boundaries and orderliness he had discovered in military school, the exactitude and rigor of mathematics. In one class session, Barrow played a recording of Claude Debussy's impressionistic *La Mer*, then asked, "Anybody here hear the sea? Well, even if you do, that's not what it's about. What the piece is about is the whole tone scale."[23]

For Sondheim, it was a life-changing declaration. "I fell in love," he later recalled. "I think it was the moment I determined I would major in music. Because he made it clear that music is a thought-out process, that it is craft, not inspiration." It was around this time that the eighteen-year-old Sondheim, well aware of the kind of music Broadway audiences wanted to hear, sent a letter to Oscar and signed it, "That renowned composer of intellectual, abstruse and unhummable music—one Stephen Sondheim." A quarter century later, less prone to self-satire, he told an interviewer that "the word hummable drives me up the wall." What mattered was much more complex than that, and Barrow led him to it. The syllabus for his class addressed the diatonic scale, the rules of harmony, the precise demands of counterpoint—in a word, the technique of composition. "It was about how you put an F-sharp next to a G because it resolves that way and here's why . . . ," Sondheim said. "It had nothing to do with the romance of making music." It was a puzzle to be solved, a process to comprehend—arguably, a way to find a path out of the hovering sense of alienation that would sometime seize him.[24]

He committed himself to Barrow's bloodless approach to writing music. It wasn't that the young Sondheim composed without passion; while fulfilling his requirements as a music major, said a classmate, he "left shards of his piano sonata in every practice room." But the passion was devoted to the very idea of work: the hard labor one needed to master a challenge, the more challenging the better. For Sondheim, imagination was a secondary muse, and inspiration not even that. "Putting It Together," from *Sunday in the Park with George*, contains a phrase that came from deep inside his creative core: *Art isn't easy.*[25]

In the summer after Sondheim's freshman year at Williams, Oscar offered him his first professional job in the theater, as a gofer on his new show, *Allegro*, scheduled to open that fall. Pumped up from the enormous success of their first two shows (*Oklahoma!* and *Carousel*), Rodgers and Hammerstein now felt they could experiment. *Allegro* called for a cast of sixty-six, a set requiring forty stagehands, a Greek chorus, and twenty-one musical numbers. The chorus was as much Brechtian as it was Greek, commenting on the action as it unfolded, and addressing both the characters on stage and the somewhat befuddled audience. Awash in cynicism and disillusion, *Allegro* centered on an idealistic young physician who abandons his best self and becomes corrupted by money and status. It couldn't have been more different from anything either Rodgers or Hammerstein had ever done in their careers, either separately or together.

It proved to be a catastrophe. In the entire Rodgers and Hammerstein catalog, only one show (*Pipe Dream*, 1955) had a shorter run than *Allegro*. Agnes DeMille, who had created the revolutionary "dream ballet" for *Oklahoma!*, was director as well as choreographer; a few weeks before opening, she was fired as director because of her rudeness and insensitivity. Sondheim, stunned by what he witnessed, later referred to DeMille as "a horror" and "a terrible tyrant." As opening night approached, Hammerstein, who was not a director, took over as director. One would not consider this the best way for a young man to be introduced to Broadway.[26]

In fact, for Sondheim it was. His first exposure to bad behavior among a show's creative team that summer helped him realize that what one saw from the orchestra seats was an illusion in more ways than one. He learned as well that the most celebrated talents could produce a flop. And, despite the show's failure, its experimental nature inspired him. More, though, *Allegro's* dramatic theme—what Hammerstein described as the dangers of "losing sight of who you are"—lingered in his mind, and his work, for decades.[27]

Sondheim graduated from Williams in 1950, near the top of his class. He wasn't voted Most Likely to Succeed, but he made a respectable third place showing (the winner became a prominent New York lawyer; second honors went to a young man who would validate his classmates' judgment by introducing Pepperidge Farm Goldfish to the American market). More importantly, he won a fellowship Williams granted annually to a graduating senior working in the creative arts.

The prize money gave Sondheim a seat on a piano bench next to Milton Babbitt, who might have seemed the least likely tutor for a young man with his eyes set on Broadway. Babbitt was a composer, a theoretician, an ultra-modernist. He hadn't yet devoted himself to electronic music (he became one if its pioneers), and it was long before he wrote "Transfigured Notes," a piece so dense, complex, and indescribable that Gunther Schuller, the conductor who first recorded it, declared it "pointless for the listener to try to ferret out conventional melodies and harmonies, for there are none." But Babbitt was already moving in that highly abstracted direction, as his academic pedigree suggested he would: he had been appointed to the Princeton faculty in 1944 as a professor of mathematics, and only later switched his professorship to the music department. He spent the rest of his life immersed in both disciplines.[28]

How could Sondheim resist, entranced as he was by the kinship of math and music? There was also a bonus: Babbitt happened to be a true aficionado of Broadway musicals and American popular song. If someone was to guide Sondheim through the elements of composition the same way Oscar led him through the technical aspects of writing lyrics, how fine it was that Babbitt was similarly generous, similarly kind, and, by virtue of the Williams fellowship, similarly available.

The most important element of Babbitt's once-a-week tutelage was the analysis of musical form, as expressed in, say, the music of Jerome Kern, and even more so in Bach and Beethoven. The fruit of this analysis was what Babbitt called "long-line composition," a method of thinking about a song that calls for the establishment of a motif that, manipulated along the way, carries the listener to a predetermined end point. As Sondheim himself put it, "small musical ideas are expanded into large structural forms," able to sustain a single number for two minutes or for twenty; Bach, Babbitt said, could "build a cathedral" out of just four notes. It applied to the composition of individual songs as it did to entire scores. Just as the indelible opening measures of Beethoven's Fifth establish a specific rhythmic pattern repeated, revised, and reshaped throughout the entire symphony, the arpeggios that open *Sunday in the Park with George* establish the chords that suffuse the entire score. So do the opening gestures of *Sweeney Todd*, sequentially transformed but nonetheless inescapable, or the brief melodic strains that reemerge over and over in the score of *Merrily We Roll Along*.[29]

"Composition is about development," Sondheim told an interviewer in 1993, "not about repetition. You move a motif along just the way you move a character." It was an idea neatly parallel to what he had learned from Hammerstein about lyrics—that they should express character while simultaneously moving the story forward. Oscar had taught him "a song should be like a play," Sondheim said in 1961. "It should have a beginning, a middle, and an end. It should have an idea—state the idea, and then build the idea and develop it and finish. And at the end, you should be at a different place from where you began." It was essentially what Babbitt taught him about musical form. In their specific vocabulary and emotional content, the lyrics Stephen Sondheim would write couldn't have been further from Oscar Hammerstein's earnest sentimentality, nor could his music have been more dissimilar from Milton Babbitt's seeming cacophony. Yet the way that both men stressed the primacy of narrative development was essential to his creative growth.[30]

Sondheim never really graduated from the School of Oscar; until Hammerstein's death in 1960, he would rely on him for career advice, and for the rest of his own working life he would employ principles of lyric writing that stressed the methods of storytelling and character development that Oscar had taught him. Babbitt was never the "surrogate father" (a term Sondheim occasionally used) that Oscar was; he was (another Sondheimism) "everybody's Jewish Uncle Milton," who remained a friend and mentor nearly until his death, at ninety-five, in 2011. But, to Sondheim, neither of those familial terms was as pertinent or as potent as one that he explained in 1995: "The word 'teacher,'" he said, "usually brings tears to my eyes, because teachers saved my life."

2

Climbing High

Shortly after graduating from Williams, Sondheim finished the last formal assignment Oscar had given him, *Climb High*. This was a complete show—book, music, lyrics—and it displeased Hammerstein; the characters, he said, "all seem shallow wisecracking young people," which was not far from the truth, and also should not have been entirely unexpected. (At one point, the main character describes a group of his parents' friends as "this collection of large wallets and tiny minds.") For his part, Sondheim would archly dismiss the show as "a four-hour summation of my views on life, ambition, morality, theater, and art, with a passing swipe at love." He was not inaccurate.[1]

In later life, Sondheim was embarrassed by *Climb High*, and after his death his estate continued to follow his wish, denying a request in 2025 to quote a fairly lengthy section of its lyrics. But you can hear two of the songs, "When I Get Famous" and "Where Do I Belong?" on *Sondheim Sings, Volume II:*

1946–1960, issued—with Sondheim's permission—in 2005 by PS Classics. (A jazzed-up version of the former is also available on *Cyrille Aimee: Move On*, released in 2019.) Perhaps he allowed the release of these particular songs, conveyed in his less-than-perfect voice, because they would tell people what kind of songwriter he was in his early twenties. But they tell more than that. "When I Get Famous" is an account of what he called the *secret dream in my heart*, as expressed in the song's title. After the opening verse, the character—the Sondheim stand-in—sings, *When I get famous, I'll be free/On my own, you wait and see.* In "Where Do I Belong?," he expresses the wish to *be part of something/Someone/Somewhere?*[2]

Throughout the years of his success, the connection between Sondheim's work and his life was a subject that alternately annoyed him, wearied him, or made him squirm uncomfortably. But it was addressed directly and eloquently by his friend the writer Frank Rich, at the memorial service in 2022 celebrating Sondheim's life. "Steve never stopped insisting there was none of him in June and Louise, in Fay in *Anyone Can Whistle*, in Leona and Bobby, and Ben and Sally, and Fredrik and Désirée—all those characters yearning to connect," Rich said. "There was none of his destructive mother in Mama Rose or Mrs. Lovett. And no, you must never superimpose him on George, hiding behind his canvas."* Later in the eulogy, Rich said, "that was Steve's story, and he was sticking to it."

As dubious as "Steve's story" may have been, it was certainly his privilege to believe it—or, perhaps, profess to believe it. But that privilege does not survive him. Sondheim's dismissal of *Climb High*'s grandiosity half a century after the fact may have

* For readers who may not be familiar with all of Sondheim's characters, members of this lineup appear in *Gypsy* (June, Louise, and Mama Rose), *Do I Hear a Waltz?* (Leona), *Company* (Bobby), *Follies* (Ben and Sally), *A Little Night Music* (Fredrik and Désirée), *Sweeney Todd* (Mrs. Lovett), and *Sunday in the Park with George*.

been entirely appropriate, but in this one instance, his acknowledgment of the show's inseparable connection to his own life and thoughts turns these lyrics into notes from an autobiography. It was, he said in an interview in 1969, "what I had learned about life at the age of 21." *When I get famous,/I'll be free* and *Why can't I be part of something*—as Sondheim sought the path that would lead him from alienation to connection, these two notes would play like underlying harmony to most of his adult life, as dissonant as it was persistent.[3]

Back in New York at twenty-one, sleeping in Herbert and Alicia's dining room, Sondheim relied on Oscar even for the beginnings of a social life—which, in midcentury New York's middlebrow creative community, was all but indistinguishable from its professional life. It was at Oscar's suggestion that Donald Klopfer, the co-founder of Random House, invited him to a party, where Sondheim met the screenwriter George Oppenheimer. Soon Sondheim showed Oppenheimer a script he had written, and just as quickly Oppenheimer invited him to Los Angeles to co-write the television series *Topper.* Sondheim knew he was well suited to a half-hour situation comedy because of its rigid framework—"like a sonnet or a lyric," he said. The two men knocked out twenty-five scripts in six months, each of the four required acts crammed into twenty-two and a half limiting minutes. With six thousand Hollywood dollars in his pocket, Sondheim immediately moved back to New York.[4]

The money enabled him to abandon Herbert and Alicia's dining room for a one-room rental of his own near Madison Avenue and East Eighty-third Street. There was sufficient space for a bed, a few chairs, a kitchenette, and the essential piano. Ready to make his musical mark, he wrote a song for the NBC children's show *Kukla, Fran, and Ollie;* it was rejected. He did an arrangement for the national tour of an Alfred Lunt–Lynn Fontanne vehicle called *I Know My Love;* it was accepted, but the credit in *Playbill* read "Clifford Sondheim." In 1953, identifying him (while misspelling him) as the protégé of Oscar Hammerstein, *Variety* reported that "Steve Sonheim" was sailing for Italy "to put the finishing touches on a new musical for which he has written the book, music and lyrics." Not quite: on a lark, he was travelling to the Amalfi coast with a pal for a gig as clapper boy on the John Huston film *Beat the Devil.* The best part of the job was playing blindfold chess with the film's star, Humphrey Bogart—no board, no chessmen, each player announcing his move as both of them retained an image of the board in his head. Sondheim said Bogart was better than he was.[5]

Mostly, these were the years of "opening doors"—in *Merrily We Roll Along,* the title of the one song he always admitted was "me, writing about me." "Opening Doors" vivifies the experience of the show's three main characters, who represent, at the dawn of their careers, Sondheim, producer-director Harold Prince, and the composer and fiction writer Mary Rodgers. Lengthy, kinetic, and event-filled, the song is a witty (and, like so much Sondheim, at times agonizing) chronicle of auditions, rejections, callbacks, petty triumphs, and rude awakenings. Soon his relationship with Prince and Rodgers was augmented by the playwright Arthur Laurents; together, these were the individuals who, more than anyone else, would enrich Sondheim professionally and engage (and in the case of Laurents, enrage) him personally for more than four decades.[6]

Mary Rodgers met Stephen Sondheim at Highland Farm, Oscar's place in Doylestown. He was fifteen and, at first, remote; she was fourteen, and bedazzled. He was simply that much more intelligent, that much quicker, that much funnier than anyone she had ever known. As Richard Rodgers's daughter, she had from birth been familiar with the brightest lights in the Broadway community, but Sondheim nonetheless provoked what she called a "magical adoration" that persisted for most of her life. "I wasn't up to his standards," she would recall. "But nobody was." She may not have been a match for Sondheim's brilliance, but she too was quick of wit and sharp of tongue, and as such all the more appreciative of her thrilling new friend. She could look past his occasional chilliness and evident impatience, or the snappishness that at times suggested he felt superior to his contemporaries. Near the end of her life she said, "I thought I would never be as infatuated with anyone again. Which turned out to be true."[7]

By Sondheim's own judgment, he outdid her in at least one fashion: he thought Mary's mother was a horrible person—"a great monster," in fact—but she had nothing on his own mother. Foxy Sondheim tried too hard, her neurotic attachment to her son and her unceasing rage at his father congealing into a caricature of the overbearing, out-of-control mother. Dorothy Rodgers didn't need to try: her husband had been one of Broadway's crowned heads for two decades, and she was his imperial, and imperious, consort. Cold and self-involved, to Mary she was emotionally unreachable and pitilessly dominating. Sondheim said Dorothy Rodgers was "one of the most awful people who ever existed," but, when comparing the two women for Mary's benefit, he added a qualifier: "She doesn't run a race with my mother, but she does come in second."[8]

It would be too simple to suggest that the Sondheim-Rodgers relationship was built on their mutual loathing for their mothers. Both wrote music, both had their eyes set on Broadway, and both were part of the extended family that gathered around Oscar at Highland Farm. But their similar family dynamics did provide them with a form of tacit understanding that lasted the rest of their lives. Dorothy and Foxy, said a mutual friend, "gave them something to talk about forever."[9]

"He is the only person in the world who can profoundly upset me if he's angry at me for any reason," Rodgers, in her mid-sixties, told Meryle Secrest. Once, bruised by that anger, she sent him "a large porcelain serving piece" by way of apology.

Accepting the apology, he wrote, "thanks for the platter, but where was my mother's head?"[10]

Sondheim said he met Hal Prince for the first time at a party Mary Rodgers gave for Prince in the early 1950s; both Prince and Rodgers, who introduced them, said it was 1949, at the opening night of Rodgers and Hammerstein's *South Pacific.* (Hal and Mary dated for two years in their late teens.) All three were in the bright dawn of their careers—their "opening doors" phase—and the door that opened first was for Prince. The director (and Broadway monument) George Abbott took him on as a gofer; by the time he was twenty-two Prince was assistant stage manager on Abbott's production of *Call Me Madam.* When Prince was twenty-five, Abbott installed him as stage manager on *Wonderful Town.* At twenty-six, *The Pajama Game* opened on Broadway—Harold Prince, producer. Abbott, who spent seven decades acting, writing, directing, and producing on Broadway (he lived to 107) didn't produce his own first show until he was forty-five.

Prince's energy and single-mindedness, and the eye he kept trained on opportunity, all burned fiercely from the very start of his career. Rodgers said he was "born clasping a list of people he wanted to meet." Sondheim, reflecting on a professional relationship with Prince that lasted nearly half a century—and that for two decades formed the most important creative collaboration in his life—said, "I'm a low flame, and he's a high flame." Prince would push and push, and Sondheim would offer various forms of passive resistance until Prince compelled him to action. Prince said Sondheim "writes in pencil—with an eraser. He doesn't want to commit. I write in ink." Prince's fervor was a necessary element of their partnership, even if at a very few junctures it would trigger discord. James Lapine, who followed Prince as the essential figure in Sondheim's creative life, said of

Sondheim's work with Prince, "In any relationship one is bound to be more of a leader, and I guess Steve needed to be led."[11]

The third long-standing professional and personal relationship Sondheim forged in the early 1950s was with Arthur Laurents. "Forged" may not be the right verb, as it suggests a solidity and permanence the two men could not sustain. In 1971, after three collaborations, two of them hugely successful, Sondheim told Prince that he really, truly, finally could no longer be friends with Laurents—yet in the 1990s, the two men were, by Laurents's account, closer than ever. In 2008, Sondheim told Laurents that he treasured their collaboration; the same year, Laurents berated Sondheim for directing a "vicious attack" at him. Throughout, people who knew of their relationship would ask, "Do Arthur and Steve love each other these days, or are they hating each other now?"[12]

The fruitful, antagonistic, jagged association that unspooled over a period of more than half a century couldn't have begun more auspiciously. Laurents, who was thirty-eight, met the twenty-five-year-old Sondheim at a party at the home of the producer Martin Gabel and his wife, actress Arlene Francis (one of the few celebrities, Sondheim said, who would come to parties he gave in his one-room apartment). What happened next, at Laurents's urging, was chronicled in the diary of Leonard Bernstein in November of 1955: "A young lyricist named Stephen Sondheim came and sang us some of his songs today. What a talent! I think he's ideal for this project, as do we all."[13]

The project was a gestating musical called *West Side Story*.

When Flora Roberts became Stephen Sondheim's agent, he was twenty-four, and had written precisely nothing for the professional stage. But she was impressed by his talent, charmed by his smile, and touched by his shyness. She wasn't exactly a mother substitute, which he might have wished for—Roberts was only nine years older than Sondheim—but it wasn't entirely wrong to characterize their relationship that way. It also would not be off the mark to call her his counselor, confessor, and champion. "Writers are causes," Roberts once said, and for nearly forty-four years, without a written agreement of any kind, she campaigned for Stephen Sondheim. At the time Roberts took him on, Sondheim had in hand three songs for a show called *Saturday Night.* He'd written them on spec—plus a courtesy fee of one hundred dollars—at the request of Lemuel Ayers, a celebrated set and costume designer about to embark on a career as a producer. Ayers was pleased, made a deal with Roberts, and went hunting for investors. This put Sondheim uncomfortably on display, singing and playing the songs from the score through a painful series of eight backers' auditions, those small gatherings of wealthy people who assemble in expensive homes to smell the aroma of Broadway without necessarily buying the merchandise. Roberts said Sondheim shied away from gladhanders, and the audience at these events were gladhanders who were all too ready to dismiss his work. Sondheim could sing on key but his range was limited, and his tone tended to cramp when he was compelled to perform. Just before one audition, the zipper in his pants broke and, in a panic, he sent Mary Rodgers to his father's apartment, where he was still living, to fetch his only suit. At a similar gathering, prefiguring a scene that would appear twenty-seven years later in *Merrily We Roll Along*, the invited audience of forty (at the home of the president of the Bronx Zoo) was so uninterested that Ayers considered dropping the project altogether.[14]

After Ayers died of a blood disorder during pre-production for *Saturday Night*, a complete set of Sondheim's first commissioned songs disappeared into a file cabinet for more than forty years (he did authorize recordings of a few of the songs, on their own, in the intervening years). He long refused to license a production of the show, then finally gave his assent to a British production in 1997; it made its first American appearance two years later, in Chicago. The plot, based on a play by Julius Epstein (a co-author of the screenplay for *Casablanca*), was a stale boy-meets-girl contrivance rooted in 1929 Brooklyn, with some uptown Manhattan glamour implausibly tossed in. There was a lot of 1920s pastiche in the music, a lot of coy winking and leering in the Epstein script, and a series of missteps in the lyrics that made Sondheim wince later in life—misplaced rhythmic stresses, unnatural diction, redundant adjectives, and various other offenses. There's only one real "long-line" composition in the piece, a labored number called "At the Movies"; the thinness of the story probably couldn't have borne the weight of much more than that. A few of the songs are excellent, though, including "What More Do I Need?," simultaneously a rousing declaration of love and a satiric hymn to New York: *My window pane has a lovely view:/An inch of sky/And a fly/Or two./Why, I can see/Half a tree/And what more do I need?* It was likely one of the *Saturday Night* songs written while he was still in Los Angeles, missing the city he loved.

Sondheim would long be proud of the harmonic structure of one *Saturday Night* song, the jazzy "Class," which in 1998 he considered "very advanced for 1955," even as he admitted that the words he wrote to accompany it contained "a treasure trove of lyricists' sins." Nonetheless, it was the show's lyrics that impressed Laurents, much more than Sondheim's music. One suspects Laurents was struck not only by their strong characterizations and clever rhyming but also by the ease of Sondheim's cultural ventriloquism as he set aside his uptown 1950s sensibilities to speak in the idiom of lower-middle-class 1920s Brooklyn.[15]

A small, lithe man, successful as both a playwright and a screenwriter (Alfred Hitchcock's *Rope* was one of his early film credits), Laurents found Sondheim personally "unprepossessing," specifically noting his "indoor complexion" and his "droopy clothes." But the *Saturday Night* lyrics stayed in his head, and when they met at another party a few weeks after the Gabel-Francis event, he realized that Sondheim might be the right man for the musical version of Romeo and Juliet, transposed to contemporary New York, that he had been developing for nearly six years with the director-choreographer Jerome Robbins and composer Leonard Bernstein. They thought they had the right lyricists—Betty Comden and Adolph Green—but other commitments intervened, and Laurents recruited Sondheim to make his Broadway debut as a lyricist.[16]

In that era, there was nothing deemed anomalous (except by Sondheim himself) about a show largely centered on Puerto Rican street culture being created by four Jews. (When Steven Spielberg's remake of the film version of *West Side Story* appeared in 2021, the gender politics of another era led some to express their dismay that four gay Jews had combined to portray the extremely heterosexual passions of a Puerto Rican gang.) "I've never even known a Puerto Rican," Sondheim said to Flora Roberts, but she persuaded him to sign on, a recommendation that had Oscar Hammerstein's concurrence as well: How could he not take the opportunity of working with such collaborators? Laurents was well established on Broadway, but Robbins and Bernstein, both thirty-seven, were stars. Robbins had choreographed thirteen Broadway shows, directed five, and won a Tony Award. Bernstein was not only the composer of two Broadway successes (*On the Town* and *Wonderful Town*) but had also conducted both the New York Philharmonic and the Boston Symphony, written an opera broadcast on national television, and become widely popular as a cultural commentator on the CBS program *Omnibus*.[17]

West Side Story, which because of its filmed versions is almost certainly the best-known show Sondheim was ever involved in, was also his first true collaboration. Despite Robbins's famously volatile temper ("I was very frightened" of him, Sond-

Leonard Bernstein, Sondheim, and Arthur Laurents, at the opening night party for *West Side Story*, 1957

heim said in a Dramatists Guild talk in 1978), Laurents's frequently tactless criticisms, and some creative differences with Bernstein that were not easily bridged, it worked—not just creatively, but personally. As Sondheim said many times over the years, he had learned that collaboration created, for him, a facsimile of the family he had never had. Part of the family feeling was warm and embracing. Another part, he admitted in that same Dramatists Guild speech, was the fact that "I enjoy the abrasion of collaboration."[18]

Robbins's behavior, even two decades after his death, is still considered the most extreme expression of Broadway abrasiveness. He was as widely detested for his combative conduct and his acidulous candor as he was celebrated for his creative brilliance. Late in life, Sondheim described him as "really mean, an awful man," but despite Robbins's coldness, his stubbornness, his acts of cruelty, Sondheim believed he was the one true genius he'd ever worked with. Laurents was a masterful librettist, a superb teacher, and also a troublemaker and a gossip and a needler; when he perceived a sleeping dog, he kicked it. But Sondheim's primary *West Side* collaborator, the man whose music would provide the scaffold for Sondheim's words, was Bernstein.[19]

Although Bernstein welcomed him warmly—he referred to him as "a charming gifted boy"—Sondheim was put off by some lyrics that Bernstein himself had already written, finding them self-consciously "poetic." Either working together (as Bernstein, both needy and gregarious, preferred) or separately (Sondheim's preference, by far), he found the collaboration with Bernstein "a generally terrific experience." But he was repeatedly exasperated by Bernstein's habit of picking apart his lyrics word by carefully wrought word, compelling him to "argue and defend every point," and would later regret defending himself with a hostile sarcasm. But in most instances the collaboration dissolved into the twenty-six-year-old novice's decision, even if through gritted teeth, to defer to his celebrated colleague. Even though he'd written it himself, Sondheim decided he just couldn't abide one phrase, *today the world was just an address*, in "Tonight." But he capitulated when Bernstein insisted he keep it in the song.[20]

An exception to his resentful acquiescence marked their disagreement over the lyric Bernstein had written for a song he called "Once in Your Life." It began *Once in your life, only once in your life/Comes a flash of fire and light/And here stands your love,/The harvest of your years.* Sondheim dug in; he just couldn't imagine those words coming from the mouth of a Puerto Rican teenager. He discarded Bernstein's words and the moist concept behind them, instead transforming the song into the somber "I Have a Love," the last number in the show. Yet he was very proud of "I Feel Pretty"—until, on opening night, his friend Sheldon Harnick (later the lyricist of *Fiddler on the Roof*, among other shows) pulled him aside and convinced him that *It's alarm-*

ing how charming I feel was similarly inappropriate for Maria's character. Not even halfway through *West Side*'s original run, Sondheim told the syndicated columnist Phyllis Battelle, "I plead guilty to writing one essentially dishonest song," he said. "I'm embarrassed by it." But even though it was his privilege to do so, Sondheim never changed the lyric for any subsequent productions. Half a century later, when Lin-Manuel Miranda was translating some of the show's lyrics into Spanish for a bilingual production staged by Laurents in 2009, he asked for Sondheim's advice. "If you could write new lyrics for 'I Feel Pretty,'" Sondheim said, "you'd be doing me a favor."[21]

Laurents was astonished by Sondheim's approach to most of the songs. "Before Steve wrote a lyric, he had to know the characters, their diction, the situation," he recalled. "That known, he wrote lyrics that could be sung only by the characters they were written for at that moment." In other words, he did precisely what Oscar had taught him to do. But in one instance, he was stumped by the challenge of writing a love song about someone whom Tony, the male lead, has just met, and about whom the audience knows absolutely nothing. Bernstein had placed the word "Maria" on the first three notes of the song; Sondheim took it from there, eschewing characterization entirely to write what he described as "a love song about the name, and not the girl": *And suddenly I've found/How wonderful a sound/Can be.*[22]

Other songs called for different strategies. A technique that Sondheim learned while working on *West Side Story*, and that he would employ several times throughout his career, was what Laurents called "raiding the dialogue"—that is, lifting language directly from the book and building a lyric around it. In one of the opening scenes, Laurents had Tony declare that he felt something coming "around the corner or whistling down the river." Sondheim lifted these and some adjacent lines ("Could be, who knows?"), adjusted them to suit the arc of Bernstein's music, added a series of crackling, vivid images, and launched the Tony character into the audience's consciousness.[23]

"One Hand, One Heart" and "Gee, Officer Krupke" were repurposed tunes Bernstein had written for (and cut from) his score for *Candide* (1956), and that Sondheim now had to transpose from eighteenth-century Westphalia to twentieth-century Manhattan. (Going in the other direction, Bernstein's tune for "Oh Happy We" from *Candide* was originally intended for a Tony-and-Maria duet in *West Side Story*'s bridal shop scene.) Sondheim considered "One Hand, One Heart" "a song of limited passion," his lyrics for it "bloodless." "Gee, Officer Krupke," he thought, was inappropriate for its place in the show, coming as it did immediately after a shocking double murder, and he wrote it, he said, "under duress." At some unconscious level, that might have been one of the reasons he willfully sought to be the first lyricist to use the words "Fuck you!" on the Broadway stage. Or maybe it was simply the puerile ambition of a smart-ass twenty-six-year-old.* But after the producers of the planned original cast album objected, Bernstein leaned in and, making what was possibly his most vital contribution to the show's lyrics, substituted two words that provided an efficient, and apt, exclamation to the end of Sondheim's first comic masterpiece: *Gee, Officer Krupke/Krup you!*[24]

By the time *West Side Story* encountered paying audiences at the National Theater in Washington on August 19, 1957, nearly half a dozen producers had attempted to get it off the ground or had rejected it outright. As Deborah Jowitt wrote in her biography of Robbins, "A musical with corpses was a hard sell." Bankrolling the show proved arduous and frustrating; Cheryl

* That urge was still part of him even in his seventies, when he briefly considered reinstating one of his original ideas for a lyric in a revival of *Sunday in the Park with George:* "There are worse things than staring at the water as you're posing for a picture after sleeping on the ferry" was almost ". . . posing for a picture after fucking on the ferry."

Crawford, one of Broadway's leading producers, made a sustained effort and "raised not a cent," Robbins recalled. Richard Rodgers and Oscar Hammerstein, who were nearly as successful as producers as they were as songwriters, considered it but declined. Hal Prince and his producing partner, Robert Griffith, fresh off their big successes with *The Pajama Game* and *Damn Yankees*, took a pass. In his son's telling, even Herbert Sondheim, who had put together a group of friends to make a small investment in the show, turned "ashen" when he read the script, and paled even more when he heard the jagged dissonance of some of Bernstein's music.[25]

But some bridge money from the producer Roger Stevens kept the show alive, Griffith and Prince (after a fairly desperate personal appeal from Sondheim) decided to take it on after all, and the show soon arrived in Washington for its pre-Broadway tryout. The critical response was ecstatic, but incomplete: The lyrics at that point were credited to both Bernstein and Sondheim, yet Sondheim's name appeared nowhere in any of the reviews. In an act of generosity that couldn't be more uncharacteristic of the usual Broadway credit mongering, Bernstein, recognizing the disparity in their contributions, decided that the lyrics should be credited solely to his young collaborator.

West Side Story sailed into New York on excellent advance word, further buoyed by a chorus of enthusiastic reviews; the one notable exception, by Harold Clurman in the *Nation*, led Sondheim to cancel his subscription and urge Bernstein to do the same (for both of them a substantial sacrifice, given their devotion to the magazine's cryptic crossword puzzles). But even an excruciating moment at the opening night party—Foxy, remarried and living in Los Angeles, had come to New York for her son's Broadway debut, where she came face to uncomfortable face with Herbert—did not dim Sondheim's sense that he had, at twenty-seven, arrived. Still, despite the change in the credits, Sondheim wasn't even mentioned in Brooks Atkinson's review in the *New York Times.* There were no separate Tony Award categories for music or lyrics that year, and the Best Musical award went to *The Music Man. West Side Story* was a respectable hit, but less than a smash. Even though the show ran for 732 performances, Sondheim—whose tendency to see the glass as half-empty was chronic—remembered that when the show returned to Broadway after a "national" tour that turned out to be only notional (it had to fold its tent after it played one city), *West Side* spent its last six months on the life support provided by the sharply discounted tickets known as "twofers." After the show finally closed, there was no road company. And in an era when Broadway was still a productive source of pop hits, Sondheim said with evident dismay in later interviews that there were only two recordings of the show's songs—"Tonight," recorded by Dinah Shore, and "Maria," by Johnny Mathis. In fact, there had also been recordings by Vera Lynn, Jill Corey, Rosemary Clooney, and Sammy Davis Jr., but as was often the case Sondheim's memory was both selective and ungenerous to himself.[26]

It was not until the release of the movie version in 1961 that *West Side Story* really entered the broader American consciousness. The film was a gigantic commercial success, won eleven Academy Awards (including Best Picture and Best Music), and yielded a soundtrack album that remained number one on the Billboard chart for a record-demolishing fifty-four weeks—a record not even approached by the Beatles or Michael Jackson and still in place more than sixty years later. (Jackson's *Thriller* from 1982 is a distant second, at thirty-seven weeks.) Sondheim didn't like the movie—he told an interviewer it had "no style"—but he could hardly object to the royalties it brought him. He also did not object, in the end, to the various complications and exasperations he had endured in his working relationship with Bernstein.[27]

"Dear Lenny," he wrote on opening night, "You know—only too well—how hard it is for me to show gratitude and affection, much less commit them to writing." And, "Friendship is a thing I give or receive rarely, but for what it's worth, I want you to know you have it from me always." Years later, as their professional trajectories crossed near the end of Bernstein's career and during the prime of Sondheim's, the friendship would endure, but in a different and eventually darker form.[28]

"How hard it is for me to show gratitude or affection"—it was a self-appraisal that even those closest to Sondheim would likely not have contradicted. His friends knew how to accept his diffident manner and to navigate his dark moods and his occasionally corrosive wit. Sondheim considered "clever" one of his least favorite words, implying as it did a sacrifice of meaning in the service of preening wordplay. But in conversation he could be clever, at times woundingly so. He could also seem remote, or at least detached, closing his eyes or looking away even when talking with a close friend.[29]

But although he told Bernstein that friendship was something he gave or received rarely, the evidence contradicts it. He had plenty of friends, most of them show business contemporaries who had come to New York for the same reason Sondheim had returned to his hometown after college. From St. Louis, the songwriter John Kander; from Chicago, the play- and screenwriting brothers James (a future Sondheim collaborator, on *Follies*) and William Goldman; from Hartford, his Williams pal Dominick Dunne. Mike Nichols came from the University of Chicago to a nightclub on East Fifty-fifth Street, where Sondheim met him as he was polishing his act with Elaine May. And, of course, there were his fellow native Manhattanites Hal Prince and Mary Rodgers. Talent draws talent, and this was a talented bunch.

For Sondheim, the years of "opening doors" were over; with *West Side Story* he became the first in his group to find major success for a creative effort (Prince was a producer, and had not yet directed a show)—the first to be "popping their cork," as the song from *Merrily* would have it. Even though his earnings from *West Side* did not begin flowing liberally until 1961, he was bringing in at least enough from other gigs to enable him to move into somewhat more comfortable quarters, an apartment in a rowhouse at 11 East Eightieth Street, just steps from the Metropolitan Museum of Art.[30]

Given his salubrious experience with *Topper*, Sondheim saw the ravenous medium of television as a convenient and accessible outlet for at least some of his talents, if not the ones he particularly cared about. This was work he took on to make a living. He was one of the original writers (credited as "Steve Sondheim") on the probably-too-erudite-for-television *The Last Word*, a game show for grammar geeks, word fiends, and other language zealots—or, as *Billboard* said, "Clearly for egg heads." (Guests included the novelists Katharine Anne Porter and Aldous Huxley.) He wrote a script for a CBS drama series produced by another Williams friend, Howard Erskine; it was based on a *New Yorker* short story by Roger Angell in which a young bride learns things about her new husband that put her in fear for her life. Angell's story was filled with ominous forebodings and a scary event on a half-frozen river, but Sondheim amped up the horror: a wastepaper basket set on fire by a carelessly discarded cigarette, a razor blade left in a perilous place, at the end the sudden and unexplained death of the young husband. The accompanying music wasn't written by Sondheim, but it was definitely in the creepy-eerie mode that he admired so much in the work of Bernard Herrmann. He wrote other teleplays in this period, mostly on spec; *In an Early Winter*, broadcast in 1958, was the only one that made it to screen.[31]

It was around this time that Sondheim first entered psychoanalysis, encouraged by Arthur Laurents. He didn't feel an urgent need for it, but this was a time and a place and a social milieu in which psychoanalysis was almost as conventional as, say, working with a physical trainer would become half a century later. Even before beginning his therapy, Sondheim had written a few songs for an unproduced musical based on a bestseller about psychotherapy called *The Fifty-Minute Hour.* His own analyst was Jean Jameson, a Columbia-affiliated psychiatrist who was an adherent of a field of analytic therapy called adaptational psychodynamics, which addressed the patient's present circumstances in addition to the more conventional Freudian focus on infancy and early childhood. Sondheim may not have perceived a specific crisis in his life so much as he anticipated that one was lurking in his future. He told Meryle Secrest, "I thought, Gee, someday I'll be upset because clearly I'm not attaching myself to anybody and I thought, am I that different from everybody else that I'm not getting into a one-on-one relationship?" If he hadn't consciously thought of the Bobby character that he would later create with librettist George Furth for *Company*, in some corner of his psyche he had already discovered him.[32]

At a more immediate level, his Williams friend Howard Erskine sensed, the therapy was working. Erskine had seen Sondheim explode into rages when people at a party asked him to play the piano and then proceeded to ignore or interrupt him (this was the humiliating basis of a particularly powerful scene in *Merrily We Roll Along*). But at one post-therapy event, a man interrupted him mid-song and asked if he knew "My Melancholy Baby." The pre-therapy Sondheim, Erskine said, would have gotten up from the piano and stormed out of the room. But on this occasion he "went right into 'Melancholy Baby' and played the whole thing," then simply returned to the song he'd been playing before. The event was a backers' audition for *Gypsy*, and Sondheim, still not yet thirty, would soon have his second great success.[33]

* * *

"There's probably no such thing as a perfect musical," Jack Viertel wrote in *The Secret Life of the American Musical.* "But when fanatics gather to compare notes, the most frequently mentioned candidate is undoubtedly *Gypsy.*" To say the show was nominally based on the autobiography of the stripper Gypsy Rose Lee is an insult to the phrase "based on." It was Arthur Laurents, in his libretto, who invented Mama Rose, whom Viertel called "the greatest show business mother-monster of all time," a woman whose monomaniacal influence over her daughters had little to do with them, and everything to do with Rose herself.

In the spring of 1958, Laurents recruited Sondheim for the show, and Jerome Robbins, already on board as director, lobbied producers David Merrick and Leland Hayward to hire him to write both music and lyrics. "Steve will do *anything* to do *Gypsy,*" Robbins told Hayward. But because Sondheim had begun work on what would become *A Funny Thing Happened on the Way to the Forum,* Robbins introduced a note of realism into his colloquy with Hayward. "Steve cannot do two shows at once," he wrote. "Who can?" This was twelve years before *Company* and *Follies* opened in consecutive seasons.[34]

When Robbins said that Sondheim "will do *anything*" to be part of the creative team, he was either dissembling or operating in the dark. After—or, better still, despite—his success with *West Side Story,* Sondheim was determined that he was done with writing lyrics for someone else's music. He thought of himself as a composer first and a lyricist almost incidentally, and was being only partly playful when he added the legend "Beautiful Music Since 1956" to the lower left-hand corner of his business card. For Sondheim, writing music was a calling, a passion; writing lyrics was "emotionally frustrating" and "bloody hard work . . . just pushing and pushing until you think you're going to drop dead from exhaustion." Yet he was awfully good at it, and he knew that the right words could enhance his music.

If he decided to join Laurents and Robbins to create *Gypsy*, he would write both.[35]

But Ethel Merman, the star around whom the show was constructed, declared that she didn't want the producers to hire a composer she deemed a beginner. Songs for the enormously successful shows she had starred in over the previous quarter century featured music by George Gershwin, Irving Berlin, and Cole Porter. But as much as she lacked faith in Sondheim's music, Merman liked his lyrics. To Sondheim that was irrelevant, and he resolved to decline the lyrics-only commission. Then Oscar Hammerstein, abetted by Flora Roberts, turned him around by transforming Merman's lofty dismissal of Sondheim's music into a plus: if he was really going to make it on Broadway, he told him, he would have to learn how to write for a star, and there were few stars as starry as Merman. It would be the difference, as Sondheim later put it, between writing Mama Rose, and "writing Mama Rose as played by Ethel Merman." He spent a summer weekend with Mary Rodgers visiting Laurents at his house in Quogue, on Long Island, and came back to the city for a final meeting with Merman and took the job.[36]

His partner this time was Jule Styne, who had initially rejected Laurents's suggestion that he collaborate with Sondheim. Styne, the composer of such successes as *Gentlemen Prefer Blondes* and *Bells Are Ringing*, was astonishingly prolific, and turned out to be entirely amiable. He always had at hand a rich supply of "trunk songs"—tunes that had been dropped from one show but were available to be called into service for another—and at least one of them, "You'll Never Get Away from Me," found a permanent home in *Gypsy*. In his book *Finishing the Hat* (the first of two volumes that together became known as the "Hat Box"), Sondheim wrote, "Jule Styne and I were not only a generation apart, we were different species, coming as we did from different musical-theater traditions, he the spontaneous 'tunesmith,' as he called himself, and I the austere revolutionary."[37]

"Lyric writing is too hard to do it for someone else," Sondheim said in 2000. But in 1958, it could not have been less difficult, at least while working with Styne. "We never had a bad week," he said. "We never had, I would say, maybe even a bad day." Styne said that Sondheim's gifts as a composer "drew more out of me than the average lyricist could. I felt I was working with a genius." Meanwhile, Laurents was still bristling over some of Robbins's behavior during the making of *West Side Story*, and Leland Hayward was worrying about some of the spikier aspects of Laurents's own personality ("the great advantage of Steve," Hayward had told Robbins early on, "is that he can work with Arthur Laurents"). But the Sondheim-Styne collaboration brought comfort and conciliation to the four collaborators. (Actually five: Sondheim's close friend composer John Kander wrote the dance music for *Gypsy*—his first music to be performed on Broadway.) It took all of four months for Styne and Sondheim to complete the entire score, and only two more than that to get to opening night.[38]

Sondheim's lyrics for *Gypsy* came as easily as they did for a few reasons, and not just because he was no longer a Broadway newcomer. He didn't have to begin with his writing partner's own lyrics, as he'd done with Bernstein on *West Side Story*, or contend with the nitpicking he felt he'd been required to endure. Unlike the street language of *West Side Story*, the backstage vaudeville argot of the 1920s that *Gypsy* demanded was not so far removed from the showbiz language of the 1950s that was familiar to him. And, following the lead of Cole Porter, one of his heroes, he had begun to write out "the rhythms and the rise and fall" of the words so that they would "sit on the music" as comfortably as they did, without the strain of misplaced accents or tangled syntax.[39]

In the largest sense, Sondheim's greatest achievement in his *Gypsy* lyrics was the title phrase of Merman's big number just before intermission, "Everything's Coming Up Roses," which went straight from his imagination into the English language. (When Robbins first heard the phrase, he asked, "Everything's coming up Rose's *what?*") Considering his reputation for rhymes that dazzle and flash, Sondheim's solution for Styne's placid, tender "Small World" could not have been less Sondheimian: in the entire song, there are only two rhymes, both in the bridge. At the other end of the rhyming spectrum: when Sondheim, Styne, and Merman visited an ailing Cole Porter and performed the score for him, the quadruple rhyme in "Together Wherever We Go" elicited a gasp of delight. (*Wherever I go, I know he goes/Wherever I go, I know she goes./No fits, no fights and no egos—/Amigos,/Together!*) "Anytime I need an ego boost," Sondheim wrote in *Finishing the Hat*, "I conjure up that gasp; it may well be the high point of my lyric-writing life."[40]

In fact, taking into consideration the situation, the performer, and the purpose of a song, *Gypsy*'s astonishing eleven o'clock number, "Rose's Turn," may have been the actual high point, at least in dramatic effect. Alone on a spotlit stage, the increasingly dislikable character at the center of the show concludes her time in the literal spotlight with a mid-song nervous breakdown. Although they admired Merman's work ethic and her talent, the show's creators had much less respect for her intelligence. At the time, Sondheim referred to her as "a talking dog," and four decades later he told an interviewer that "Ethel's imagination and brain were not great." The famous anecdote about Merman's preparation for the emotionally devastating and complex song is true. Midway through the piece, the unhinged Rose breaks into a pathetic and wrenching stammer—*M-M-Momma—/M-M-Momma* . . . Merman had only one question: "That Momma stuff—is that on the upbeat or the downbeat?" Sondheim once described Merman as a "loud, vulgar, cheap, small-eyed lady." For this role, she was perfect.[41]

Gypsy was already in rehearsals when Sondheim and Robbins created the harrowing number—one of the greatest moments in the history of musical theater—late at night, in an empty theater illuminated by a single, small light. They combined some of the striptease movement and rhythms from the show with fragmented lyrics lifted from songs heard earlier, with additions and variations that Sondheim—uncharacteristically—improvised on the spot. It was almost an inverted overture, its themes turned inside out and rendered not to entice the audience but to shock it. The darkened theater, the dramatic moment, the unintentional enactment of a Hollywood-like fantasy version of artistic creation—for Sondheim, "I couldn't wait to tell my friends that I had lived that dream."[42]

Rose's self-gratifying domination of her daughter was Laurents's invention, but as the show developed, Sondheim, in both his lyrics and his contributions to the book, was integrally involved in both the story and how it was told. The two men spoke at least twice a day over the four months that preceded rehearsals, together creating the monster that was Rose, a mother whose manipulations of her child Louise were unthinking, instinctual. The actual subject of the show, Jack Viertel concluded, is "the crushing damage that a parent can inflict on her children." At the curtain, Louise is at last free of her mother, and the audience could leave the theater feeling rather good. If he thought about that in the context of his own life, as he must have, Stephen Sondheim probably felt pretty good himself.[43]

3

On His Own

In june of 1961, Richard Avedon took a photograph of Stephen Sondheim, who was thirty-one but didn't look it (frontispiece). It's hard to imagine a more appealing picture of someone who had already seen so much success at so young an age. His hands are clasped behind his back. His eyes are bright, his face lit up in an uncharacteristic open-mouthed smile. He's looking not at the camera, but at something over the photographer's left shoulder—as if he was anticipating some point in the future, which he knew was going to be wonderful.

It would, of course. But not right away. Sondheim had been working on the show that would become *A Funny Thing Happened on the Way to the Forum* when Oscar Hammerstein died, on August 23, 1960, at sixty-five. The final Rodgers and Hammerstein show, *The Sound of Music*—which was also the first Rodgers and Hammerstein show for which Oscar didn't write the book—was nine months into what became a run of three and a half years. The last song Oscar had completed with Rodgers was "Edelweiss," its lyric as dewy-eyed as anything he'd ever written, and as distant from the sensibility of his protégé as midtown Manhattan was from the Austrian Alps. Just as the show was beginning rehearsals, Oscar was operated on for the stomach cancer that would kill him nine months later. He knew he was dying, as did those who were close to him.

When the moment arrived, Sondheim told Hal Prince that he was pained not just by Oscar's death, but by his own reaction to it. Because he'd "lost something" so valuable to him, an agitated Sondheim said, his genuine sorrow was tainted by "self-pity." Unable to see that mourning is always as much about the mourner as about the mourned, he excoriated himself for a perceived selfishness. He had it upside down. A month before his death, Oscar had inscribed a photograph of him, "For Stevie, my friend and teacher," an artifact Sondheim treasured for the rest of his life. It was a breathtaking declaration of Oscar's regard for the young man whose career—and in some ways, whose life—he had set in motion.[1]

After Ethel Merman vetoed Sondheim as the composer for *Gypsy*, both she and the show's producers were still so eager to have him as lyricist that he asked for—and received—a share of the royalties larger than a lyricist's usual allotment. "I was not proud of my own work in *West Side Story*," he said in 1982, "but I was proud of being connected with the show," even if he considered the movie version "a mess." But with *Gypsy*, "I was proud all the way through. And I started to make money." The sale of the movie rights enabled him to buy the house he would live in for the next six decades. He paid $115,000 for the five-story townhouse at 246 East Forty-ninth Street, just next door to Katharine Hepburn; as well off as he was, his father nonetheless had to co-sign the mortgage. (The amount he paid was the equivalent of $1.54 million in 2023, when his estate sold the house for $7 million.) Apart from its size, the house was fairly unprepossessing from the street, but revealed its wonders in back, where it shared the lush, block-long Turtle Bay Gardens with nineteen other fortunate homeowners.[2]

Until he took on a "house man" in the early 1970s, Sondheim lived on the lower two floors of his new home (tenants occupied an apartment on the top three). But shortly after he bought it, he came very close to taking on a roommate who was much more than a roommate. In his version of one of the odder events in his adult life, he and Mary Rodgers had grown "moderately serious" about each other. In her version, they in fact conducted a trial marriage. Both accounts converge on the central fact that, for a time, they lived together at 246 East Forty-ninth.[3]

Rodgers was divorced, with three children, and was engaged to marry someone else. It was right around the time that Sondheim's unwillingness to commit was the focus of his psychotherapy with Dr. Jameson, who urged Rodgers not to proceed with the marriage. Sondheim was searching for someone to love, and Rodgers had loved him since they'd met as teenagers. "So we would get into the same bed, side by side, frozen with fear," Rodgers wrote in her memoir. "We just lay there. We didn't discuss anything; we didn't do anything. If we touched, it was *en passant.*" That doesn't quite jibe with his version—or at least not with his choice of adverbs: Sondheim said the relationship was "virtually non-sexual."[4]

Who can know what that modifier meant to him? He had long believed he was gay, but he had also made various efforts to engage with women romantically. By the evidence, sex of any kind wasn't yet a big part of his life. Sondheim told Secrest that "you didn't have sex in those days." Rodgers even speculated that he was celibate. What both knew was that the arrangement was a charade. It became clear to Rodgers that Sondheim was completely ignorant of just what constituted a relationship when she called him from London, where her show *Once Upon a*

Mattress had just been mauled by the critics, and asked him if he would pick her up at the airport when she landed in New York. As she wrote in her memoir, "He said, 'Meet you at the *airport?*'—as if I'd asked him to eat the leg of a piano." When Rodgers suggested they end their experiment, Sondheim showed no emotion at all—no sorrow, no joy, just passive acceptance. "People need to have a happy ending, or a sad one," he told an interviewer in 1976. "Usually I'm neither happy nor sad. I'm ambivalent about most things."[5]

At twenty-four, fresh from the Juilliard School of Music, where he had received a master's degree in composition, Jonathan Tunick heard the first few notes of the overture of *A Funny Thing Happened on the Way to the Forum* and was astounded. He had thought Sondheim "was a lyricist who wrote some tunes, but I was amazed to find out that he was really a composer." Thomas Z. Shepard was a twenty-six-year-old refugee from the Yale School of Music who had just taken a job at Columbia Records. When he first heard *Forum,* "the music just bowled me over," he said. "Oh my god, this man is a great composer." Both men's lives would be profoundly affected by the experience: Shepard went on to produce the cast albums of nine Sondheim shows, and Tunick orchestrated dozens of distinct productions of them.[6]

Forum was the product of Sondheim's collaboration with his friend Burt Shevelove and the television writer Larry Gelbart. "Larry Gelbart is the funniest man you'll ever meet," Sondheim said in 2004, "but Burt was, perhaps, second." Gelbart had emerged (along with Mel Brooks, Carl Reiner, Neil Simon, and Woody Allen) from Sid Caesar's writers' room when he, Sondheim, and Shevelove began work on the show in 1958. (Fourteen years later, Gelbart made *M*A*S*H* one of the greatest successes in television history.) Shevelove, who had met Sondheim through Dominick Dunne, was a man of startling wit and broad erudition who had made a quiet reputation for himself as a television writer and on the fringes of Broadway. His particular attachment to the Greek and Roman classics was as noteworthy as a general quickness of mind comparable to Sondheim's own. They bonded over their shared interest in the theater, but also through a passion for word games, particularly acrostics, a complex crossword variant that calls upon a contestant's vocabulary, definition-solving ability, familiarity with the rules of syntax, and the consequent conjuring of an unfamiliar quotation. With two copies of the most recent issue of the *Saturday Review* in hand, "We would each open a copy to the acrostic," Sondheim said. "No pencils. We'd just look at it. There'd be silence, and then one of us would read the answer quotation out loud."[7]

Forum's roots were ancient, and they were enduring. In adapting a handful of works by the Roman playwright Plautus from the third century B.C.E.—much as Shakespeare had done by turning Plautus's *Menaechmi* into *The Comedy of Errors* (which Richard Rodgers, Lorenz Hart, and George Abbott later turned into *The Boys from Syracuse*)—Gelbart and Shevelove employed Plautus's use of colloquial language, witty wordplay, and constantly changing rhythms of speech. All, of course, were modes that Sondheim would exploit in nearly every one of his shows over the next half century. In *Forum*, he assembled a delicate accretion of startling imagery in "Pretty Little Picture" (a song he worked on for most of a year) and displayed his dazzling rhyming facility in "Everybody Ought to Have a Maid." In the first, Sondheim wrote of a bride and her beau in a bed on a boat as they *Feel the roll of the playful waves,/See the sails as they swell./Hear the whips on the galley slaves—/Pretty little picture?/Well.* In "Everybody Ought to Have a Maid," he assembled a glittering chain of seventeen rhyming gerunds—fluttering, shuttering, cluttering, buttering, puttering; pattering, chattering, clattering, flattering, and so on—to convey the personalities of the show's four lead characters, supported by a playfully simple (and notably hummable) tune. It's an ideal representation of how a lyricist who is also a composer can create words that sit so comfortably on the music you would think they were written simultaneously—as they were.

By 1958, when Gelbart, Shevelove, and Sondheim began working on *Forum*, Shevelove had become one of Sondheim's closest friends, and except for one severe rupture—provoked, in fact, by *Forum*—they would remain so until Shevelove's death in 1982. "Of all the people in my life," Sondheim said thirteen years later, "Bert is the one I miss the most." In addition to their professional interests and personal hobbies, they also shared a calculated, even heartless, attitude toward creation and revision. Shevelove once said about the process of rewriting, "Well, I'm polishing a little here and polishing a little there. The trouble is, the more you polish shit the more it looks like shit." Sondheim demonstrated a stoic dispassion whenever he sacrificed his personal devotion to a song that might have been a success on its own but wasn't working in the context of a show. Always, the show came first.[8]

At no time in Sondheim's career did this become more apparent than in the spring of 1962, when *Forum* was staggering through a dreadful tryout run at the National Theater in Washington. Hal Prince, producing, had hired George Abbott to direct. The most successful director of musicals and comedies Broadway had ever known, Abbott was also a celebrated play doctor whom producers would recruit to salvage a troubled show with the default injunction, "Call in George Abbott." *Forum*, which had been rewritten eleven times in its four-year journey to the Washington tryout, was in such severe trouble it was about to self-immolate. As hostile audiences and brutal reviews in Washington augured a death more merciful than premature, the creative team looked to Abbott to provide a life raft that might save their four years of apparently fruitless labor. "I

Mary Rodgers, for many years Sondheim's closest friend, here in 1959 with George Abbott, who said Sondheim "didn't trust me at all"

don't know," Abbott said. "I guess we'll have to call in George Abbott."[9]

Sondheim considered these the only amusing words Abbott ever uttered. In fact, he said that this most revered of theatrical figures, whose successful comedies and musicals stretched from a play called *Broadway* (603 performances) in 1926 to *Fiorello!* (795 performances) in 1959, had neither a sense of humor nor any apparent talent other than the ability to keep things organized. Sondheim said that he, Gelbart, and Shevelove had to explain the show's abundant jokes to him. Gelbart remembered that "Mr. Abbott," as everyone on Broadway referred to him, never cracked a smile when he heard the show's score or read its book. He did say, when Gelbart asked if he could call him "George," that yes, he could—and when Gelbart asked him why everyone called him Mr. Abbott, he said, "Damned if I know."[10]

When the show was dying in its tryout in Washington, Sondheim suggested that Abbott's work could benefit from a little doctoring itself. The emergency physician in this case was Jerome Robbins, who famously created "Comedy Tonight," a new opening number that told the audience they were about to witness an uninhibited, knockabout farce. Abbott liked the idea. He had already rejected Sondheim's original opener, "Invocation"—for much of its length a droning incantation that sounded vaguely (if artificially) "Greek"—and Robbins recognized that *its* replacement, a light wisp of froth called "Love Is in the Air," was pale and ineffectual. But for Sondheim, there was more sweat than magic in the creation of the number that saved the show. In 1972, Robbins told an interviewer that he was able to pull "Comedy Tonight" out of Sondheim only after many grueling hours in his hotel room, "making him stick to the subject and helping him get over whatever was blocking him." It was, Robbins said, characteristic behavior: "He's a procrastinator and he'll do everything he can to put up a wall of huge insurmountable problems in front of himself and then conquer them at the last minute." But then, he said, the words and music all come together "when the chips are down and he has to come up with something." Robbins "could work with Sondheim, which I couldn't," Abbott told an interviewer in 1983. "Sondheim didn't trust me at all."[11]

In a functional sense, the Gelbart-Shevelove book and the Sondheim lyrics were largely out of a pre–Rodgers and Hammerstein Broadway, where a song could be dropped into a script for reasons no more complex than a hunch that the audience would be ready for one. (Another difference: Gelbart said he wanted to fill the "vulgarity vacuum" left behind by Hammerstein's lofty sentiments.) In a narrative sense, the songs in *Forum* were placed where they were in order to slow down the show's plot, not to advance it—to give the audience respite from the hectic, intricate, and very funny farce that surrounded each number. In 1978, Sondheim said that the audience didn't really have to pay close attention to *Forum*'s lyrics, as they had so little to do with the plot. Much of the music, though, was something new. Commenting on "Pretty Little Picture," record producer Thomas Shepard marveled at "the quirkiness of the melody [and] the harmonies underneath it." That it may have taken a trained ear to notice the novelty of the song was beside the point; Sondheim knew that he was going in a new direction, in some instances to such a degree that he later came to regret it. "A song like 'Pretty Little Picture' has absolutely unnecessary dissonances in it," he told Mark Eden Horowitz in *Sondheim on Music*, "because I was so afraid of writing a triad." Leonard Bernstein, who was a master at the integration of dissonance and melody, had criticized him for the willfulness of *Forum*'s dissonances, and it took decades for Sondheim to admit Bernstein was right. "It's essentially a musician's score," he told a friend. Which was another way of saying, "I was showing off"—for his peers, not his audience.[12]

However much Tunick and Shepard appreciated his musical innovation, it sailed past the audience and barely stirred the reviewers. Sondheim's tolerance for critics had already been tested when Harold Clurman sneered at his lyrics for *West Side Story*. Now that his music was on display for the first time, he went into a defensive crouch, training his eyes and his anger on anyone who didn't appreciate his "musician's score." Even after his extraordinary string of critical triumphs in the 1970s, neither his rage nor his resentment over the *Forum* reviews had subsided.

In fact, the only undiluted pan came from Norman Nadel in the *World, Telegram & Sun*, who said it "would have been a second-rate score even in 1940," and the *Journal-American* was barely more positive. But the two reviewers who truly mattered were pleased. In the *New York Times*, Howard Taubman praised "Everybody Ought to Have Maid," said that "Lovely" was "romantic and pretty," and, in the only phrase that could possibly be considered negative, described "Comedy Tonight" as "relentlessly snappy." Walter Kerr in the *Herald-Tribune* said Sondheim's music started off oddly, but then it "begins to pay off . . . The score is in and out but wins out."

It's true there were few outright raves, but other reviewers called the score "modest but pleasant" (*New York Post*), said it "falls pleasantly on the ear" (*New York Mirror*), and characterized it as "jaunty" (*Christian Science Monitor*). Yet Sondheim wasn't listening. In a series of for-the-record interviews with Columbia University's Oral History Project in 1982 that were not to be cited until after his death, he almost sounded like a trauma survivor. The music for *Forum*, he said—entirely inaccurately—had been "universally panned and trounced on and slandered and kicked around the block." Wounds hadn't healed; they'd festered. *Forum*'s reception provoked the beginning of a career-long sensitivity to even the mildest demurrers, and a consequent loathing of most reviewers. "Musicals are the only public art form reviewed mostly by ignoramuses," he wrote in 2010 (by which time he had composed seventeen of them). They "know nothing, of course, about music." And music was what he cared about most.[13]

The critics' praise for Abbott's direction only compounded Sondheim's displeasure. In a letter to a friend, he said he'd known that the "bungling" Abbott was inept, "but the enormity of his ineptness is unbelievable." He wasn't much happier that the show's star, Zero Mostel, also received great notices. Years later, he described Mostel, who had an uncontainable penchant for improvisation and other crimes against the show and its script, as "fucking impossible." After the passage of another twenty-five years, when Sondheim completed the *Forum* chapter of *Finishing the Hat* and gave it to Peter Gethers, his editor, Gethers asked if he'd really meant to write about the show without even once mentioning its award-winning, audience-thrilling, ticket-selling star. Sondheim answered with a single word: "Yes."[14]

The greatest injury came when the Tony Awards nominations were announced. *Forum* received eight—but none for its score. (The nominees for musical score were *Stop the World—I Want to Get Off; Little Me; Bravo Giovanni;* and the eventual winner, *Oliver!*) Six of the show's nominees won, including Abbott for best direction, and Mostel for best actor. And when the night's biggest prize was announced, Prince, Shevelove, and Gelbart ran to the podium to accept the Best Musical award with the expected giddy joy. Yet none of them even mentioned Sondheim, much less thanked him. It was a deeply hurtful moment. Prince at least called the next day to apologize. Shevelove did not, and it led to a rupture between the two men that lasted for months.[15]

Despite the show's enormous financial success (much more than even *Gypsy*, *Forum* became Sondheim's primary source of income well into the 1980s); despite his having achieved his boyhood dream of writing both music and lyrics for a Broadway show; and, the behavior of his colleagues aside, despite the Tony Award for Best Musical for something that was indeed *his*—despite all that, it was not enough. In a letter to a friend, written months before the crushing blow of the Tonys, Sondheim said that working on *Forum* was "the bitterest experience" he'd yet had.[16]

His despair at a time of great success evoked another incident on the show's journey to becoming a huge financial success for Sondheim. When Shevelove said he wanted him to write songs that didn't advance the plot, he explained that it was necessary for the audience to have the opportunity to "savor the moment."

Remembering the conversation more than twenty years later, Sondheim said, "I'd never savored a moment."[17]

In the early 1960s, Sondheim's world was both expanding and contracting. He gave more and more interviews and enjoyed his growing celebrity. He traveled more, the European hotels getting finer and more expensive with each trip, the people he met along the way getting more and more famous. In London, he had lunch with Princess Margaret (who asked him to make a martini for her), then spent a weekend at Dirk Bogarde's estate in Buckinghamshire. In Madrid, he joined Mike Nichols and Leonard and Felicia Bernstein for lunch with Ava Gardner.[18]

But in New York, he was settling into a firm and somewhat insular position in a well-defined circle created by the Bernsteins. More than two decades later, he would lampoon that circle in "The Blob," an ensemble number from *Merrily We Roll Along* that poked slightly malicious fun at an air-kissing, gossip-swapping, bitchiness-wielding collection of the people who *write the books/ And put on the shows/And run the saloons/And design the clothes* and who see themselves as *the most important people/In the most important city/In the most important country/In the you-know-what!* It would take a much-too-long paragraph to list the original Blob's many members, but you could construct a representative sampling with Mike Nichols, Lauren Bacall, Lillian Hellman, William Styron, Isaac Stern, Richard Avedon, and their various wives, husbands, and lovers. They may have flinched at their eventual—and gentle—come-uppance in "The Blob," but Sondheim didn't wait as long to offer his own self-satire, which he put forth (unintentionally, he claimed) in 1970. Mary Rodgers was convinced Sondheim was a version of Bobby, the disengaged main character in *Company*, an emotional cipher defined by his popularity among his friends, and by his own alienating lack of commitment. "That's exactly what [he] was like; he was Bobby," said Rodgers. In their social circle, the unattached, unemotional, sexually unresolved Sondheim was the magnetic core. "Our whole world revolved around Steve," she said.[19]

And why not? He was, of course, successful; in such a crowd, that was a prerequisite. But his particular popularity arose from a combination of verbal brilliance and, like Bobby, the singleness that made him available to everyone. His quickness in conversation left his friends slack-jawed in wonder. "He was madly witty," Bernstein's daughter Jamie recalled, "often slouched on a couch, squinting through his cigarette smoke, and making cutting remarks." But those who might be subject to his sarcasm didn't see malice in it—or, at least, chose not to. "Snark was his kingdom," Jamie Bernstein said, and it was an honor to be welcomed into it.[20]

But there were plenty of reasons why Stephen Sondheim in his early thirties was not the likeliest figure to be the object of such affection. His personal habits were deplorable; Rodgers said "he was a pig" who "never washed, never shaved." That was no doubt an overstatement, but it wasn't far off. Although he could clean up for a public appearance (or an Avedon portrait), his hair was lank, often filthy. Indifferent to fashion or even conventional notions about physical appearance, he cared nothing about what he looked like, describing himself as "one of nature's slobs." A scenic designer who worked with him said, "You could tell he wasn't visual just by looking at him." Others reported that he looked "neglected," carried himself with "determined dishevelment," and wore black socks at the beach. The actor-writer Simon Callow called his style "unsmart casual." Friends chuckled when Annie Leibovitz photographed him for an American Express advertising campaign in the late 1980s; her stylist dressed him in linen slacks and shirt, bow tie, and suspenders, holding a straw hat. In one frame, Leibovitz actually had him perch, in all his risible finery, on the limb of a tree.[21]

But even those who knew him well could be astonished by his reaction to the slightest hint of familiarity. Remembering herself as a child, Jamie Bernstein said, "you wouldn't want to go over and climb in his lap," as she would some other close friends of her parents. "You wouldn't dream of it." Documentary filmmaker (and Blobster) Ofra Bikel told friends about a party at the Bernsteins' where she encountered Sondheim, leaned over to greet him with a kiss on the cheek, and he cried out "Don't touch me! Don't touch me!" Mary Rodgers connected his personal hygiene to this distancing instinct, believing that his appearance was a form of declaration: "Stay away from me."[22]

In the fall of 1962, when Hal Prince married Judy Chaplin, Sondheim was the best man. (The wedding announcement in the *New York Times* identified him as "Stephen Sendheim.") His relationship with Prince was long, wide, and intricate. They worked together, off and on, for half a century, and even when they weren't working together—after the debacle that was *Merrily We Roll Along* in 1981, until the comparably ill-fated *Bounce* in 2003—they remained close. The six shows they created between 1970 and 1981 (an astonishing three of them in consecutive years) represent a creative efflorescence that no Broadway songwriter-director team has ever enjoyed.

At Sondheim's memorial service in 2022, the Princes' daughter Daisy said that as great as the friendship between Hal and Steve was, "the deeper friendship" was with Judy. She was a show business baby, daughter of the songwriter, arranger, and producer Saul Chaplin, who composed several hits (including "Dedicated to You" and "Bei Mir Bist du Schoen") and was musical director and associate producer of the film version of *West Side Story*. Notoriously private, for decades she never gave interviews. In his conversations with Meryle Secrest in the 1990s, Sondheim would occasionally suggest that she might be able to answer a specific question or relate a particular anecdote, but it was "too bad Judy Prince won't talk to you." To Sondheim, though, she was always available. Her urge for privacy was so strong that in the more than nine hundred pages of *Finishing the Hat* and *Look, I Made a Hat*, Sondheim loyally obliges her, bringing up her name just once, and even then only to provide the reader with an I.D. for the "Jude" referenced in a fiftieth-birthday song he wrote for Hal. But she was the intentionally unnamed person whom he refers to, in *Finishing the Hat*, as "my real-life Muse." In her book, Secrest said he told her that Judy was "very, very smart." For a man acknowledged by most who knew him to be brilliant, it was a high compliment. But Secrest's version, a perfectly sensible edit of what he said, missed a nuance: on tape, he said she was "very, very, very, very smart." For a man obsessed with words, the quadrupled version suggests a meaningful intensity.[23]

The screenwriter and playwright Peter Stone said Sondheim "could almost not function without her." Mutual friends believed they spoke every day. In the one known—but never published—interview she did give, to Mel Gussow of the *New York Times* just before *Company* opened in 1970, she said only one thing about Sondheim: When they met, he was her husband's best friend. Hal Prince said, "I'm certain that the nature of his relationship [with her] is different from anybody else's. And far different, certainly, from my relationship."[24]

* * *

There was much that was, and remains, unknowable about Sondheim and women. What definitely *is* known is that his attachments to women were emotionally intimate. Mary Rodgers and Judy Prince (who would become sort-of rivals for his attention in the 1990s) were at the top of the list. Others included the actress and activist Cynthia O'Neal; *fashioniste* D. D. Ryan; Leonard Bernstein's wife Felicia; and Mary Ann Madden, the longtime puzzles editor of *New York* magazine, whom he met through his friend, journalist Gloria Steinem.

Another was *Vogue* cover girl Nancy Berg, a dark-haired beauty who, she told a reporter, "wanted to live my life grandly" (and who at least once appeared in *Vogue* in a Herbert Sondheim dress). Berg later acknowledged that she drank too much, partied too much, relied way too much on amphetamines. She claimed a roster of beaux that, she said, included John F. Kennedy, Frank Sinatra, and Orson Welles. Like Sondheim, Berg despised her mother, which no doubt helped them form a bond. Some of Sondheim's friends believed they were truly a couple, despite his no-longer-hidden homosexuality (he didn't advertise it, but he also didn't deny it; Rodgers said "he was surrounded by people who were at the very least not emanating a lot of masculine hormones in the direction of women"). In 1964, the syndicated entertainment columnist Earl Wilson reported from the opening night party for *Anyone Can Whistle* that "Nancy Berg and Steven [*sic*] Sondheim weren't concealing a thing from anybody." Berg said she was "quite mad about him," but also "terribly jealous"—of actress Lee Remick.[25]

Sondheim met Remick in London in 1963, when the British production of *Forum* was under way. She was twenty-eight, already a star, celebrated for her work in *A Face in the Crowd* and *Anatomy of a Murder*, and for her harrowing Oscar-nominated performance in *Days of Wine and Roses.* Sondheim never denied that he was in love with Remick and would comfortably say

Vogue cover model Nancy Berg in 1964, around the time she was dating Sondheim

that "it was a romance." She was married (though separated) at the time; he was having an affair with press agent Paul Solomon, whom he had met in his Broadway social circle. But at least within the confines of the Blob it became more and more apparent that Remick and Sondheim were in love. Cynthia O'Neal recalled them sitting on the couch at parties, holding hands, "very much a couple." When they appeared on the television game show *Password*, she certainly looked like she was in love with him, her glowing eyes and ardent smile coming from somewhere beyond acting school.[26]

Remick and Sondheim retained a form of emotional connection until her death from kidney cancer in 1991, at fifty-five. In the 2000s, collecting various videos and films in which he had appeared, he told Jane Klain of the Paley Center for Media that the *Password* episode was "the holy grail." (After years of searching, she found a copy in 2020; Sondheim was thrilled.) Back in the mid-1960s, when his romance with Remick

Sondheim, Lee Remick, and *Password* host Allen Ludden. Their friends considered Sondheim and Remick "very much a couple."

had come to an end, he stopped dating women. To friends like O'Neal, it was a relief. To Arthur Laurents, it was inevitable. Sondheim had been involved with women, Laurents believed, "because he hoped."[27]

It was in 1982 that Sondheim, during his Columbia oral history interviews, made the comment about being trounced and slandered by *Forum*'s critics. By then, he had enjoyed success sufficient to dilute the agonies and anger that he had gorged upon twenty years earlier. *Forum* was a miscalculation; he had expected the critics to applaud it, and when, by his judgment, they hadn't, he "really wanted to prove that I could do something that they would like." He chose an odd path for the effort. "That's when I went to Arthur and said I wanted to do something with really a lot of music in it," something, he continued, "really weird." The result was *Anyone Can Whistle*, the strangest, most oblique, and least successful show of his career—

but, musically, the first forging of the style he would expand, refine, and strive to perfect for the rest of his life.[28]

Laurents was the obvious person for him to turn to. It was Laurents who had brought the twenty-five-year-old Sondheim to Leonard Bernstein and Jerome Robbins as *West Side Story* was beginning to take shape. Late in his life, Laurents said Sondheim had been his best friend. It was a friendship further enhanced by their shared success on *Gypsy* and deepened by the byplay of two brilliant theatrical minds, demonstrated both in their work together and in their personal lives. For years they shared long letters about shows and movies each of them had seen—acutely detailed accounts that, collected, would make an indispensable primer for anyone studying stage or film production. The letters might also be considered fairly scandalous. About Barbra Streisand, with whom he would collaborate happily and productively many years later, Sondheim was unsparing. After attending a benefit performance in 1968, he told Laurents how, in "her form-fitting, sequined dress, double chins and one hand on hip, she was indistinguishable from Sophie Tucker." She "doesn't have one sincere moment left inside her." He cited her "movie-star narcissism" and "contempt for her audience." Finally, "the voice is still there, but nothing else."[29]

At the same benefit, he told Laurents, Joel Grey performed "embarrassingly." At a performance of *Hallelujah Baby* (libretto by Laurents), Leslie Uggams was "unintelligible" and repeatedly "dropped out of character." At Harold Pinter's "latest disappointment"—*The Homecoming*—"the most exciting part is the intermission." The candor expressed in Sondheim's letters to Laurents suggests the intimacy and trust that undergirded their friendship.[30]

But at the same time, their relationship would be shaken, and eventually shattered, by periodic eruptions over the course of more than fifty years. It must be said that Laurents, for all his theatrical gifts, was for decades one of the most widely disliked people in the theater business. (Mary Rodgers was concise: Laurents, she wrote in her memoir, was "a little shit.") Unlike Sondheim, he did not keep his opinions shrouded in private correspondence but would use them as weapons.* His gossip was often malicious, and he considered candor a cardinal virtue, even when it was wounding. Sondheim told an interviewer that he and Laurents had a productive "mesh" when they worked together, but you wouldn't know it from the shrapnel that littered their work on *Anyone Can Whistle*. During the show's tryout run in Philadelphia, Sondheim confronted Laurents directly in three pages of dudgeon and ire. "I am sick and tired," he wrote. "You said 'a lot of people' think I'm trying to destroy the show. Would you like to hear what 'a lot of people' . . . have said about you?" He cited Laurents's "tantrums," his "intolerance," his "tactlessness." In another letter, Sondheim told Laurents that his "grumpiness and insinuations . . . anger and upset me [and] paralyze me." Even when they were getting along with each other while developing the show ("I love you, I love your work," Sondheim told him in a letter of apology), there was a tartness in their relationship. This was evident when, during the development of *Anyone Can Whistle*, Sondheim said to Hal Prince that because Laurents disliked John Osborne's *Luther*, "I can't wait to see it."[31]

In the summer of 1971, just weeks after praising Laurents's work from the stage at the 92nd Street Y's "Lyrics and Lyricists" program, Sondheim told Prince about the "horrendous" week-

* Sondheim did step out into the public arena for one battle around this time. After Meredith Willson, creator of *The Music Man*, published a piece in the *Herald-Tribune* attacking playwrights who insist on writing about "abnormal people whose lurid behavior [has] never been considered suitable for the stage," Sondheim roared back. Willson's view, he said in a letter to the editor, was "insufferable," "intemperate," "senseless," and "ruinously narrow." He ended by mentioning both the specific play Willson was attacking and Willson's own most recent effort, saying: "*Who's Afraid of Virginia Woolf* is bringing back audiences that *The Unsinkable Molly Brown* drove out."

end he had just spent at Laurents's beach house and the "final phone conversation" that followed. "I mean final," he told Prince. "It only took me 15 years to wake up." But for another four decades their peculiar entanglement, when unknotted, resembled a sine wave, as they repeatedly vibrated from friends to enemies to friends to enemies again. When Sondheim was developing *Passion* with James Lapine in 1994, he asked Lapine, who was directing, if Laurents could attend a workshop performance; he valued his opinion. Lapine's consent was reluctant—what director wants another director in the room when he's working?—but he found himself unable to reject Sondheim's earnest request to bring in his old collaborator. When the workshop was over, Sondheim happened to be out of the room. Laurents unloaded on Lapine. He did not hold back; he thought the show was terrible. After he left, Sondheim returned and eagerly asked Lapine, "What did he say? What did he say?" Lapine told him. "Steve went berserk, absolutely berserk," Lapine recalled. "I just thought, what is this relationship these people have with each other?"[32]

In 1962, when their relationship had not yet begun its wild yawing between love and loathing, both men took Sondheim's wish to be "weird" in his next show far too seriously. Despite Sondheim's smash success with *Forum* and Laurents's own impressive credentials, they had to go through more than thirty backers' auditions to raise the production budget for their new show. It's easy to understand why. Were it possible to summarize the plot they cooked up for *Anyone Can Whistle*, the show might have had a chance to run longer than its nine flaccid performances. Sondheim later called it "extreme satire"—"extreme" being an understatement, "satire" being news to the befuddled audience. One effort at a summary (origins unknown) might explain the problem: "There's a rock in the middle of the town and they build a pump inside of the rock and they have it discovered by a very strange child that's wandering around the city. Meanwhile, there is on the hill outside the town something called the 'Cookie Jar' which is an asylum." And it goes on from there in a dizzying, allegory-riddled spiral intended to make the then popular point that the insane can sometimes be saner than the sane (see *King of Hearts* and other films of the period). Choreographer-director Michael Bennett, with whom Sondheim later shared great creative success in the 1970s, had it right when he dismissed *Whistle* as "pure complicated, intellectual Sondheim left to his own devices." Laurents was similarly unburdened; Sondheim himself said that the fact that Laurents both wrote and directed meant there was no one to take issue with their bad ideas. Years later, Sondheim likened *Whistle* to "a show written by the two smartest kids in the class from the back row. It's just so condescending and smart-ass."[33]

The main character, played by Angela Lansbury in her first appearance in a stage musical, was the town's mayor; her first reaction on reading the script was, "I thought it was nuts, crackers." Sharing top billing, and appearing in her first (and last) stage musical: Lee Remick. The leading ladies' lack of musical experience may have contributed to the tense atmosphere that beset the production on its way to Broadway. Lansbury had appeared in film musicals, but in several of them her voice had been dubbed. At one point, her inability to provide what Sondheim wanted—or, perhaps, his inability to explain what he wanted—led to an ugly confrontation reverberating through two flights of a backstage staircase. "I remember screaming my ass off," Lansbury once said. "I remember yelling, 'I don't know what you want. What the hell do you want me to do? Tell me and I'll try to do it but for god's sake let's get on with it!'" Like Lansbury, Remick was a talented actress, but even though her singing was undistinguished, she and Sondheim managed to avoid confrontation. Engaged as they were in what Sondheim considered a romance, he had specifically asked to be left out of the discussion if she had any substantial differences with his and Laurents's view of the role.[34]

When *Anyone Can Whistle* opened at the Majestic Theatre on April 4, 1964, the reviews were pitiless. (Howard Taubman, in the *New York Times*, said "there's no law against saying something in a musical but it's unconstitutional to omit imagination and wit.") After Sondheim got extremely drunk on opening night, and after he and Laurents agreed to forgo royalties in an effort to keep the show open, and even after they had put up their own money for an ad in the *Times*, their creation was clearly beyond salvation. The investors lost every cent they had put into it. Among all of Sondheim's Broadway shows, it remains one of two that have never had a Broadway revival (the other is *Passion*, from 1994). The only balm Sondheim may have found for the entire experience was his ability to deflect: In response to an opening-night telegram from Hal Prince, he wrote, "WELL, THEY THREW CABBAGES AT STRAVINSKY."[35]

But there was one rave review, from Norman Nadel of the *World Telegram & Sun*—the same critic who had said that Sondheim's work for *Forum* "would have been a second-rate score even in 1940." Now he recognized a different Sondheim. He called the *Whistle* score "spectacularly original," even "remarkable." The overture alone thrilled him, with its "intriguing, mild dissonances [and] scant, pleasantly tantalizing fragments of themes." Did Sondheim note that Nadel was not one of the musical "illiterates" and "ignoramuses" in the critics' seats—that he was, in fact, a classically trained musician who had founded the Columbus Symphony Orchestra?[36]

Maybe not. But Sondheim did live long enough to see *Anyone Can Whistle* become what Frank Rich would call "a cult flop." Goddard Lieberson of Columbia Records had considered the score of such value that he went ahead with a cast recording despite the show's dismal failure. A few of its songs have entered the standard Sondheim repertoire; the title song alone has been recorded by performers as disparate as Mandy Patinkin, Nancy Wilson, Judy Collins, and the jazz trumpeter and opera composer Terence Blanchard. However "crackers" the show's book might have been, however stressed the backstage atmosphere definitely was, however thoroughly the show failed, Sondheim's work on it established his musical signature. Instead of the show's songs providing respites from the action, as they'd done in *Forum*, they simultaneously commented on the action and moved it along. Employing a number of principles he'd learned from Milton Babbitt, particularly long-line composition, he was able to integrate song and spoken dialogue in numbers such as "Simple," which traverses thirteen minutes of stage time before the first act curtain, incorporating along the way ten different characters and a few crucial plot points. And, not dissimilar from what he later did in *Sweeney Todd* and *Sunday in the Park with George*, he built all of the show's music on its four opening notes and their interrelationships. He said, "All the songs are based on seconds and fourths and the relationship between a D and an E and a C and an F." Audiences certainly didn't notice this, but it was the kind of musical organizing principle that Sondheim wanted.[37]

Just as much as his structural devices, what also marked his work in this peculiar show was how closely it connected, in both content and style, with the Sondheim yet to come. He wasn't writing for Puerto Rican teenagers, monomaniacal stage mothers, or ancient Roman *farceurs*. As tedious and off-kilter as the plot and premise of *Anyone Can Whistle* were, there was room in the book for songs about people with conflicting emotions, people confronted by difficulty, people in love. And, inescapably if unintentionally, about Sondheim himself. The closing number, "With So Little to Be Sure Of," conveys in music as well as lyrics a level of genuine emotion he had never before approached, much less achieved.

That was even more the case with the title song. In 1963,

during the show's development, Sondheim had recorded himself singing and playing a demo version of "Anyone Can Whistle," which has been widely considered (despite his vociferous denials) as close to an autobiographical song as any he would ever write. The closing lyrics echo some of those he'd written for the admittedly autobiographical *Climb High* during his time at Williams. In "Where Do I Belong?" the twenty-one-year-old Sondheim had asked, *why can't I/Be part of something/Someone/Somewhere?* Somewhat modified by more than a decade of adult life, it was a sentiment contextually reprised in "Anyone Can Whistle," which ends with *Maybe you can show me/How to let go,/Lower my guard,/Learn to be free./Maybe if you whistle,/Whistle for me.* On the demo version of the song, the lyrics accompanying the bridge seem even closer to his image of himself at thirty-three. Sondheim's voice almost imperceptibly cracking on the final word, he asks, *It's all so simple/Relax, let go, let fly./So someone tell me why/Can't I?*

Around the time that he was working on *A Funny Thing Happened on the Way to the Forum* with Sondheim and Gelbart, Bert Shevelove ran into Oscar Hammerstein. "You know," Oscar told him, "Steve won't really be a member of the working theater until he has a flop." Now he had one.[38]

Especially if one takes into account his view that *Forum* was his "bitterest experience"—or, as he called it in a milder usage, "the *Forum* tsuris"—the 1960s were not good to him. He began a collaboration with satirist Jules Feiffer that produced one song before the project fizzled. He wrote another for a Mary Rodgers show that folded after forty-three performances. He spent three months working with librettist Abe Burrows on *How to Succeed in Business Without Really Trying* before they mutually decided that their visions for the show were in conflict. He soon entered into the most fraught collaboration of his career, an experience that would make both *Forum* and *Whistle* seem like picnics. The stinging comments of reviewers (he tried to dismiss them, but never really could); the pain—and perhaps humiliation—of *Whistle*'s failure; and the clouds brought on by his chronic detachment made Sondheim ripe for a return to psychotherapy.[39]

The proximate cause of his entry into a full-blown psychoanalysis with Milton H. Horowitz, a prominent semi-Freudian, was romantic confusion. Remick was not yet gone from his romantic life, and his love affair with Paul Solomon was on the rocks. In those years, when the closet door was still locked from the inside, "I was never easy with being a homosexual," he told Secrest, whose exploration in the mid-1990s of this subject and his psychotherapy in general will doubtless remain the primary source for anyone delving into her subject's inner life.[40]

Horowitz, who became president of the New York Psychoanalytic Society in 1983, favored patients involved in the arts. He told one of them, "hang around here long enough and you'll see everyone you know." Bizarrely, that included Leonard Bernstein, a longtime patient whose close friendship with Sondheim didn't appear to trouble Horowitz. Yet more bizarrely, both men welcomed the personable Horowitz into their social lives. Bernstein referred to him as "Uncle Miltie." James Lapine, Sondheim's collaborator on three shows between 1984 and 1994, said Sondheim "palled around and was friends with the psychiatrist; he came to [Sondheim's] parties. He should have had a good psychiatrist who was not his friend." But Sondheim remained attached to Horowitz, continuing in therapy with him for twenty-five years and, in his will, endowing the Horowitz-Sondheim Clinic for Theater Artists at the New York Psychoanalytic Institute.* Among many other things that appealed to

* Another sociable psychoanalyst of the era who was popular among various celebrities—including Sondheim's friends Mike Nichols and Anthony Perkins—was Mildred Newman, co-author with her husband, the analyst Bernard Berkowitz, of the gigantic bestseller *How to Be Your Own Best Friend.* Newman was

Sondheim was Horowitz's view of Foxy. Sondheim told Secrest, "I am happy to say, I proudly say, even my shrink said, 'That's the creepiest mother I've ever heard of.' 'Creepy' was the word he used."[41]

Horowitz later wrote two papers that provoked attention in the psychoanalytic community. One was called "On Revenge," the other "Revenge and Masochism." In them, he suggested that the revenge instinct was related to the unconscious fear of what he called "deep loneliness." He also emphasized "the need to connect," and said "the patients I have seen to be most suffering are the unattached, the unconnected." There's no reason to believe that Horowitz drew substance for these papers from his therapeutic experience with Sondheim. There's also no reason to believe that he did not.[42]

Foxy moved back to New York after her second husband died in 1959. Her son had visited her a few times in California, and they continued to have at least a facsimile of a decent relationship after her return to the city. He had his life and she had hers, which included a successful new career as an interior designer (one of her clients was Sondheim's old friend Dominick Dunne). Mother and son exchanged gifts, talked occasionally, and managed to retain a surface calm. He didn't rant about her to his friends, mostly making use of her as a punchline. They even collaborated on the never-published *Stardom*, a board game that, Sondheim said, was about "how to fuck your way to the top" in Hollywood. Foxy handled the design, Stephen the words; one instruction he worked into it read, "Foxy likes you. Lose a turn." (Another one was: "Go see JOAN CRAWFORD on Sunset

so comfortable among Manhattan's glittering elites that she tried to recruit Sondheim as a patient, calling him on the phone and asserting, "I think maybe I could do you some good, Mr. Sondheim." He later told an interviewer that he considered Newman "a danger to humanity."

Boulevard, W. She needs some help in beating her children.") After seeing an unsuccessful musical called *Foxy* in 1964, he told Hal Prince "I liked my mother better." When Jerome Robbins sent him a Christmas gift (they exchanged them annually), Sondheim said, "The pillows couldn't be better—they made my mother furious."[43]

In addition to its exploration of his relationship with his mother, Sondheim's psychoanalysis would eventually lead him to recognize that his feelings about his father required reconsideration. But he never modified his fundamentally positive view of him. By 1964, women's styles had changed; Herbert Sondheim, Inc., had not. The company soon failed, and Stephen paid off his father's debts. When Herbert died two years later, at seventy-one, the *Times* referred to him as "the old pro of Seventh Avenue." The last time Stephen saw him, as he was dying, Herbert told his son, "It's going to be all right."[44]

In 1964, just two weeks after *Anyone Can Whistle* came to the end of its brief and painful run, Sondheim told Hal Prince about his next show. "The project represents everything wrong: my reverting to just lyric-writing (which I loathe), an adaptation of a play (which I disapprove of) and a successful one (which I really disapprove of), and working with Dick (whom I both loathe and disapprove of)." "Dick" was Richard Rodgers. The show was *Do I Hear a Waltz?* Sondheim concluded his explanation to Prince with the words, "BURN THIS LETTER." Prince filed it.[45]

Sondheim always gave three reasons for agreeing to write lyrics to Rodgers's score for this musicalization of Arthur Laurents's play *The Time of the Cuckoo.* It was a favor for his dear friend Mary, who had recognized that her father, at sixty-four, was professionally fading and personally lost. It was also a favor, in the form of a memorial, for Oscar; in their last conversation before his death, Hammerstein had beseeched his protégé to find a way to work with his longtime partner. And Laurents, who would direct as well as adapt his script for *Cuckoo*, convinced him that riding on the wave of Rodgers's music would be profitable. "I wanted to make a lot of money," Sondheim wrote in an early draft of *Finishing the Hat*. Burt Shevelove had a word for that last reason: "It was streetwalking."[46]

Rodgers was an alcoholic, a womanizer, a bully, and not only the show's "muscle"—the member of the creative team with the greatest influence over the results—but also its producer. He was the most successful man on Broadway; if you factor in his work with Lorenz Hart as well as with Hammerstein, he was the most successful man in Broadway history. He began his collaboration with Sondheim not long after *The Sound of Music* concluded its three and a half years in the Broadway Alps. Sondheim's most recent show had staggered through nine performances; Rodgers's most recent, *No Strings*, cantered through 580. The collaboration was asymmetric. The material—American spinster in Venice swept off her feet by Italian hunk—was clichéd. For Sondheim, the experience was disastrous.

There's a familiar quotation from Richard Rodgers about Sondheim, often invoked when people discuss *Do I Hear a Waltz?*: "I watched him grow from an attractive little boy to a monster." The context, however, suggests it was said in a jocular fashion. Four months before the show opened, Sondheim and Rodgers were sitting among the Renoirs and Matisses in Rodgers's apartment on Park Avenue, talking to a reporter from the *Times*. Recalling having met the twelve-year-old Sondheim when he and Hammerstein were completing *Oklahoma!*, Rodgers made the statement, the reporter wrote, "with a mischievous gleam." Sondheim showed no displeasure. The headline on the piece read, "Long Time Friends Aim for Broadway Early Next Year."[47]

But Rodgers's impish gleam could not be long sustained. One particular incident embodies their entire collaborative experience. Sondheim had concocted notably acidulous and ironic lyrics for a lively, sparkling Rodgers melody, "We're Gonna Be All Right." The song could have served as an early test run for the stinging ironies of *Company*. A married couple invokes the horrors of their union as they chirp their way through the buoyant tune behind perky smiles and good cheer. It's a jaunty chronicle of infidelity, excessive drinking, the husband's occasional homosexuality, the wife's intellectual torpor, and the way they manage to hide it all:

Bury everything, learn to smile.
Happy couples can stay in style
Just by practicing charm.
All is well,
Least as far as their friends can tell.
Please ignore the peculiar smell,
There's no cause for alarm.
Mildew
Will do
Harm.

Sondheim, Laurents, and Mary Rodgers all said Dick loved the lyric. Usually chilly, at best formally accommodating, Rodgers was so pleased he embraced Sondheim and smiled broadly when he heard it for the first time. The next day, however, he tore up the lyric sheet in front of the cast and called it "a piece of shit." His even chillier and far less accommodating wife, Dorothy, had weighed in, and wouldn't have had to spell out the parallels to their own marriage embedded—and exposed—in the song (the homosexuality excepted). A disemboweled version ended up in the show, completely stripped of its wit, its ironies, its very meaning.[48]

Rodgers felt no better about the collaboration with Sondheim and Laurents than they did. "The more we worked on the show, the more estranged I became from both writers," he wrote. "Any suggestions I made were promptly rejected, as if by pre-arrangement. *Do I Hear a Waltz?* was not a satisfying experience." When Rodgers, as producer, closed the show after a tepid six-month run (for a Rodgers show, an abysmal failure), Laurents accused him of acting "out of personal vindictiveness." Sondheim, who had taken to calling Rodgers "Godzilla" behind his back, said the show "deserved to fail."[49]

But unlike *Anyone Can Whistle*, this failure, for Sondheim, was a huge success. Battered and buffeted by the experience, he was liberated. He vowed that he would never again write lyrics only, even turning down the chance to work with Jule Styne again, on *Funny Girl.* Never again would he take on a project out of a sense of obligation, or because of the prospect of a financial killing. "I was brought up on the swiftness and insubstantiality of musicals," he said—and now made his break from the insubstantial with shows devoted to urban alienation, shattered dreams, arrant revenge, the hallucinatory nightmares of childhood, presidential assassinations, and obsessive love. After *Do I Hear a Waltz?*, Sondheim was a free man.[50]

He began his liberation by breaking his ties to Laurents, over lunch at the Russian Tea Room. "There was no leading up, no chitchat, no warning," Laurents wrote in a postscript to his memoirs. "Well-rehearsed, he went right into it: I was too strong an influence and he had to stop seeing me, our friendship was kaput." Sondheim swerved away from the stage for a moment to collaborate with the playwright James Goldman on *Evening Primrose*, a one-act television drama-with-music that included two of Sondheim's most haunting songs ("Take Me to the World" and "I Remember"). Both arise naturally from a plot about a young man who willingly removes himself from society; they drew so little attention that neither would be released on a studio recording for another thirteen years. For a brief time he suspended his new rule about not writing lyrics for someone else's music, joining Bernstein, Robbins, and playwright John Guare on a futile adaptation of Bertolt Brecht's *The Exception and the*

Rule, a polemic about class warfare that was suited to Sondheim only in the sense that the material was so unlikely. He hated Brecht's work in general, which didn't help. He was also not charmed by Robbins doing a Robbins: One day during auditions, he excused himself and, without a word to any of his collaborators, took a cab to the airport and simply disappeared. Out of this ill-considered adventure came eight Bernstein-Sondheim songs, none of them ever recorded, all of them secured under legal lock and key by the Sondheim estate. (Three years later, Bernstein reused some of his music from the Brecht show in the "Prefatory Prayers" section of his *Mass*.) "Both of us were thrilled" when the Brecht show fell through, Guare remembered. "The only thing I missed was those late-night talks with Steve."[51]

Do I Hear a Waltz? closed on September 25, 1965. The only new Sondheim work the world would hear until April 15, 1970, were the four songs from the one-night, here-and-gone telecast of *Evening Primrose* in 1966. On his fortieth birthday, his entire body of recorded music consisted of twenty-eight songs from the cast albums of *A Funny Thing Happened on the Way to the Forum* and *Anyone Can Whistle*. Then came the first preview of *Company*, and Sondheim's life changed utterly and forever. So did the history of the American musical.

4

The Hal-Steve Thing, Part 1

They met when Sondheim was not yet twenty. A few years later, while Sondheim was writing the stillborn *Saturday Night*, Hal Prince, at twenty-six, was already a successful Broadway producer. His first hit was *The Pajama Game*, and along the road that led to their eventual partnership were two of Sondheim's own initial successes: *West Side Story*, which Prince produced with his partner Robert E. Griffith; and, after Griffith's death, *A Funny Thing Happened on the Way to the Forum.* Following the disappointment of *Anyone Can Whistle* in 1964 (produced by Kermit Bloomgarden), Sondheim began to talk with Prince about two new musicals. One would become *Company*, the other *Follies.* During the late '60s, as both shows moved from concept to opening night, Prince's theatrical vision and Sondheim's creative imagination became as connected as language is to thought.

Hal Prince's attention span was short, his patience limited.

He vibrated with energy, with ideas, with ambition. He was as decisive as Sondheim was ambivalent, as dynamic as Sondheim was passive. Sondheim avoided confrontation; Prince didn't relish it (except sometimes), but neither did he flinch when he encountered resistance or disagreement. Sondheim might back off during what he called Prince's "wilder manic moments," but he didn't hesitate to let Prince fight his battles for him. They were made for each other.[1]

Early on, their lives were as intertwined as their work would become. "He was always around," Judy Prince said of Sondheim. Hal Prince referred to the three of them as "the triumvirate." Sondheim even taught Prince to drive. When Prince was thinking of directing the first production of Lorraine Hansberry's *The Sign in Sidney Brustein's Window*, Sondheim told him the play was clichéd and "hopeless"; Prince ended up withdrawing from the production. When Sondheim was considering the invitation to write some new songs for a revival of the musical *Candide* by Leonard Bernstein and Lillian Hellman, he relied on Prince's guarantee to make certain that neither Bernstein nor Hellman would interfere.[2]

For decades, friends and colleagues outside the triumvirate puzzled over the nature of the three-way relationship. Witnessing them during the development of *Pacific Overtures* in the mid-1970s, librettist John Weidman felt discombobulated. "My head was spinning around trying to figure out how they were all connected to one another," he recalled. As Judy was Sondheim's muse, Hal was part coach, part drillmaster, part handler. James Lapine, discussing what he called "the Hal-Steve thing," said, "I think Hal dominated Steve and Steve liked that. I think he needed that. It was like, 'Steve, go to your room and write.'" Sondheim would probably have agreed with Lapine's assessment. "The minute after I leave a meeting with Hal, or get off the phone with him," he said in 2002, "I can't wait to get to the piano or to writing. He inspires you." After both men were dead, Lin-Manuel Miranda said Sondheim called Prince "The Enthusiasm."[3]

It was during the run of *Forum* that Prince stepped from his producer's chair and made his debut as a Broadway director. His first big success in that role came a year later, with *She Loves Me*, words and music by Sheldon Harnick and Jerry Bock, book by Joe Masteroff, and a pair of Tony nominations for Prince, for best producer and best director. His reputation rocketed to a completely different level three years later with the revolutionary *Cabaret*, music and lyrics by Sondheim's friends John Kander and Fred Ebb, book again by Masteroff. The tone and setting—debauchery, debasement, the rise of Nazism—couldn't have been more distant from Broadway convention. It even had a downbeat ending. And, staged with breathtaking audacity by Prince, it ran for 1,165 Tony-winning performances.

It was time for Hal and Steve to begin a full collaboration.

In the winter of 1966, when Sondheim appeared on the game show *Password* with Lee Remick, the show's host, Allen Ludden, asked if he'd been working on a new musical. "Yessir," he replied, "*The Girls Upstairs*, with a book by James Goldman." That show, later renamed *Follies*, wouldn't make it to the stage for another five years. Along the way, Sondheim spun his wheels on the Brecht collaboration and briefly considered doing a musical based on the Fellini film *8½*. At the urging of Gloria Steinem, he agreed to construct a frequent (and notably diabolical) cryptic crossword puzzle for the soon-to-be-launched *New York* magazine; it was a rechanneling of the creative energy he'd long expended by creating puzzles for his friends. Arthur Laurents tried to pressure him into collaborating on a revival of *Anyone Can Whistle*, barely five years after the fatal crash of its original production, but Sondheim would have none of it. For one thing, he had come to see the show as ill-conceived and pretentious; for another, Laurents's "incoherence and hysteria" while trying to persuade him to go ahead with the revival led him to tell Prince, "I think Arthur is pushing it in order to make the next few months of my life impossible."[4]

Then Prince had an unlikely idea—taking a series of eleven short plays written by an acquaintance of Sondheim's and somehow turning them into a musical whose main character was an unattached man in modern New York. It had no plot. And the plays were mostly about married life, written by the actor George Furth, who was himself an unmarried gay man and who had never written a play. Sondheim was surprised by the idea but attracted to it in Sondheimian fashion: *A Funny Thing Happened on the Way to the Forum*, a fairly conventional musical for its time, had been his big success; *Anyone Can Whistle*, an experimental satire, had been a catastrophic flop. So, after Prince explained what he had in mind, Sondheim decided that another experimental satire, based on a libretto by a writer both untried and unknown, with no discernible narrative structure, would be just the thing.

But Sondheim and Goldman had already completed a second version of *The Girls Upstairs.* The show's forthcoming Broadway run had been announced. And even as he began to work on *Company*, Sondheim didn't know whether it was possible to extricate himself from commitments he'd made to Stuart Ostrow, the producer of *The Girls Upstairs.* Prince decided he would step in to produce and direct both shows—so long as *Company*, which he had initiated, came first. Then he made the extrication possible by having Sondheim sign a letter—"dictated word for word by me"—to Ostrow, demanding his freedom.[5]

This was the embodiment of a pattern that would recur throughout their astonishingly productive professional relationship: Prince fighting Sondheim's battles for him, while simultaneously serving as the motivating force behind the work they did together. Two of Sondheim's later collaborators, John Weidman and James Lapine, both believed that Sondheim's chronic self-doubt and indecision required Prince's forcefulness. While they were working on *Bounce* in the early 2000s, Prince enjoyed telling Weidman how he could manipulate Sondheim: "'I'm going to get him to do such-and-such,'" Weidman recalled him saying. "'Just watch!'"[6]

Prince's manipulations—and his prodding, and his decisiveness, and the sheer force of his kinetic personality—were necessary for getting the Sondheim-Furth collaboration to work. Furth was by nature fretful, frantic, and impatient. That this, his first effort as a writer, was actually heading toward Broadway may have been thrilling, but Sondheim's indecision about putting aside *The Girls Upstairs* had intensified Furth's extravagant anxiety. He all but begged Prince to intervene; he felt, he said, "panic stricken." Citing his own mental health, Furth told Prince, "I can't go on." At one point in the summer of 1969, Sondheim was ready to drop out of the project altogether. Then Prince-as-Sondheim dictated that letter to the producer of *The Girls Upstairs*, telling him he was stepping away from the project to write the music and lyrics for *Company*—and, because he was about to board the S.S. *France* for a transatlantic trip, he couldn't be reached. It was an easy way to hide.[7]

Then work began anew on what Prince would describe, just before its opening, as a show about "a man in our society who doesn't have to engage."[8]

The months before a Sondheim show began rehearsals were rarely happy ones. "The wheels that I hate have started rolling: casting, meetings, designs, orchestrations, all the compromises that make me wish I were in the dress business," he once told Jerome Robbins. In this instance, his collaborator problems supervened. Although Furth and Sondheim ultimately developed a close friendship, and a working relationship smooth enough to be renewed a decade later for *Merrily We Roll Along*, it did not start well. Sondheim's chronic pre-show self-doubt was aggravated by Furth's own disquiet. But when they finally got down to work, Furth presented an entirely new and especially exasperating problem: Sondheim always depended on a collaboration so intimate that he could call his librettist late at night to seek a reaction to a new song or to a lyric idea he was developing. In this regard, Sondheim considered Furth hopeless. "I was finally reduced to calling George last night to check out some lyric ideas," he told Prince, "and he was, as I expected, sweet and uncomprehending." It was even worse with music, as Furth was about as musical as a sofa. He never listened to music, and didn't even own a device on which music could be played.[9]

Inevitably, Sondheim turned toward Prince. As well, and as long, as they had known each other, it was this, their first creative collaboration, that forged the bond that would endure through the six defining shows they worked on together over the next decade. From *Company* forward, Prince tightened his grip on Sondheim's vulnerabilities. He was unquestionably the show's "muscle." In every Broadway production, wrote William Goldman (James's younger brother) in *The Season*, "someone has to dominate." The world would come to know the great successes arising from the Sondheim-Prince partnership as Sondheim shows, which was accurate to some extent; the music and lyrics did belong entirely to Sondheim. But in a larger sense, each of their collaborations was a Prince show. In fact, Sondheim didn't write a single note, much less a song, for *Company* until he saw the model of the set Prince and designer Boris Aronson had devised. For all but one of their joint efforts from *Company* through *Merrily We Roll Along*, the initiating idea and much of its expansion into a coherent show started with Prince.[10]

In Furth's eleven one-act plays, Prince perceived the germ of a show centered on the conflicting (and often simultaneous) joys and difficulties of marriage. Furth had written the plays for the actress Kim Stanley, who would have played all the women in it.* Then Sondheim, Furth, and Prince expanded on two of Furth's original one-acts, tossed out the other nine, created a main character (originally a woman, later a man, and fifty years later a woman again) who would blend what was essentially a series of sketches—a revue—into a coherent whole. They also added an entirely new character whom Furth specifically based on his friend Elaine Stritch—a character who elicited from Sondheim what would become the show's best-known song, "The Ladies Who Lunch." The show's title became *Threes*, and then changed to *My Married Friends* (which provided a useful hook for the climactic moment in the show's title song), before they settled on *Company*. Furth, Sondheim, and Prince considered making Bobby, the main character, gay. But (according to Furth's contemporaneous notes) the idea was quickly dismissed. "Should the man be a homosexual?," he wrote. "No, we say. If he is trapped and cannot do something positive, then that is one play. But here, if he can but doesn't, that is another play." It was 1970, when a gay character would truly have been trapped.[11]

Company (not to mention Sondheim's career) was further enhanced by a sort of package deal. He admired the pop songwriter Burt Bacharach, whose sole Broadway musical, *Promises, Promises*, was well into its three-year run as *Company* was ramping up. Prince and Sondheim recruited the *Promises* choreographer Michael Bennett, then only twenty-six, and the show's

* A decade later, when there was talk of a Hollywood adaptation, Furth had some genuinely imaginative casting ideas: each couple would be played by an actual married couple (Lee Majors and Farrah Fawcett-Majors, Richard Benjamin and Paula Prentiss, et cetera), and the unattached man around whom the movie revolves would be played by Warren Beatty. A bizarre casting decision that actually came to pass during the last six months of *Company*'s original run was the hiring of the aging Hollywood sex bomb Jane Russell as Elaine Stritch's replacement. It was the only time she ever performed on Broadway.

orchestrator, Jonathan Tunick, who was thirty. Tunick and Sondheim had met before, after Sondheim was impressed by a show in which Tunick made a six-piece band sound like a full orchestra.

What became the lengthiest and sturdiest collaboration in Sondheim's entire career began in 1969 when he and Tunick had dinner at an Italian restaurant on Second Avenue. After the two men sat down, Sondheim ordered a Scotch, and so did Tunick. Sondheim ordered another Scotch, and so did Tunick. But, fearful of saying something foolish in front of someone he so admired, Tunick demurred at Scotch number three. And four. And however many more Sondheim consumed. "That's all right," Sondheim said, "no one can keep up with me. I just love to drink!" Tunick told this story at a private memorial service for Sondheim fifty-three years later, and when he quoted that last comment, he said it was "the first of many understatements" his friend uttered over the length of their relationship. Sondheim's friends and colleagues erupted in laughter. It was the sound of recognition.

By any definition of the word, Stephen Sondheim was an alcoholic. When the singer and pianist Michael Feinstein said as much on a New York radio broadcast about a year after Sondheim's death, some of the fans who populate the various websites, Facebook pages, and Reddit chats devoted to Sondheim and his work responded with dismay and denial; they were unfamiliar with what his friends and collaborators knew so well. "He just drank, beginning in the afternoon," James Lapine said. "Shots of vodka that he sipped as we worked." Lapine also said, "He was an alcoholic. No question about it." Sondheim's friend Cynthia O'Neal, who knew him from the time of *West Side Story* until their last conversation a few days before his death, simply said, "He was an addict."[12]

Not only an addict, but beyond reform. John Guare, Sondheim's collaborator on the failed effort to turn the Brecht play into a musical, tried to get him to join Alcoholics Anonymous, as did George Furth. After his first meeting, Sondheim told Furth that AA was "a place for angry, lonely people to go." He never returned. At the first public performance of *Follies*, colleagues saw him wandering the rear of the theater, a bottle of bourbon in hand. He'd drink his way through opening nights, he said, "because of the tension," often retreating to a limo outside the theater during intermission to drink with friends. The first time he met producer André Bishop, who nurtured *Sunday in the Park with George* until it was ready for Broadway in 1984, Sondheim drank "a million martinis." He was in his eighties when the show had its French premiere, and his Parisian producer watched him guzzle seven drinks during an evening meeting in his office.[13]

While working, Sondheim would drink to loosen up, to break through his inhibitions in an effort to combat what he called his "mental censors." On the road, the private shot glass of vodka during work sessions could be augmented by long sessions at the hotel bar. John Weidman said that when *Pacific Overtures* was in its out-of-town tryouts Sondheim would do his rewriting in the bar, and write until—and this was Sondheim's own expression—he was "sodden."[14]

What astonished nearly everyone close to him was how little the drinking appeared to alter his demeanor. Friends evaluated his vast capacity for liquor with a combination of dismay and something like awe. Lapine said, "I never saw him intoxicated as we were working; he had an amazing metabolism." Before visiting Michael Feinstein's house one evening, Sondheim got a call from Feinstein's secretary, who asked him what he wanted for dinner. According to Feinstein, he replied, "vodka, vodka, and more vodka!" People who didn't know him well could be alarmed by the quantity he consumed and simultaneously astonished by what one dinner guest—Adam Moss, editor of *New York* magazine—called his "extreme control."[15]

But not always, especially as he got older. When Sondheim was in his sixties, John Guare encountered him in a moment of such crippling despair that he was curled up on the floor in a fetal position, clutching the bottle he'd been drinking from. Around the same time, Mary Rodgers noted how his "drunk highs" would lead to wildly enthusiastic behavior that he wouldn't remember in the morning. In Sondheim's seventies, John Weidman once saw him so inebriated at a cast party that he had to be helped down a flight of stairs by two people, one holding on to him on each side.[16]

It would be easy to say Sondheim drank so much because of psychological demons, or his relationship with his mother, or with women, or with producers, or investors, or critics. Robert Hurwitz, who supervised the recording of ten Sondheim cast albums for Nonesuch Records, thought "his incredible gifts enabled him to use the pain in his life" in his work. Yet, he added, "millions of people" endured similar pains, "but very few could write *Sunday in the Park with George* or *Company*."[17]

Maybe the drinking (along with his periodic engagements with cocaine and a long-standing attachment to marijuana) truly helped him do that. Only Sondheim himself could say whether it was worth it, but one suspects he would have said it was.

Prince described the character of Bobby—"the beige hole at the center" of *Company*—as "a bit of George, a bit of Steve, a bit of me." The bits of Prince and Furth may have been hiding somewhere in the fog of Bobby's anomie, but shards of Sondheim were glaringly present: the uncommitted man at the heart of his social circle, a man fearful of attachment and perpetually ambivalent. Because Sondheim knew nothing about marriage from his own experience, he interviewed Mary Rodgers at length for her insights. (Among the show's entire creative team, only Prince and designer Boris Aronson were married.) Because Sondheim knew everything about the absence of commitment and the evanescence of resolve—he was engaged, he said at the time, in "a constant series" of relationships—he likely wouldn't have felt the need to study those things at all. "Ambivalence is my favorite thing to write about," he once said, "because it's the way I feel, and I think the way most people feel." This ambivalence was expressed most viscerally in "Sorry-Grateful" and "Marry Me a Little," two songs that are well summarized by their titles. To Rodgers, who knew him as well as anybody, the role of Bobby was close to autobiography. Over the years, pressed as he was by friends, reporters, and others to acknowledge this, the most he would concede was that Furth had picked as his subject "a world that I understood." Judy Prince found the characters and their circumstances—married couples attached to an uncommitted friend—so familiar that she said, "I really expected it to open in our living room."[18]

Her husband may have thought that was a notion too close to the depressing reality: the show's advance ticket sales amounted to a very thin $175,000. (Prince's most recent production, *Zorba*, had opened eighteen months earlier with $2 million already in the bank.) But when the curtain came up at the Alvin Theatre on April 26, 1970, Prince's instincts, amplified by Sondheim's talent, were proven right. *Company*'s pallid advance indicated how low were the expectations for a show with music and lyrics by a man who had had only one success as a composer, eight years earlier. Clive Barnes's review in the *New York Times* was snippy and dismissive ("the show will be particularly popular with tourists"). But Walter Kerr, his colleague at the *Times*, was completely undone: He called it "brilliantly designed, beautifully staged, sizzlingly performed," and said "Sondheim has never written a more sophisticated, more pertinent, or—this is the surprising thing in the circumstances—more melodious score; and the lyrics are every bit as good." But: Kerr also called it "misanthropic," "jaundiced," "middle-aged mean," and said it "stare[s] contemporary society straight in the eye before spitting in it."

With Hal Prince on the opening night of *Company*, 1970. Sondheim later said that without Prince, "I would not have been possible."

Mike Nichols told Prince that in five years, people would insist that the *Times* had loved it.[19]

There were raves in *Newsweek*, *Time*, and elsewhere, but Douglas Watt of the *Daily News* (who happened to think the show was great) covered both sides of the argument when he characterized *Company*'s impact as "a shock wave." Broadway had never encountered anything quite like it: No overture, no chorus, and—centrally—a relentless storm of irony replacing any hint of sentiment. Larry Kert, who had played Tony in *West Side Story* and stepped into *Company* as Bobby early in the run, said the show revealed "the acid in the sponge cake." Sondheim said his own goal for the show was to have the audience "sit for two hours screaming their heads off with laughter and then go home and not be able to sleep." If Oscar Hammerstein had been the tree, this apple had landed in a different universe. Richard Rodgers noted this in a surprisingly positive letter to Sondheim, in which he praised both the music and the lyrics and added, "I think *Company* is to cynicism what *The Sound of Music* is to sentimentality." From Rodgers, there could have been no higher compliment.[20]

Alan Jay Lerner, the lyricist of *Brigadoon*, *My Fair Lady*, and *Camelot*, reacted to the show more personally. When he came home from the opening night performance, he broke into tears and told his wife, "My way of writing musicals is over."[21]

When *Company* was in its pre-Broadway tryout in Boston, a reviewer for *Variety* had savaged it (using language unhappily reflective of the era): the show "as it stands now [is] for ladies' matinees, homos, and misogynists." It was in Boston that Prince determined that the closing number, a bitter song for Bobby called "Happily Ever After," was a "downer" that would displease audiences. Sondheim said that would be "perfectly fine with me, but not for [Prince]." Just before *Company* decamped for New York, Prince demanded a more positive closing number. Written under the pressures of an impossible deadline, "Being Alive" came out of Sondheim so easily it was almost as if it had been sitting inside him, waiting for its opportunity. It was an anthem for Bobby that suggested that this particular unattached man knew he needed to find someone to make his life complete—but couldn't quite get there. The song was "positive" in that it suggested the character's potential for transformation, but cautionary in its wavering resolve. Sondheim interpolated into the song a spoken line from Furth's script that, he said, gave him chills: "Blow out your candles, Robert, and make a wish. *Want* something. Want *some* thing!"[22]

Sondheim's insistence that *Company* was not autobiographical led him to grow touchy and resentful when people suggested otherwise. Let's take him at his word. But let's also conduct an exercise of reverse engineering: consider an unmoored character without a meaningful one-to-one relationship; who is beloved by (yet often detached from) his friends; who is made uneasy by what he perceives as pressure to commit; and who finally does want something that's missing from his life, namely someone who could *crowd me with love* and *force me to care*. That character may indeed not be Stephen Sondheim. But he's awfully close to a mirror image.

Company broke through all sorts of musical theater barriers, pushing forward with its subject matter, its brittle tone, its abstracted structure. It also, for the first time, earned Sondheim meaningful notice as a composer. From *West Side Story* and *Gypsy* through *Forum* and, to a lesser degree, *Anyone Can Whistle*, he had been known as a deft and original lyricist. For the latter two shows, he had essentially been regarded—and often dismissed—as a lyricist trying to write music. Always thinking of himself as a composer who just happens to write lyrics—"There's a great joy in writing music," he said, but "there's no joy in writing lyrics"—he confronted the indifference his music elicited with a range of emotions that ran from irritability to petulance to truculence.[23]

Oddly, the musical roots of *Company* were embedded, at least in his own conception, in the pop/rock music of the day. In addition to the harmonic innovations of *Promises, Promises,* he appreciated Bacharach's polished but unconventional rhythmic style and admired the show's use of electric instruments, as well as an off-stage line of backup singers; hence the recruitment of Tunick, who included both in his *Company* orchestrations. When he was forty-three, Sondheim told an interviewer that "there's no such thing as being too old to write rock," and when he was fifty-nine he took a whack at it, writing a variant of rap for the witch in *Into the Woods* (*He was robbing me,/Raping me,/Rooting through my rutabaga,/Raiding my arugula* . . .). But his belief that some of the *Company* music was connected to rock was largely delusional.[24]

That may have had something to do with his generalized estrangement from the popular music of the era. He admired the Beatles greatly, particularly for their harmonic imagination, and once asked the lyricist-composer-playwright Leslie Bricusse to introduce him to them. They met at a raucous after-hours club in London where, Bricusse recalled, "we sat there deafened and smiling stupidly at one another, mouthing unheard niceties." Sondheim considered Paul McCartney the group's major talent, but lamented the decline he perceived in McCartney's music after the Beatles broke up. He admired much of Randy Newman's music, and nearly all of Laura Nyro's—as late as 2005, a colleague said, he was still "giving his Laura Nyro speech." Her deft key-changes and her daring willingness to alter an established musical phrase in mid-song attracted him greatly, as did many of her lyrics. Nyro's way of rocking back and forth between two chords in songs like "Stoned Soul Picnic" was very similar to what Sondheim did in *Company* with the first twenty bars of "Barcelona" (through *Put your wings down*) and parts of "Someone Is Waiting." The two of them once spent an afternoon at his house listening to and dissecting Alban Berg's modernist opera *Lulu*. A decade later he embraced the Talking Heads, and after that Radiohead. But he disdained Joni Mitchell, and in 1973 said Bob Dylan "bores me to death, and I find him pompous."[25]

Sondheim considered the popular music of the 1970s and beyond to be about the singer and not about the song; musical theater songs, he felt, were necessarily the opposite. (The same principle, he said, impeded his appreciation of opera, where the soprano is venerated more than the aria she sings.) The rise of the singer-songwriter was partly responsible for this, as was a promotion machine custom-built for performances in vast arenas, where individual songs hardly had the chance to stand on their own musical feet. Sondheim wrote—*always* wrote—for specific characters in specific situations; only once, in *Road Show*, from 2008, did he pull out a "trunk song" that had been cut from an earlier show and drop it into a new one. This focus on specific characters and their circumstances is one of the chief reasons that, except for "Send in the Clowns" from *A Little Night Music*, his music never became widely popular outside its original context.

"Ladies Who Lunch," which has at least become a fixture in what remains of the world of cabaret performance, was written for the character of Joanne in *Company*, and expressly for Joanne as played by Elaine Stritch. It embodied a heightened form of Sondheim's compositional approach: writing for a specific character, as played by a specific actor, just as "Rose's Turn" had been shaped to suit Ethel Merman's voice and her personality in *Gypsy*, or as "Send in the Clowns" would be fashioned for Glynis Johns in *A Little Night Music*.

Stritch's sardonic mien, her weary detachment, and her booze-ravaged voice (the song's original title was "Drinking Song") suited the *character* of Joanne the way a growl suits an angry hound. But Sondheim's inspiration for the *subject* of the song—those ladies of its title—came from Foxy. After his mother, newly widowed, moved back to New York from Los Angeles, her life as an interior designer gradually metamorphosed into her life as a lady who lunched, specifically at the 21 Club. Her usual companion was the elegant Molly Berns, an imposing woman whose husband Charlie had been one of 21's original owners; the rest of their crowd included fashion industry notables (Jo Copeland, Mollie Parnis) and various film stars of an earlier era (Colleen Moore, Glenda Farrell) "who married well," Sondheim said. "Picturing them, the phrase 'the ladies who lunch' just popped into my head."[26]

His acidulous disdain for his mother and her world was a part of him, packed in a deeply embedded arsenal of disapproval, disgust, and mockery. The song gave him an opportunity to cre-

The Ladies Who Lunch, at the 21 Club, circa 1948: Foxy Sondheim, unidentified, Molly Berns. Twenty-four years later, they provoked a song.

ate a memorable character delivering a potent message built on imagery that evoked a world much of his audience knew—or, almost as likely, a world they inhabited themselves: *A matinee, a Pinter play,/Perhaps a piece of Mahler's—/I'll drink to that.* The famous story about Stritch thinking "a piece of Mahler's" referred to a pastry is no invention. Sondheim told Stritch's biographer, Alexandra Jacobs, that she had said, "What is this? A *schnecken*?" As Stritch remembered it, "I thought it was referring to a bakery in New York, some sweet treat or something.

He looked at me with those eyes that can drill right fucking through you and told me it referred to 'a very significant composer.' " Then, she said, he simply walked away.[27]

Foxy apparently didn't mind the song's explicit condemnation of her world. "My mother doesn't really understand my shows," her son told an interviewer. "But she understands my notices." On March 28, 1971, when *Company* was eleven months into its eventual run of 705 performances, the forty-one-year-old Stephen Sondheim stepped onto the stage at the Palace Theatre to accept the Tony Award for best score of a musical. His hair was a mess, as if "comb[ed] with a rake," as Foxy once described it. His sideburns nearly reached his chin line, and throughout his fairly brief speech he either scratched the back of his neck, fiddled with his tie, or rubbed his chin. His characteristic lopsided smile made him appear younger than he was—it gave him the look of the wise-guy cut-up in a high school class—and along with his various nervous tics made him appear less comfortable than he probably was. He was, in fact, comfortable enough to tell the audience, "I never thought very highly of awards. But I must say, it's awfully nice to win one."[28]

Company had run the table—best musical, best score, best director (Prince), best book (Furth), best scenic design (Boris Aronson). The bitterness of eight years before, when Sondheim had been virtually the only participant in the creation of *Forum* not invited to the podium, was finally behind him. And less than a week later, as *Company* was selling out the Alvin on the strength of its Tonys sweep, *Follies* opened just around the corner at the Winter Garden.

Hal Prince had been true to his word—*Company* first, *Follies* next. During the run of *Company*, Sondheim joined the Princes at their house on Majorca to work on the show. Sondheim invited Foxy to stay with him in the house next door.

This shouldn't seem as odd as it probably does, as there was nothing about Stephen Sondheim's relationship with his mother that wasn't odd. They frequently exchanged gifts. She was there as his guest for all of his shows. He supported her financially. She decorated his house on East Forty-ninth Street, and she gave him a keychain suspended from a charmlike book with the names of almost all of his shows inscribed in it—except for *Anyone Can Whistle.* She left that one out, she said, because it was a flop.[29]

Like so many others, Hal and Judy Prince enjoyed Foxy's company—at least until (according to Sondheim's version of the tale) a fake suicide attempt that he considered a deliberate act of malice directed toward him. As Sondheim explained it to Meryle Secrest, the local doctor feared that suicide might be on her mind and had given her a few of the sleeping pills she had requested, scattered through a bottle otherwise filled with placebos. She swallowed the pills, soon recovered, and according to Sondheim said, "Oh, Steve, I'm so grateful-sorry!" Sondheim found it hilarious that she had butchered the title of "Sorry-Grateful" from *Company*. He ran next door to the Princes' and said, "I have got to tell you the most screamingly funny thing you have ever heard in your life. She fucked it up!" Hal and Judy were "rolling on the floor" with laughter. "Can you imagine," he continued, "she'd rehearsed this whole thing to make me feel terrible, and she'd screwed up the line!"

Nowhere in Sondheim's telling did he consider that if she had indeed taken the pills without knowing they were fake, she likely would have died. That, too, might have been construed as an act of malice directed at her son, but of a very different sort.

Sondheim often said that each of his shows had an underlying metaphor—something he and his collaborators never state outright, but that shapes the entire work. For *Company*, it had been Manhattan itself, which was specifically present in Aronson's metallic, impersonal, and impressively vertical set, and in the song "Another Hundred People." But in all the other songs and scenes it was visible only to the creators. As Sondheim explained, they considered Manhattan "the handiest locale for the inhumanity of contemporary living and the difficulties in making relationships."[30]

The metaphor for *Follies* was the crash of the American dream. Until the end of World War II, he said in an interview in 1985, "America was the good guy, everything was idealistic and hopeful and America was going to lead the world. Now you see the country is a riot of national guilt, the dream has collapsed, everything has turned to rubble underfoot." Elsewhere, he said "the point of the show is that you should use the past to look into the future." As T. E. Kalem put it in his review in *Time*, it was "the first Proustian musical." Kalem also wrote, "The frontier of the American musical theater is wherever Harold Prince and Stephen Sondheim are." Sondheim himself recognized that *Follies* was "a dour, experimental work. The nun doesn't escape from the Nazis in the end."[31]

For the main characters—two former chorus girls from a prewar revue based on the Ziegfeld Follies, and their husbands—their past was a time of innocence and delight, and their future, at show's end, looked as bleak as Antarctica. It hardly seemed a sensible premise for a Broadway musical, and the way Prince approached it as producer and co-director (with Michael Bennett) may have been even less sensible, at least financially. Just to break even, *Follies* would have had to run eight months with the Winter Garden Theatre filled to capacity. It did manage to last nearly twice as long as that, but for much of the run it sustained itself on sharply discounted tickets and houses sometimes more nearly half empty than half full. Reviews were mixed, some of them openly hostile (Walter Kerr found it "exhausting" and "tedious," while his *Times* colleague Clive Barnes praised the lyrics while assaulting the music for "sending shivers of indifference up your spine.") The limp applause for each number had to compete with the sound of the audience's coughing and foot-shuffling. The sounds emanating from the investors after it closed were doubtless even more depressing: like those who had bet on *Anyone Can Whistle*, they lost every penny they had put into it.

Those pennies had been expended, eight times a week, on a production that was like none that Broadway had seen in decades: a cast of forty-nine actors, an orchestra of thirty musicians, a backstage crew of twenty-eight, and a series of sets and costumes so lavish they would have shamed Florenz Ziegfeld and his original Follies. The grandeur of the production was nothing short of dazzling, and it was impossible to imagine that a producer as shrewd as Prince would have spent that kind of money on a show that he didn't believe in deeply. But there are times when belief and money and talent will not add up. Jonathan Tunick told friends that "if they missed [it], they'd never get another chance—you'll never see that kind of staging again."[32]

Sondheim's work for the show was equally elaborate. Most of the songs were pastiches based on the work of songwriters of the interwar period, put through his own particular filter. *Follies* was "a chance for me to pay homage without attitude to the genre I loved," he wrote. "Without attitude" are the operative words in that comment. No irony, no sarcasm, no implicit commentary on the composers whose styles he largely admired and, in *Follies*, thoroughly exploited. Here were Sondheimized versions of eleven composers and twelve lyricists, including Irving Berlin ("Beautiful Girls"), Rudolf Friml ("One More Kiss"), George Gershwin ("Losing My Mind"), Cole Porter ("Ah! Paris!"), and Harold Arlen ("I'm Still Here"). Arlen was a special Sondheim favorite. He considered his music "a thrill to hear and a pleasure to steal." Once again, Sondheim won the Tony for Best Score. (As co-director, Prince won again as well, as did Boris Aronson for his set.) But it took nearly fifteen years for the world to realize just how magnificent the score was. The original cast album, produced by a tightfisted Capitol Records, dropped some songs, abridged others, and generally showed even less respect for the show than audiences had. The cost of mounting *Follies* precluded revivals. It didn't even have its British premiere until 1987.[33]

But its moment would come. Stefan Kanfer, writing in *Time* in 1971, said this: "Audiences interested only in nostalgia should not see *Follies* now. Let them wait until it is revived in, say, the mid-1980s. Then this imperfect but glittering production will be an item of genuine nostalgia—the show that turned the American musical around and pointed it forward."

Kanfer was precisely right, even about the timing. The next New York production of *Follies* landed in September 1985, provoking James Kirkwood to ask in the liner notes of the subsequent recording, "Where were you on the night of September 6?" It was like asking people if they remembered V-J Day, and in terms of its importance to Sondheim's place in the cultural firmament, it would be a similarly momentous event.

It's hard to find a number in *Follies* remotely as self-referential as "Anyone Can Whistle" or "Being Alive." But one could invoke Goethe's frequently quoted aphorism that "every author in some way portrays himself in his works, even if it be against his will," to find a vivid aspect of its creator's personality. In "Buddy's Blues," the vaudeville-style expression of emotional ambivalence is taken to ridiculous, but not inapt, extremes: *Don't come any closer/'cause you know how much I love you*, or *Go-away-I-need-you,/Come to me I'll kill you.* Far more important, though, the *Follies* songs reflect Sondheim's deep appreciation for not only his predecessors but, just as much, for the era they worked in (when "America was the good guy"). Simultaneously, it posed a challenge that was central to his life: Memory, he told Secrest, "has to be separated from fact," and "that's what *Follies* is all about." Of course, he also said that "Somebody else could come out and say, 'Oh my God, his mother was a saint and his father was a bastard.'" But "this doesn't matter," he declared. "It's the way I remember it."[34]

Setting aside the brief appearance of the historical figure Emma Goldman in *Assassins*, *Follies* has the distinction of including one of only three presumably Jewish characters in all of Sondheim's work: the impresario Dimitri Weismann—Jewish by name and inferentially by occupation, and off the stage for the rest of the night after a brief speech in the show's opening scene. (By name and occupation, Mr. Goldstone, from *Gypsy*, and Joe Josephson, from *Merrily We Roll Along*, have similar pedigrees.) The young people in *Saturday Night* could have been Jewish, but only because they lived in Brooklyn and spoke a form of Brooklynese that Sondheim said he believed to be Jewish. Besides, that show was created by Julius Epstein, who had completed the book by the time Sondheim came aboard.

Sondheim was hardly obliged to put substantial Jewish characters in his work, but it's nonetheless a minor oddity. Early in his career, identifiably Jewish characters and Jewish themes or settings were common (and lucrative) coin on Broadway. For context, consider *Pajama Game*, *Bye Bye Birdie*, *Milk and Honey*, *I Can Get It for You Wholesale*, *Fiddler on the Roof*, *Funny Girl*, and *Cabaret*. All but *Wholesale* (which introduced the world to Barbra Streisand) were big hits, and even though *Birdie*'s creators gave their main character a gentile name, both his profession (songwriter) and his mother (archetypally Jewish) could not possibly have fooled New York audiences. Even half a century later, similar audiences could appreciate the reality embedded in a comic song in *Spamalot* that repeatedly insists, *We won't succeed on Broadway/If we don't have any Jews.*

In 2022, the actor Etai Benson, who had played Paul in the gender-switched *Company* that was in previews when Sondheim died, found himself in conversation with Rabbi Samantha Frank, who was on the staff of the 92nd Street Y. Benson, who considered himself a "Jewish agnostic," said to Frank, "If I could pick a religion, it would be Sondheim." And thus was born a three-session program the two of them conducted at the Y, titled "Sondheim and the Torah." It was devoted to Jewish values, said Benson, that "conscious or not, find their way into his work." These included the power of intergenerational connection, and the Jewish ideal of *tikkun olam* (repairing the world), and various other concepts. Frank said "No One Is Alone," from *Into the Woods*, "is basically chapter one of the Torah." Her syllabus for the course included Sondheim lyrics annotated with connections she drew between his words and similar concepts in the Old Testament. In "Someone in a Tree," from *Pacific Overtures*, she found parallels with Exodus, Proverbs, and Psalms.[35]

But Benson's "conscious or not" is the key concept here, resolving into an undeniable *not*. Just as it is extremely unlikely that Sondheim consciously (or even unconsciously) chose to avoid Jewish characters or topics, there's little reason that he would have been drawn to them. He was raised in a completely secular atmosphere—no Hebrew school; no bar mitzvah; no synagogue membership; a mother who came from a line of Hasidic Jews but claimed, he said, that she was brought up in a convent in Rhode Island. At Williams, he either posed as a Quaker or truly believed he was one. Leonard Bernstein taught him how to pronounce *Yom Kippur*, and invited him to his first seder, and many to follow; he never attended another one after Bernstein's death in 1990. "My attitude toward Israel is the *New York Times*' attitude toward Israel," he once told an interviewer. "Whatever they tell me about it is what I believe. I became aware of Israel because Lenny cared so much about it." (When he met Bernstein, Sondheim was twenty-five and Israel had already been an independent nation for seven years.) Arthur Laurents told Meryle Secrest, "He was not a Jew when I met him" in 1953.

But fifty-four years later, Sondheim told an interviewer that he considered his Jewish identification "very deep."[36]

How could it not be? He was raised in the garment business and spent his entire adult life on Broadway: Culturally, at least, he was saturated in Jewishness and believed that the American perception of Jewishness as a religion (as distinct from an ethnicity) was a misapprehension. He once said he "grew up thinking the Jews were the world. Everybody was just Jewish. I went to summer camps where everyone was named Nussbaum." After he graduated from the very-not-Jewish Williams College (where a gentile friend once said to him, "Your father is a Seventh Avenue cloak-and-suiter. Of course you're Jewish!"), his adult world was even more Jewish than the one he'd known as a child. Among his many librettists, across eighteen separate shows from *Saturday Night* in 1954 through the posthumous *Here We Are* in 2023, only three were gentile: George Furth (*Company* and *Merrily We Roll Along);* Hugh Wheeler (*A Little Night Music* and *Sweeney Todd*); and David Ives (*Here We Are*). Yiddish popped up in his letters and speech as frequently as if he'd spent his career as a pastrami slicer in a deli: *shiddach*, *pisher*, *chazerei*, *kvetch*, *alte kocker*. There was a reason why the bugle-playing stripper Miss Mazeppa in *Gypsy* got her name from a poem by Lord Byron about a Ukrainian military hero: Sondheim needed a rhyme for *schlepper*.[37]

Another frequent Yiddishism in Sondheim's vocabulary was the word he used to describe the show that succeeded *Follies*. He was proud of *A Little Night Music*, he told Jules Feiffer, "But I don't know if I really like it. It's so damn *goyische*."[38]

Hal Prince did not disagree. *A Little Night Music*, he said, was his "gentile musical." Prince had produced *Pajama Game* and *Fiddler on the Roof*, and had produced and directed *Cabaret*. Along the way to *Night Music*, he had done shows with characters who were Greek (*Zorba*), Victorian Londoners (*Baker Street*), and Hungarians in between-the-wars Budapest (*She Loves Me*). But "unlike most of the shows I've done, I have nothing to hang on to [in *Night Music]* for my own Jewishness." He didn't say what purported Jewish traits were missing from *Night Music*—tradition? generational conflict? devotion? anxiety?—but this show was something entirely new for both men. "It seemed so well planned and so lacking in the kind of gut excitement that both Hal and Steve are generally drawn to," James Goldman said. "There is nothing disturbing about it."[39]

For Sondheim, it was the first show that he worked on that hadn't begun with someone else's idea. He and Prince, facing some commercial pressure after the investors' total loss on *Follies*, together decided to try a farce—upbeat, funny, unburdened of psychodynamics, unhindered by meaning of any kind. They had first discussed the notion years earlier; the fate of *Follies* insisted they return to it.

After they had failed to acquire the rights to their first choice of source material, Jean Anouilh's frothy *Ring Round the Moon*, Sondheim suggested *Smiles of a Summer Night*, Ingmar Bergman's uncharacteristic (for Bergman) romantic fantasia. Bergman readily assented, on the condition that they use a different title. That was no problem for Sondheim: *A Little Night Music* had been the original title of *Evening Primrose*, and he'd long hoped to find another home for it.[40]

Raising money on the heels of a flop led Prince to harness his appetite somewhat. He limited the budget to 70 percent of what he had spent on *Follies* but, as indomitable as ever, he began rehearsals before the required capitalization had been pledged, and before Sondheim had written six of the songs that would end up in the show. Risk was rewarded: *Night Music* turned out to be the biggest hit among the seven shows Sondheim and Prince created together. According to one estimate, Sondheim's share of the gross during its initial eighteen-month run in 1973–1974 ran to more than $16,000 a week.[41]

What was not to like? The book, by Hugh Wheeler, was a worldly sex comedy, a summer-scented gathering of the coupled, the uncoupled, and the wanting-to-be-coupled in a Swedish country house at the end of the nineteenth century. Prince described the show as "whipped cream with knives," but to Sondheim's slight dismay (and, no doubt, to the box office's great benefit) the whipped cream obscured the knives. Boris Aronson's set, based at least in part on René Magritte's painting *The Blank Signature* (a ghostlike image of a woman on horseback in a grove of trees), was stylish and evocative. Florence Klotz's *fin de siècle* costumes would have suited the characters in a Swedish translation of Henry James or Edith Wharton. And, perhaps most important, Sondheim's score was the most conventionally accessible one he had created to date.[42]

This was despite the fact that a complex musical construction underlay it, incorporating (among other things) theme and variations; an intricate series of permutations of waltz time (mazurka, sarabande, polonaise, et cetera); and a trio of three very different songs ("Soon," "Now," "Later") sung both simultaneously and comprehensibly. There was no rhythm section in the orchestra, because the material simply didn't call for it; Tunick believed *Night Music* was the first Broadway musical since the 1920s that didn't have one. Glynis Johns, who played the female lead in the original production, said she once performed the show with an actor so bewildered by the score's complexities he would break into tears and flee to his dressing room. But in its melodic charms, the score seemed to reveal a composer who very much had his audience in the forefront of his mind as he wrote. During the Boston tryout, in fact, Sondheim was so concerned that the show wasn't reaching audiences that he suggested the framing device of a vocal overture (he normally eschewed that hard-sell relic of an earlier age; there was no overture of any kind in *Anyone Can Whistle*, *Company*, or *Follies*). He was not in any way selling out, only recognizing that whipped cream called for indulgence. For the first act curtain number he established the sort of earworm that would carry the audience into the intermission besotted with what they had just heard. The audience couldn't have escaped "A Weekend in the Country" if it had wanted to: the energetic main chorus repeats, with slight variation, seven times in barely seven minutes, orchestrated so deftly by Tunick that each iteration adds something new while never abandoning any of its tuneful immediacy.[43]

Sondheim often joked, "Want to hear a medley of my hit?" In his entire catalog of roughly five hundred songs, only "Send in the Clowns" bears broad recognition beyond the community of musical theater enthusiasts. The cabaret artist Bobby Short heard it during the pre-Broadway Boston run of *A Little Night Music* in early 1973, then began playing it regularly at the luxe Café Carlyle in New York. After the release of the cast album in April, Frank Sinatra immediately recognized its value as a pop song, recorded the first free-standing version that summer, then sang it live at Carnegie Hall in the fall. Soon covered by Judy Collins, "Send in the Clowns" won the Grammy Award for Song of the Year in 1975 (the last time it was bestowed on a theater song) and became a hit when Collins rereleased it in 1977. Since then, it has been recorded more than five hundred times by a range of artists that reaches from Sarah Vaughan and Bing Crosby to Bryan Ferry and Grace Jones—not to mention in a transcription for bagpipe by the Regimental Band of the Royal Scots Dragoon Guards, and (with Sondheim's full cooperation) as a duet for Krusty the Clown and Sideshow Mel on *The Simpsons*. Lin-Manuel Miranda once heard it emanating, over and over and over, from an ice cream truck in Queens.[44]

The song's success may have been an aberration, but it was

by no means an accident. For one thing, because of an extremely rare (for Sondheim) reprise, Broadway audiences had the opportunity to hear it twice—first as the quiet climax of the show and then, its lyrics altered to suit the denouement, the very last words before the curtain comes down. In the song's first appearance: *And where are the clowns?/There ought to be clowns./ Well, maybe next year.* In the reprise, following a few entirely new lines: *Make way for the clowns./Applause for the clowns./They're finally here.*

More crucially, nearly anyone who could carry a tune could sing it. Because Johns had a limited vocal range, the entire song traverses only one note more than a single octave; because her seductive, breathy voice precluded phrases of more than the briefest length, or sustained notes at the end of them, there are few to be found (although Collins did manage to stretch *Isn't it rich?* into "Isn't it *riiiii*ch?"). And because the lyric, in the context of the show, is itself a metaphor, it works equally well outside the show as it does in it; a full appreciation of the song requires no knowledge of the plot or the characters who inhabit it. Imagine Judy Collins or Frank Sinatra singing a gorgeously rhapsodic (and very hummable) song like "Agony," from *Into the Woods: I found a casket/Entirely of glass—/No, it's unbreakable/ Inside—don't ask it—/A maiden, alas,/Just as unwakeable.*" A listener could only be baffled. And in the same show as "Send in the Clowns," the lyrics of the gorgeous "You Must Meet My Wife" are so specific—and so witty, but only if you know what's going on—that taking the song out of its context and leaving it to stand on its own would be entirely bewildering. Mark Eden Horowitz of the Library of Congress, whom Sondheim said understood his music as well as anyone, said it "could be the most beautiful piece of music Sondheim has composed. I've often wished that it had an alternate, more universal lyric, simply so it could be sung more often as a traditional stand-alone love song." But "Send in the Clowns" can reach anyone, on its own terms, in nearly any emotional circumstance that isn't joyous; Ingmar Bergman even suggested he wanted the song played at his funeral. It is a contained, self-sustaining, and glorious piece of songwriting—and its composer-lyricist happened to have written it overnight.[45]

Sondheim's committed reliance on a song's context was one of the reasons he never wrote free-standing pop songs. If you asked him to write a love song, he explained, he wouldn't know where to start. "But if you say write a love song, sung by a lady in a bar at five in the afternoon on her third martini, and she's wearing a red hat . . ." He also did not venture, except on a very few occasions (for instance, the soundtrack to Alain Resnais's 1974 film *Stavisky*), to write pure music, with neither lyrics nor any particular meaning. "I express the character," he said. "Let's see what happens to him. I express it musically." He was a superb lyricist; he was a superb composer; but perhaps his greatest gift was the ability to put the two arts together to accomplish a third, which he characterized for Mark Horowitz: "I'm a playwright who writes with song."[46]

Apart from *Getting Away with Murder*, an ill-considered (and universally panned) mystery he wrote with George Furth in the late 1990s, the only plays Sondheim wrote were those Oscar Hammerstein had dismissed ("worst thing I've ever read") when he was a teenager. But in every one of his shows following *A Funny Thing Happened on the Way to the Forum*, he was in fact writing plays. They just happened to be accompanied by music and set in the context of his collaborator's libretto. Robert Hurwitz, the record producer, believed that "the most fundamental point of his music, its purpose, is to express the sentiment of the words." The two couldn't be separated.[47]

Sondheim saw many of his songs (from *Anyone Can Whistle* forward) as one-act plays that both fit the character and had a beginning and an end, with a traversing or transformative change in the middle. Together, these elements moved the narrative of the show forward. "I'm not asking [actors] to sing songs," he said. "I'm asking them to play scenes." Robert Westenberg, who played the Wolf and Cinderella's Prince in the original production of *Into the Woods*, said Sondheim wrote "entirely from the view of the character, so doing the songs is basically like doing monologues or dialogues." They were "songs that you can really act. He writes scenes, basically, that happen to be sung."[48]

Just as his songs rarely made sense outside their original theatrical context, they were usually logical necessities on stage. If you remove, say, "Soon," "Now," and "Later" from *A Little Night Music*, the narrative no longer makes sense. "A Weekend in the Country" assembles and sets up every story line in the complex second act. The song begins with a cheery maid handing an invitation to her mistress; then, over its seven propulsive choruses, the maid's delight is transformed by the various characters' mostly foreboding reactions to the same invitation. At its end, this seven-minute narrative playlet, Jack Viertel wrote, leads the curtain to fall "on a virtual orgy of expectation and suspense."[49]

Songs that perform this function are everywhere in Sondheim's work. "Chrysanthemum Tea," in *Pacific Overtures*, reveals the process of a very slow murder, and "A Bowler Hat" traverses fifteen years in the life of both a character and a nation. "God That's Good," in *Sweeney Todd*, takes the audience from an amusing party-like atmosphere through the slow revelation of a diabolical and grisly plot. "Putting It Together," from *Sunday in the Park with George*, uses nearly 47 pages in the show's 246-page vocal score to explore the relationship between talent and commerce in the art world. Even something apparently as simple as "Barcelona," from *Company*, is an example of a Sondheim one-act: Scene one, declaration (*Where you going?/Barcelona/Oh/. . . Do you have to?*); scene two, seduction (*Look, you're a very special girl/Not just overnight*); scene three, resolution (*Oh, God . . .*).

And along the way, we get to know an essential part of Bobby's character.

This is where Sondheim's early training with Milton Babbitt came into play—learning how to craft the music that would carry the words, and thus the narrative, forward. Long-line composition enabled him to hold the audience's interest for three, six, in a few instances nearly ten minutes—long enough, in other words, to support the lyrics without tedious repetition, while capturing the extended emotional development of the scene. Rodgers and Hammerstein had done something similarly audacious in "Soliloquy," from *Carousel;* for Sondheim, it was an essential element of nearly every show.

In most cases, this meant he couldn't write his songs until his librettist had given him the textual material he required. He'd often begin at the piano, character and situation in his head, and idle his way through unformed melodic ideas, rhythmic figures, and harmonic progressions that seemed appropriate in mood and tone. Sometimes he'd have a copy of the script on the piano's easel so phrases might provoke not only lyric ideas but musical ones as well. Then, he once said, "the puzzle takes over"—the task of bringing the fragments he'd assembled into a coherent whole. From Hammerstein, he had learned that before he attacked the beginning of a song he ought to know how he wanted it to end—the way, in essence, that it would either complete the song's dramatic arc, or plug into the socket of the next scene. In either case, the characteristic Sondheim song ends up in a place it did not start from. Unlike Richard Rodgers, whose melodic fertility was such that Noël Coward purportedly said "he could pee a melody," and unlike Jule Styne, whose store of "trunk songs" could be plundered for whatever show Styne was working on, for Sondheim both melody and rhythm would emerge from the harmonic accompaniment he had established (even if conditionally)—as did the lyrics, ideally in a sort of conversational tone that followed the rhythms of natural speech. Music and lyrics thus became one indivisible entity.[50]

Around the time Sondheim was working with Rodgers on *Do I Hear a Waltz?*, Rodgers told an interviewer that "Steve has a curious way of making people sing as if they were talking." That, in fact, was the point: "The way normal speech rises and falls," he once said, "suggests a melodic contour." Or, put even more simply, a song.[51]

Until the last part of his career Sondheim usually wrote late at night, alone, either curled over the piano keyboard or stretched out on a couch with a large pillow supporting his head. "I spent my life either as the letter C or the letter L," he told *New Yorker* writer D. T. Max. Sometimes loosened by liquor or marijuana, sometimes drawn into the task by a passage written by one of his librettist collaborators, he usually took a week to write a song. A few took much longer, but he generally waited for the stress of *not* writing to build up to the point where the impending avalanche of a last-gasp deadline compelled him to write. As much as he was a natural procrastinator, he was also—conveniently—someone who thrived under pressure. Thus did "Comedy Tonight" save *Forum* from death on the road, thus did *Night Music* enter rehearsals with six songs unwritten, thus did Mandy Patinkin explode in a fury when Sondheim wasn't producing the necessary material for him to sing in *Sunday in the Park with George*, even as paying audiences were already seeing the show during its off-Broadway trial run in 1983. Patinkin told an interviewer, "I said to Steve, 'please, I beg you, just write the songs, write anything for these two places, even if it's shit.'" Soon he delivered "Children and Art" and "Lesson #8," two non-shitty and absolutely crucial second-act songs—"and the whole [show] came together," Patinkin said. "It was like a magic trick." For *Follies*, Sondheim wrote seven songs when

At home on East Forty-ninth Street, working in his "Letter L" position, away from the "Letter C" at the piano (Photograph by Hans Namuth, 1960)

the show was in rehearsals, as well as the bravura "I'm Still Here" (which Tunick had to orchestrate overnight) during the Boston tryout. For *Into the Woods*, he wrote "The Last Midnight" only one week before the show opened. "Put a gun to his head," James Lapine said. When he wrote at the last minute, Lapine added, he wrote "brilliantly. He didn't have time to stew over it."[52]

Of course, the later he wrote during a show's development, the better he understood both the show and its actors. Late in *Night Music*'s rehearsal schedule, with public performances just days away, Prince called him in to watch Johns and her leading man, Len Cariou, improvise a scene in which they appraised their relationship with rueful realism, a scene simultaneously crucial, intimate, and in need of a song. Johns said, "Steve arrived at 4 p.m. and watched it. Then he went off, came back at 10 the next morning, sat down, and played 'Send in the Clowns.'"[53]

Sondheim himself said it took thirty-six hours for him to write his most famous song, an extraordinary feat. "Probably one of the most frightening things in the world is staring at a blank sheet of paper wondering how you're going to fill it," he said. "But somehow you do." A decade earlier, when he had conjured the over-the-weekend wonder that was "Comedy Tonight," he had joined his extraordinary capacity for imaginative rhyming with the fairly simple technical tools needed to produce the song's bouncy rhythm and jaunty tune. Its content was also straightforward, uncomplicated by any need for greater meaning—or, really, meaning of any kind. "Send in the Clowns," however, was a far more complex undertaking. It was essential to the show's plot, and it had to express the interior emotions of the well-defined characters who sang it. "Comedy Tonight" was all surface; "Send in the Clowns" had to go deep. Sondheim's lyrics for the song were clothed in metaphor and imagery, and his music embodied the song's emotional content with a complex melding of rhythmic and melodic elements, set against an accompaniment of ambiguous chords and brief moments of expressive dissonance. For instance, the music behind the phrase *Sure of my lines*—it's profoundly unsure.[54]

Just six simple rhymes edge the song forward ("Comedy Tonight" has more than twenty), all of them unexceptional monosyllables or iambs (pair/air; approve/move; doors/yours; flair/there; fear/dear; queer/career/year), suggesting that Sondheim was entirely focused on other aspects of the song's compelling texture. The composer and writer Rob Kapilow has provocatively argued that the pressure to produce this critical song in such difficult circumstances might have led Sondheim to plumb emotional territory he otherwise would not have been able to reach and thereby find the song's emotional heart. "Written in a single night," Kapilow wrote, "in a state of near-exhaustion, after the show was nearly complete, under the pressure of a deadline, constrained by the limitations of Johns's vocal abilities, it is possible that the song bypassed some of Sondheim's famous self-censorship and self-criticism and accessed emotional aspects of his carefully controlled musical personality that might otherwise have been unavailable."[55]

If this was indeed the case, it either eluded Sondheim, or he forgot about it, or he chose to distance himself from it. He was proud of the song, and he doubtless appreciated the perpetual cascade of royalties that emerged from it. But its singular success nagged at him, too. In 2004, he told an audience that "the 90th time you hear—I won't even mention it!—it's like, fuck, give me something else."[56]

A Little Night Music opened on Broadway on February 15, 1973. Critics loved it, audiences rushed to see it. (Although, in *Finishing the Hat*, the one review Sondheim chose to cite was Peter G. Davis's brutal pan in *New York* magazine, which was still setting his teeth on edge thirty-seven years after the fact.) Five weeks later, Sondheim won his third Tony for Best Score. The word "unprecedented" would be too faint a modifier—all three were for shows that were produced in three consecutive Broadway seasons. A few weeks after the Tonys, he appeared on the cover of *Newsweek*, which called him "a national treasure."[57]

Not one, however, that most Americans had heard of. Broadway was much more culturally relevant in 1973 than in its twenty-first-century form. But even then the public was more invested in the Broadway of Carol Channing belting "Hello, Dolly" than it was in Glynis Johns whispering "Send in the Clowns." Sondheim remained a cult figure—but to him, the cult that cherished him most was the cult that mattered. On a warm, muggy night two weeks before the Tony winners were announced, fifteen hundred people filled the Shubert Theatre for a black-tie event called "Sondheim: A Musical Tribute." Burt Shevelove directed. Angela Lansbury, Chita Rivera, Len Cariou, and thirty more stars from Sondheim shows performed forty-two Sondheim songs. The speakers—Leonard Bernstein and Jule Styne among them—were Broadway eminences. The tickets had sold out in a week, at prices that ranged from the 2025 equivalent of $180 up to $725). "All of Broadway turned up to pay homage," the *Times* said. "Those who were not on stage seemed to be in the audience." (One who didn't show up was Zero Mostel, who was dissatisfied with the amount of stage time he'd been allotted. Craig Zadan, one of the evening's producers, said Mostel "wanted to do the show—all of it.")[58]

The music critic Alan Rich said the show "ran for over three hours and seemed to have lasted just about eighteen seconds." To fifteen-year-old Corby Kummer, who had come with his father from eastern Connecticut, the evening remained, half a century later, "the most exciting night of my life, even in retrospect." Kummer, later a prominent magazine editor, was already a Sondheim pen pal in 1973 and was still in touch with him when he died. Twenty-four-year-old Jack Viertel, who had discovered Sondheim's work a few years earlier as an undergraduate, had never met him but would eventually work with him on revivals in the early 2000s. "Steve's genius was eventually embraced by the world at large," he recalled half a century after the tribute. "But for those of us who had been at the Shubert that night, it was already old news."[59]

In later years, Sondheim became a virtual harvesting machine of gala tributes and official honors, but the 1973 salute remained the one that meant the most to him, he said, because it was "the first public appreciation by my peers." At the after-party, Bernstein asked Sondheim's mother, "Foxy, aren't you proud?" And Foxy said, "He belongs to the ages."[60]

The show had concluded with Sondheim alone on the stage. He had chosen "Anyone Can Whistle" for this climactic moment. Apart from his voice and the piano, the Shubert was silent, enrapt. And just as it had happened in the demo he had made ten years earlier, there was a barely perceptible catch in his voice when he got to the song's final word: *It's all so simple:/ Relax, let go, let fly./So someone tell me why/Can't I?*

5

The Hal-Steve Thing, Part 2

In 1958, Columbia Records issued a two-record set of the Paul Weston Orchestra playing the music of Jerome Kern. The writer of the liner notes made a valiant effort to say something about each song but, in his opening comments, seemed to acknowledge that he was on his way to failure. "If music could be described in language," the twenty-seven-year-old Stephen Sondheim wrote, "there would be no need for it."

More than forty years later, his extraordinary (if frequently technical) conversations with the Library of Congress musicologist Mark Eden Horowitz demonstrated the problem. "Music is a foreign language, which everyone knows but only musicians speak," Sondheim said in 2011. Here's an example from his dialogue with Horowitz: "Musical harmony, as you know, moves by bass line," Sondheim began. Then he continued:

> That is the motive that changes things. And it doesn't matter how you screw around with the notes on top; if the bass

> remains solidly consistent, it's going to sound that way throughout. So, if you want to stay in C major, and you want some variety, why not go to a C I^6? Now the instability of first inversions is something that's very hard to deal with when you're so used to block harmony. I get scared sometimes when I use a I^6 that it's all going to fall apart. Because, you know, it's so easy and satisfying to pound away at the I-V-I-V-I-V, as most songs do. But when you get to the I^6, it becomes a little more interesting. Because the I^6 chord tends not to want to go back to the V, but to lead to a IV or even, sometimes, to a VI chord.

Point arduously proven. Technical analysis may work for musicians and musicologists, but for the rest of us it is at best opaque, and often incomprehensible. It's easy to talk about lyrics: we use words to discuss words. But "the problem when you describe music in words," said Anthony Tommasini, the longtime classical music critic for the *New York Times*, "is that whatever you say invites more words, more detailed explanation."[1]

The distinctiveness of Sondheim's music that made Tommasini consider him a genius—"a word I never use," he said—has also made a portion of the musical theater audience dismiss him as unmelodic, complicated, hard to penetrate. As much as he detested the word "hummable," the element many found missing in his work, he nonetheless recognized the difference between his songs and what the musical theater audience of the 1950s and '60s wanted to hear. Taste is inscrutable, and some people will never be convinced, but the mistake many may be making is a simple one: they're not really *listening*. The verbal dexterity of Sondheim's lyrics is so captivating that a listener's focus is immediately and inevitably drawn away from the music to the words. But that listener should keep in mind a double truism: Music exists to say things that can't be expressed in words, but when the two are carefully plaited, the music makes the words even better. The great lyricist Yip Harburg said, "Lyrics make you think thoughts, music makes you feel a feeling." But when artfully combined, a song "makes you feel a thought."[2]

Virtually from the moment he imagined a career on Broadway, Sondheim knew it would be as a composer. What got in the way was that facility with lyrics, so stunningly revealed in *West Side Story* and then *Gypsy* when he was still in his twenties. When he stepped out as composer as well as lyricist in *A Funny Thing Happened on the Way to the Forum* and *Anyone Can Whistle*, he had to refute the critics who considered him only a lyricist—in over his head in his music, presumptuous in his claim to musicianship. But even as late as 1973, with two Tonys for best score (*Company* and *Follies*) in his pocket and a third, for *A Little Night Music*, about to join them, Sondheim told an interviewer he still bristled when commentators dismissed him as a lyricist who happened to write music. The Tony victories should have proved he had been certified by the Broadway community as a composer. But his lingering sense of grievance suggests that the earlier dismissal of his music was an affront he was unable to put behind him. Others did not stop hinting at it, either. As late as 2017, the *New York Times* ran a headline identifying Sondheim as "theater's greatest living lyricist."[3]

Writing music was a thrill, a reward, an exalting experience. At its best, writing a lyric was like solving a puzzle—a form of wordplay on steroids. But at its much more frequent worst, he found little pleasure in writing lyrics, which he called "a tiny little craft." He seemed to dismiss his own thrilling wordplay, his ironic wit, the delight (or sorrow) evoked by his imagery. He said it was like "making pewter ashtrays when I was in camp. You get your piece of pewter, and day after day you work on it, and then eventually you have an ashtray with a lot of holes, and you give it to your parents, and they say it's terrific." Writing lyrics, he said, was "a matter of sweat and time consumption" that required finding the right word, chasing it through his rhyming dictionary, excising syllables to make it match the rhythm of the music, then "making sure it fits the singer's tongue and teeth."[4]

From the beginning of his career audiences were thrilled by his lyrics. Fans could quote them at length, masticate their meaning, express amazement at their complexity and their content, argue whether his most astonishing talent was represented by the deft wit of *We've no time to sit and dither/While her withers wither with her* (from *Into the Woods*) or the wrenching pathos of *You take your road,/The decades fly,/The yearnings fade, the longings die./You learn to bid them all goodbye* (*Follies*). But in an interview in 1982 he referred, generically, to "those goddamned lyrics" that "are just so unbearably difficult to write." Earlier in his career, he'd said "it's a job that I find so difficult and takes so long that it's hardly worth the result." Near its end, several years after his last show had opened on Broadway, he simply said, "Lyric writing is, for me, hell."[5]

Music was different. Music consumed him. He insisted he rarely read books (which was not quite true—he admired Wallace Stevens and E. B. White, among many others). The novel, he said, was "the most boring art form in existence," and despite growing up within a mile of the Metropolitan Museum of Art, he never entered it until he was in his twenties. He knew the Museum of Modern Art somewhat better, but only because he went there to see movies. "I just had no cultural background at all," he said. "I didn't know what I was missing."[6]

In 1996, following a fire at his house on East Forty-ninth Street and during the necessary renovations, Sondheim donated his entire collection of roughly twelve thousand records to the Library of Congress. The library received three thousand index cards as well, all of them neatly typed, arranged alphabetically, and collectively providing the best possible evidence of both his desire for order and the intensity of his passion for music.

Each card had the name of a composer at the top and a list of recordings of the composer's music in Sondheim's enormous collection. The first one was headlined, "ABBASOV, A."; Sondheim's only recording of music by this obscure Azerbaijani composer was "Suites No. 1 and No. 2 from the ballet *Chernushka*." Eighteen cards in the collection were crowded with the works of Chopin, who tied for the lead with Prokofiev. It took seventeen cards to contain all of his Stravinsky, sixteen for Debussy, fifteen for Brahms, fourteen for Bach, and so on.

In a way, though, Abbasov was representative of the range of Sondheim's musical interests, one entry on a lengthy roster of other composers interred in similar obscurity: Flagello and Frumerie; Holmboe and Husa; Moniuszko, Rubbra, Schibler, and hundreds of others of comparable insignificance. But not to Sondheim. Each of the seven lesser luminaries listed here, and many others of equal lack of renown, required at least two cards to enumerate his or her recorded works stored (in part) on the long wall of bookshelves in the house on East Forty-ninth Street, stripped of their album covers and clad only in their protective sleeves (a space-saving idea he picked up from Leonard Bernstein).[7]

It would take someone with Sondheim's unimaginably broad and deep musical tastes to know what he learned from Ashraf Abbasov or Gunnar de Frumerie or Stanislaw Moniuszko, but the traces of better-known composers that he particularly cared for are vividly present throughout his music: in *Sweeney Todd*, he drew on Igor Stravinsky, Bernard Herrmann and Gregorian chant. Aspects of *Sunday in the Park with George* were heavily influenced by Benjamin Britten (who "just kills me," he said). *A Little Night Music* evokes Chopin ("Later," "In Praise of Women"), Schubert (the slow sections of "The Miller's Son"), and Rachmaninoff ("Send in the Clowns"). In *Company*, he drew on Erik Satie ("Barcelona"), but also, for the title number that opens the show, on the unlikely Harvey Schmidt, best known for *The*

Fantasticks. Sondheim detested Schmidt's subsequent show, *Celebration* ("just as disgusting, coy, characterless, gooey and pretentious as" *The Fantasticks*), but he told John Guare that its title song helped him "know what to do with 'Company.'" It was, he said, "the sound I was looking for," apparently referring to the repeated phrase behind the words *I want to celebrate!*, which follows the same musical contour as *In comes company!* and similarly punctuates the song.[8]

More than any other composer, Maurice Ravel was everywhere in Sondheim's work, especially in *A Little Night Music*, *Sweeney Todd*, and *Into the Woods*. His attachment to Ravel (whom Sondheim considered his favorite composer) may have gone deeper than his intense appreciation of the composer's ravishing harmonic innovations. In the conversation with Sondheim for the Columbia Oral History Archives in 1982, the interviewer surprised him with this quote, from an unnamed source: "He avoided his admirers, maintained a well-protected barrier of personal intimacy. [He was] an independent innovator, an explorer in vast fields of music, a sensualist." The interviewer went on to say, "that sounds to me like a description of Stephen Sondheim," but then revealed it was in fact a description of Maurice Ravel. "Really?," Sondheim replied. "It's nice. It's too good for me. But I understand the point. I would like to believe that. Thank you."[9]

Even while Sondheim was working on *A Little Night Music*, his creative restlessness drew him toward two unrelated projects. With his friend Anthony Perkins he wrote the screenplay for a murder mystery called *The Last of Sheila*, and at the request of the French director Alain Resnais he composed the soundtrack for *Stavisky*, a film about a Parisian con man in the 1930s. The *Stavisky* score incorporated a number of melodies that had been dropped from *Follies*, while *The Last of Sheila* was essentially a narrative version of the Murder Game, a house party favorite of Sondheim's, tricky and playful and almost hopelessly complicated. Rex Reed's review in the *Daily News* said the film "requires a postgraduate degree in hieroglyphics to figure out," and that was one of the nicer things he had to say. Sondheim was less than pleased with the production process; he found the women in the glittery cast—Raquel Welch, Dyan Cannon, most especially Joan Hackett—"horrific," entangled as they were in "talking about their fucking characters and what the motivation was." (Welch, he said, insisted that she didn't want "my public" to see her smoking marijuana, as the script had specified.) Among the cast, Sondheim said only James Mason understood that the movie "was about clues, not about character."[10]

But *Sheila* was also, he said, one of the two "really happy writing experiences" he'd had up that point. The other was the simultaneous creation of the score for *Stavisky*. What the two movies had in common was the absence of lyrics. "Not having to write lyrics made it like a vacation," he said. For *Stavisky*, it also freed him from another burden: he said it was the only music he ever wrote without resorting to the disinhibiting effects of drugs or liquor. "Pure music," he said, "doesn't require the kind of help" that he needed when he wrote lyrics.[11]

After *A Little Night Music* closed in August 1974, Sondheim still had a presence on Broadway. The revised lyrics for *Candide* that Hal Prince had commissioned, notably for the show's opening number ("Life Is Happiness Indeed"), helped the show become a hit in its 1974–1975 version. As Prince had guaranteed, both Leonard Bernstein and librettist Lillian Hellman stayed away. Except for a few never-recorded birthday songs and the like, this was the last time Sondheim wrote lyrics for someone else's music. He loved Prince; he loved Bernstein's music for the show; and, most important, he had no emotional investment in the work. Thus, no pain in the lyric writing.* He had simply done a favor for a friend.[12]

As he did with his next piece of work, although this time the favor was much more substantial. Burt Shevelove (whose engagement with the classics had blossomed into *A Funny Thing Happened on the Way to the Forum*) asked him to write music and lyrics for an adaptation of *The Frogs*. Shevelove had presented a version of the Aristophanes play at Yale in 1941, and the current director of the university's drama school, critic Robert Brustein, asked him to bring it back. As in 1941, it would be presented in and around the Olympic-sized swimming pool in Yale's Payne Whitney Gymnasium, again with a cast largely drawn from the drama school (among them Sigourney Weaver and Meryl Streep) and the Yale swimming team. Shevelove asked Sondheim to provide music and lyrics; they gave themselves four weeks to write the show and four weeks to rehearse (and, of course, rewrite) it before a planned run of eight performances in May 1974. Sondheim recalled, "I thought it would be a lark."[13]

It had its moments. Sondheim writing music for a Greek chorus was odd, but mildly successful. One song added for a subsequent production had lyrics unlike any he'd ever written: "Fear No More" was a speech lifted intact from Shakespeare's *Cymbeline* (if Sondheim was going to collaborate, Sondheim devotee Michael Mitnick said many years later, "it would of course only be with the best"). His own lyrics for the show were nicely decorated with some charming jokes, resulting in what Mel Gussow in the *New York Times* called "amusingly adulterated Aris-

* Prince and the author of the revised book, Hugh Wheeler, may have endured at least a flicker of pain when they received a letter from Hellman several years later, in response to a royalty check Prince had sent her: she had decided to accept the check but to donate it to charity. She said, "I want you to know that I will have no part of the money for what has become a piece of trash." This *Candide* ran for 740 performances and won four Tony Awards; the numbers for Hellman's version had been 73 and none.

tophanes." But the setting was, in fact, ridiculous. Jonathan Tunick hadn't been able to accommodate the reverberation in the swimming pool, which made the music sound, he said, as if it were being performed in a urinal.[14]

The entire affair led to an intense and durable loathing: for the rest of his life, Sondheim despised Brustein, who provided one-stop shopping for Sondheim's twinned abhorrence of critics and academics. Brustein's reviews in the *New Republic* had been generally chilly toward Sondheim's work, and what Sondheim himself called his own "snappish intolerance" was amplified by an aspect of Brustein's personality that few except his dearest friends and relatives (and not even all of them) would dispute. As Bruce Weber characterized it in his obituary for Brustein in the *New York Times* in 2024, he had "the moral certainty of a martyr."[15]

It was not a formula designed for cordial collaboration. Sondheim said Brustein's arrogance was "palpable." After one session with cast and crew, he blasted Brustein for not thanking the chorus and the orchestra and subsequently declined to take part in any meeting with him. Scheduled for only eight performances, the show was beset by the mechanical and aural difficulties the swimming pool presented, and the planned dress rehearsals had to be skipped. Sondheim remembered being furious that Brustein did not postpone opening night, instead exposing the show to the New York critics in its first full performance.[16]

To Sondheim, both at the moment and in his memory, the lark he had anticipated had been transformed into a monstrous raptor, forever circling his recollection of the *Frogs* experience. Twenty years later, in an entirely different context, Sondheim brought up a negative review of *Forum* "written by Robert Brustein, that asshole." Twenty years after that, in his eighties and by then universally recognized as the most accomplished composer and lyricist on Broadway since at least the 1950s; winner of eight Tony Awards, seven Grammys, and an Oscar; recent recipient of a Presidential Medal of Honor bestowed by Barack Obama—Sondheim was sticking to his story: "Brustein hated my work, and did everything he could to destroy my career."[17]

At the memorial service for Sondheim in 2022, Jonathan Tunick said, "He was deeply sensitive and mercurial and could boil over at the slightest perceived offense." With those close to him, Tunick added, such perceptions were rare and soon forgotten.

With others, less so.

Apart from Sondheim's tangle with Brustein, one other memorable episode occurred during the week of *The Frogs*, this one more comic than not, but nonetheless freighted with something ominous. Foxy, who never missed an opening night, had come to New Haven with some friends, but she encountered a bureaucratic fumble: Her tickets had not been set aside. Enraged, she berated the box office clerk. As her anger (and no doubt her humiliation) mounted, she expressed it by shouting at the clerk, *"I'M MRS. STEPHEN SONDHEIM!"*[18]

Sondheim told this story years later, after his relationship with his mother had settled into a form of cold war. But, by his account, even that took considerable forbearance on his part. Sometime in the middle 1970s, they apparently had a terrible fight, cause unknown. Out of that arose the letter from Foxy that became the heart of perhaps the most familiar (and definitely the most horrifying) anecdote about Sondheim's personal life. Going into the hospital for what she called, in her self-dramatizing way, "open heart surgery"—actually, the installation of a pacemaker—she cranked up the drama to a histrionic level in an effort to inflict shame, pain, or some other undefinable wound on her only child. The letter, written in the hospital and hand-delivered at her request, said that she wanted him to know that "the only regret I have in life is giving you birth."[19]

After Sondheim described the letter to Michiko Kakutani

of the *New York Times* in 1994, the story popped up in every Sondheim biography, and in every article that sought to explore his personal life. His own role in disseminating the story added to its impact, as he repeated it in many print and television interviews, at times with dramatic emphasis but just as often as something offered almost in passing, as if he were describing a bad stretch in high school, or a mildly knotty moment in the creative process. The letter became The Letter, a proper noun that, among Sondheim followers, needed no further explication. People hunted for traces of it in his work. In *Pacific Overtures*, the shogun's mother murders her son. (Sondheim in fact called it "essentially a Jewish mother song.") In *Into the Woods*, the tables are turned as the mother is crushed beneath a falling tree.[20]

Maybe. And in 2024, a further "maybe" was introduced into the tale, perhaps inaccurately but nonetheless in the public record. In *Sondheim: His Life, His Shows, His Legacy*, by Steven Silverman, the author wrote that an unnamed "close work associate" of Sondheim's offered a different version of The Letter's origins. In 2022, the source asserted that Sondheim had told him it never existed, that it was simply a story he'd invented. Unfortunately, Silverman died just before his book was published; there could be no effort to press him to identify his source, or even to find out how and when he or she fit into Sondheim's life. But if Foxy indeed wrote The Letter, it tells us a lot about her son's relationship with her. And if she didn't, but her son told the world that she did, it tells us just as much.[21]

In a way, though, he did tell the world, even if unintentionally. In 2025, a year after Silverman's book was published and just as this book was going to press, a photocopy of his apparent response to The Letter—four snarling and accusatory pages—turned up in Mary Rodgers's newly opened archives; he had given it to her in 2013, during one of their whose-mother-was-worse moments. ("Dear Mary," his cover letter said. "Just pretend

I'm writing to your mother.") But in this version of his original response to The Letter, apparently represented to his oldest friend as definitive, the word "regret" is absent. The phrase he attributes to Foxy is "the only guilt I can think of is giving you birth."[22]

There's a mile of difference between regret and guilt, but it was a distance that Sondheim could not navigate.

However much Prince considered *A Little Night Music* his "gentile musical," and to whatever degree Sondheim fretted that it was "so damned *goyische*," *Pacific Overtures* went so far beyond *fin de siècle* Sweden that it might as well have been set on Neptune. It's difficult to imagine Prince presenting the show to potential investors. Did he say it's a show "about Japan's encounter with Commodore Matthew Perry and the U.S. Navy in 1853, with music derived from the Japanese pentatonic scale, lyrics that evoke haiku, and a visual style derived from kabuki, with a little bunraku thrown in"?

Sort of. Prince and Sondheim held backers' auditions, where the voluble Prince outlined the story and Sondheim sat at the piano and performed several songs. That was something he'd been doing since *Saturday Night* in 1954; he had even done it to raise money for *West Side Story*, when he insisted on performing Leonard Bernstein's music. ("God only withheld one musical talent from Lenny," he later explained. "He gave him the voice of a frog.") Sondheim's own singing was limited by his occasionally wobbly intonation and minimal range, but his pianism was dynamic. It was also innovative: To suggest the metallic, percussive sounds of Japanese instrumentation, he attached thumbtacks and paper clips to the piano strings. At one backers' audition for *Overtures*, some of the songs received polite applause, and a few that he played and sang with exceptional fervor (notably "Someone in a Tree") had lifted the invited audience to near rapture. But that was almost beside the point. Sondheim and Prince had seized the Broadway musical and turned it in new directions; if they were ready to take another unexpected swerve—this time to mid-nineteenth-century Japan—so were their investors.[23]

The material that became *Pacific Overtures* was born in the library of the Yale Law School in 1972, where John Weidman was a third-year student trying to distract himself from his last exams (and from the looming possibility of a career as a lawyer) by writing a play about the opening of Japan to western commercial interests. Weidman had majored in East Asian studies at Harvard, so he knew the material. His father, the novelist Jerome Weidman, had written the book for the Pulitzer Prize–winning *Fiorello!;* Hal Prince had co-produced the show, which gave his son enough of a connection to get his script, which had been conceived as a straight play, into Prince's hands. Then Prince decided it should be a musical and presented it to an extremely reluctant Sondheim, who agreed to proceed only because of his faith in Prince's judgment. Once in, though, Sondheim was captured. "What's interesting to write," he said a few years later, "is something you haven't done before."[24]

To Weidman, Prince was "the essential artistic engine" behind the show. But Prince's energy, his fire, and his visual imagination created a template that an excited Sondheim could adapt in ingenious ways for the words and music. The central metaphor lurking behind their work on *Pacific Overtures* was an imaginary Japanese playwright who comes to New York, sees a Broadway musical, then goes home and writes one about Commodore Perry coming to Japan. For Sondheim, it was a solidly functional idea that he would play out in reverse: He spent two weeks in Japan with Hal and Judy Prince absorbing the sound of Japanese instruments. He adapted his compositional style to the pentatonic scale by locating its connection to Spanish guitar music, which he loved. And he found himself composing in minor keys, which he had seldom done. (While writing the verse for "The

Miller's Son" in *A Little Night Music*, "I thought: 'Oh look! I'm writing in a minor mode!' ") He wrote much of the music in his letter L position—on the couch—to avoid the familiar rhythmic patterns that he might lapse into if he were writing in letter C (hunched over the piano, hands on the keyboard). To achieve the facsimile of authenticity in the lyrics, he eschewed Latinate words in the first act and let them creep into the second act only in appropriate places, once the four admirals bring western idiom into Japan (and into the show) in the Gilbert and Sullivan pastiche "Please Hello!" There were few rhymes in the show's lyrics, and a lot of simple subject-predicate syntax: "a kind of translator-ese," he said. The one song entirely in modern, western idiom was the curtain number, "Next." By then—he usually wrote in chronological sequence—Sondheim had been so thoroughly immersed in Asian sounds that he may have needed a writer's crutch: this "onomatopoeic blast," as he called it, was a rhythmic and programmatic derivative of his own "When," from *Evening Primrose*.[25]

The Prince-Sondheim-Weidman collaboration was not without its snags. On the way to Broadway, a savage review in the *Boston Globe* was a gut punch. The critic Kevin Kelly said the book was "a stilted cartoon," the music was "extremely wearisome [as it] goes in one ear and stays there like a plug," and the entire enterprise "was bad from the very beginning: that is, the concept." Frantic writing and rewriting and re-routining preceded the show's New York opening (the ten-minute "Chrysanthemum Tea" was born in Boston). So did backstage tension. The Steve-Judy-Hal "triumvirate" produced its own particular anguish when, in the midst of the creative complications, Prince learned Sondheim was in his hotel room with Judy, auditioning "I Never Do Anything Twice," a song he was writing for the film *The Seven-Per-Cent Solution*. Exasperated that Sondheim was devoting his time to another project when their joint effort was flailing, Prince may also have been resentful of the intimate bond shared by his wife and his best friend. Nothing about this three-way relationship was simple.[26]

Pacific Overtures was a flop. As with *Anyone Can Whistle* and *Follies*, every cent of its capitalization sank into the mire of contradictory love-it-or-hate-it reviews and indifferent audiences. But out of it came some of Sondheim's most striking work, including "Someone in a Tree"—of everything he wrote, the song he remained proudest of for the rest of his life.

That was not the only extraordinary number in *Pacific Overtures.* For "A Bowler Hat," Weidman wrote a series of letters encompassing fifteen years in the life of a samurai as he slowly adapts to westernization. Prince said, "Steve will inhale the letters and exhale them as a song," which he did not only in the rhymeless lyrics, which he wrapped around Weidman's words, but also in the music: Although its six choruses are melodically identical, each expressed to the syncopated plucking of a *samisen*, the accompaniment moves from eastern to western modes over the course of the five-minute song. The modest, haiku-like phrases of "Poems," which seem simple to the ear, build dramatic power through melodic units so exquisitely measured that each time some of them reappear, a single, critical note has been changed. Even as the two characters alternate singing on the repeated cue *Your turn*, the rests leading into the phrase are as varied as they are precise: The first lasts four and a half beats, the second five beats, the third half a beat, the fourth one beat. Performers struggled with the song; for those who could grasp its subtleties, doing so was sufficient reward.[27]

But for "Someone in a Tree," Sondheim dug as deeply—into the music, the lyrics, the storytelling, the intimations of his own life—as he did in virtually any other song he wrote (its one competitor is "Finishing the Hat," from *Sunday in the Park with George*). Weidman, who had suggested the idea for the song, wrote a five-page narrative that, in Sondheim's adaptation, told two stories: how the Japanese and the Americans negotiated an extended and tense encounter, and how the event was perceived by a ten-year-old boy who climbed a nearby tree so he could overhear the conversation. Sondheim said his pride in the song was variously due to "the poetic Orientalism of the lyric"; or "its attempt to collapse past, present, and future into one packaged song form"; or the "swing and relentlessness of the music." The restlessness was induced by an unexpected compositional tactic from a master of complex harmonies: The song relies on just two chords for its entire seven-plus minutes.[28]

But in the one show that was furthest from his own experience and from the world he lived in, Sondheim also found a profound personal connection. When he asked Weidman to come to his house to hear him play "Someone in a Tree" for the first time, Sondheim later said, "I was so emotional about it I thought I couldn't possibly play it for him." He started to cry before his hands touched the keyboard. Weidman found the expression on his face "extraordinary." He said Sondheim was "just completely undone by it."[29]

Sondheim cried often. He told the playwright Claudia Shear that her show *Blown Sideways Through Life* "left me hyperventilating and sobbing so that I could hardly get out of my seat." He cried whenever he read his favorite poem, "Love Note to a Playwright" by Phyllis McGinley. He cried when he first saw Gershwin's original manuscript for *Porgy and Bess*. He cried when holding babies, when talking about teachers and teaching, when reading *Henry IV* or the first sentence of *The Catcher in the Rye*. He admitted that he cried while watching *Animal Planet*. "Drop a hat," he said. "I'm an easy crier."[30]

But even into his late eighties, listening to "Someone in a Tree" would make Sondheim weep as no other song did. It was one of the two songs that he wanted to be part of his memorial service (along with "So Little to Be Sure Of," from *Anyone Can Whistle*). What was ostensibly a song about Japanese history was also a song about an outsider—and about a young boy trying to connect to something larger than himself.

John Weidman said that Sondheim was extremely proud of the way he had solved a dramatic problem with "Someone in a Tree." "But," he added, "that doesn't make you cry thirty years later."[31]

In January 1976, shortly before *Pacific Overtures* opened, Sondheim sat for an interview with the *New York Times*—what the news business refers to as a "walk-up," a journalistic ritual performed in anticipation of a coming event. For the Broadway audience, it's one of the first times the public learns something substantive about a show that's about to open. For Broadway producers, publicists, investors, and others who have a stake in the show, a *Times* walk-up could inspire people to buy tickets, and at the very least initiate the chit-chat and buzz and heightened anticipation that would prefigure success.

Not this time. The paper's editors assigned the piece to Clive Hirschhorn, the well-established theater critic of London's *Daily Express*. His piece was headlined "Will Sondheim Succeed in Being Genuinely Japanese?" but could just as appropriately have been called "Does Sondheim Think He's Better Than Everybody?" The article contained several factual errors, including the assertion that Sondheim had a Chinese servant named Loo, when in fact his house man was a Hispanic American named Luis Vargas, called Lou, who had become a close friend. Vargas cooked for Sondheim, tailored his clothes, cut his hair, and generally ran the household. He was a "servant" whose name was on the door: an entry buzzer for his own apartment in the townhouse was posted outside, along with Sondheim's.[32]

The piece infuriated Sondheim. In direct quotation, Hirschhorn had him belittling *A Chorus Line* and its director, Michael Bennett, who had choreographed *Company* and co-directed *Follies*. Hirschhorn also quoted him snarling at the songwriters

Marvin Hamlisch and Cy Coleman, who "talk about me all the time and it irritates the hell out of me." And in a generalized blast at the industry, per Hirschhorn, Sondheim said "there's very little I admire" on Broadway. "For me, [admire] means something I'd like to sign my name to, and I see very little I'd like to sign my name to that I haven't already signed my name to, if you know what I mean." What he meant: My work is worthy, unlike everybody else's.[33]

After the article was published, it was difficult to tell who was angrier—Sondheim, or nearly everyone else on Broadway. The Hirschhorn piece, he said, "meant to damage, and meant to wound, and that's what it did. I think it was entirely an act of malice." In a letter to the *Times*, he complained about the characterization of Vargas, the absence of his comments supporting subsidized theater, and the way Hirschhorn had turned his praise for *The King and I* into a putdown. (Notably, Sondheim did not retract or correct his statements regarding the contemporary Broadway theater.) In the British magazine *Plays & Players*, Hirschhorn defended his reporting and described how much he admired *Pacific Overtures*. He also said he'd had to pay for his reviewer tickets, because before previews began (but after his "walk-up") the production had struck his name from the press list. Many who had previously resented Sondheim's recent dominance of the Broadway musical felt justified; many who had been neutral became resentful. Six years later, in his Columbia oral history, Sondheim said he had been "so severely misquoted" by Hirschhorn that "I've never given an interview again."[34]

Except he had. Sondheim gave a substantial interview to the British *Gay News* just months after the Hirschhorn debacle, when he was in London promoting *Side by Side by Sondheim*, a three-performer revue. (The paper said he was "a very attractive, cuddly man with pleated brown eyes, a pudgy nose, and a sad-cheeky expression.") He talked to the *Times* again at length for two separate pieces on *Sweeney Todd* in 1979. (The show, he said in one, "has a creepy atmosphere"—not exactly a ticket-selling description for a musical.) By the mid-1980s, he opened up more broadly. He simply couldn't resist it, and over time he would come to have excellent relations with most of the press (critics aside). He was usually genial, always polite, and never uninteresting; he was, in nearly all settings, a wonderful talker.[35]

Of course he faced the same questions over and over, and of course he developed neatly packaged and freely repeated answers. He told the story about lyric-writing and making a pewter ashtray at summer camp to Mary Ellin Barrett (as it happened, Irving Berlin's daughter) in *Good Housekeeping* in May 1959, and told it again, using virtually the same words, in *The Dramatist* in the autumn of 1978. The eternally repeated comment about his relationship with Hammerstein ("If Oscar had been a geologist, I would have become a geologist") was a familiar rerun as well. A brilliant piece of film editing in James Lapine's documentary *Six by Sondheim* (2013) reveals how the pre-ordained answers worked. In the film, Sondheim narrates the Hammerstein section in six separate interviews, spliced together in such a way that if you just listen to the audio, you would think it was from one uninterrupted conversation. But if you're watching, you see a variety of Sondheims—bearded, clean-shaven, suit and tie, red sweater, blue shirt, younger, older, and so on—telling the tried-and-true story across the years without so much as a pause.

From the late 1980s forward, he agreeably offered live access to magazine and newspaper reporters, to radio and television interviewers, to authors and documentarians and, it sometimes seemed, anyone who happened to own a tape recorder. But the access was not entirely unlimited. In 2017, he allowed a writer working on a profile to accompany him to a benefit dinner, where they were joined by Meryl Streep. "I was introduced to someone who Steve said was writing about him," she recalled. It was a code, she recognized, for "don't say anything fun."[36]

* * *

When *Sweeney Todd* opened on March 1, 1979, it broke several molds. For the first time in Sondheim's career, the idea for the show was his alone. For the Broadway musical theater, traditionally built around various degrees of conventional romantic attachment or comic distraction, it was even more unlikely than *Pacific Overtures* had been. Though flecked with some of the broadest humor to appear in a Sondheim show, it was at core not just a tragedy but a disturbingly blood-splattered one. On first hearing the idea, Len Cariou, who would play the lead role in the original production, thought that Sondheim and Prince "have lost their minds completely." (Sondheim, who admired Cariou, told the writer Laurie Winer that the actor was the perfect Sweeney because "Len Cariou could actually kill someone.") The show's central theme was based on Gregorian chant. The music didn't stop when the characters hit their buttons at the end of their songs; as a result, nearly all the dialogue was colored by potent underscoring that intensified the drama and propelled it toward its concluding tragedy (a technique Sondheim consciously adapted from the way horror films employed music to sustain tension). More than three decades later Sondheim's own comments on *Sweeney* revealed the presence of his own life in the show—his experience, his unconscious mind, and how they augmented each other in his creative process.[37]

Sondheim's love for the macabre dated back to his childhood. In his teens, he made five-minute horror movies. In college, when he played the murderous psychopath in the student production of *Night Must Fall*, it had been the "only part I ever wanted." The Murder Game in *The Last of Sheila* was the same unnerving, lights-out amusement he liked to indulge in with friends. Horror intrigued him, and it motivated him. On a trip to London, when he saw Christopher Bond's modern adaptation of the nineteenth-century play *The String of Pearls: A Domestic Romance* (retitled *Sweeney Todd, The Demon Barber of Fleet*

Street), he knew he had found the musical he longed for: "I'd love to sing that," he said.[38]

The String of Pearls, first performed in 1847, was a product of the English "bloodbath theater" of the period, a penny-dreadful mix of melodrama, terror, and shock. No other Sondheim show had so improbable a premise: A deranged barber slits the throats of his customers and hands their bodies over to a collaborator so she can stuff their remains into the meat pies she sells to unsuspecting customers. Complications—and genuine tragedy—ensue. Revised at least seven times over the decades, turned into two films, several books and, in 1959, a dance version for the Royal Ballet, the *Sweeney* story had terrified generations of British children. According to Hugh Wheeler, the London-born librettist of the Sondheim version, the warning that "Sweeney Todd will get you if you don't watch out!" was "more than enough to send countless thousands of recalcitrant children scurrying to finish their porridge and jump into bed."[39]

The Sondheim-Prince-Wheeler version shocked audiences right from the outset. At a backers' audition, Prince was so voluble and upbeat as he began to explain the plot one could almost think he was describing a knockabout farce. But once Sondheim started singing and playing the score, no one could think this was anything but a horror show. When he began to play the ominous, rolling accompaniment to "The Ballad of Sweeney Todd," his foot heavy on the sustain pedal, the demonic dissonances artfully intensified, the effect was frightening. When he got to the phrase *Swing your razor wide, Sweeney!/Hold it to the skies!*, his hands attacked the piano with such force he could have been hammering daggers straight through the keyboard. Two songs later, as Sweeney, Sondheim sang *There's a hole in the world/Like a great black pit/And it's filled with people/Who are filled with shit.* He may have failed with "fuck" in "Gee, Officer Krupke," but years later he said that he had been pleased to be the first person to use a four-letter word on the musical stage.

(Perhaps referring to Sondheim's determination to do so, Richard Barr, the lead producer for *Sweeney Todd*, later described Sondheim as "a mature little boy.") He was surely less pleased by the initial reaction to the rough audition of his daring show. Facing a Broadway season in which *Annie*, *Grease*, a revival of *Hello Dolly!* (with Carol Channing back above the title), and another of *The King and I* (Yul Brynner, likewise) were regnant, Barr and the other producers (this time, Prince was solely the director) had so little luck with potential backers that they took the radical step of placing an ad in the *Times* headed, "NEW STEPHEN SONDHEIM MUSICAL OPEN FOR INVESTMENT." A share—one of 500—could be had for as little as $1,800, and in time 271 people provided the necessary $900,000. *Variety* believed an investor roster that lengthy was a Broadway record.[40]

The pervasive sense of impending doom embodied in the opening number was what Sondheim had been seeking from the moment he began to think about the show. He had also imagined it as nearly a miniature—Grand Guignol, as he had told Judy Prince when he first played some of the songs for her. But Hal Prince found in the *Sweeney* story something vastly larger, both physically and emotionally. At first he'd imagined a "black box"—just a velour backdrop and focused lighting. However, seeking to turn it into a parable of class conflict at the beginning of the Industrial Revolution, Prince wanted more scale, more menace, more bleakness (all of which cost the investors a $200,000 budget overrun). Scenic designer Eugene Lee found the set in Rhode Island—a decrepit iron foundry that Prince bought (for $7,000), shipped to New York (for $100,000), and installed in the cavernous Uris Theatre at additional budget-breaking expense. Audiences encountered the gruesome, menacing set on entering the theater—Prince's way of telling the ticketholders where he wanted to take them. Barely thirty seconds after the lights went down, a bleak organ prelude was impaled by the ear-splitting, blood-boiling blast of a steam whistle. This told them what Prince wanted them to feel. In Sweeney's first song, when he declares that the world is . . . *filled with people/Who are filled with shit*, Sondheim was telling them, he later said, that the evening wasn't going to be a version of Masterpiece Theatre.[41]

Perhaps even more startling than *Sweeney* itself was Sondheim's reaction to Prince's staging. Two years after the show closed, he said he admired the craftsmanship, but thought the scale overwhelmed the show—"drowned" it, he said—when he had simply imagined "a little horror movie." In fact, elements of the movie-on-stage that he had hoped for survived in Sondheim's music: the extensive underscoring, the repeated use of the failsafe spine-chiller he called "my Bernard Herrmann" chord, and the omnipresence of the opening measures of the "Dies Irae." (For readers with a keyboard handy, the notes of the "Bernard Herrmann chord" are D/E-flat/G-flat/B-flat.) Conceived sometime between 1100 and 1300, the brief sequence of notes that make up the theme of the "Dies Irae" has been used in more films than one can count, whenever the composer or director wishes to suggest dread or terror. Fritz Lang used it in *Metropolis* to intensify the film's apocalyptic symbolism; Stanley Kubrick opened *The Shining* with it, setting the mood for everything that was to follow; and Frank Capra even brought it into *It's a Wonderful Life*, as George Bailey contemplates jumping to his death from a bridge. But however effectively film composers used it in the background to accompany something sinister in the action, Sondheim got much more out of it: He used it to define a person. Drop the first syllable in the phrase *Attend the tale of Sweeney Todd* and you have a variation of the theme—the "Dies Irae"—that accompanies the Sweeney character throughout the show. It's there, harmonically transformed, when the chorus sings *Swing your razor high, Sweeney;* it's in the accompaniment to "Epiphany"; it's even hinted at in the first four notes of the phrase *Nightingale, blackbird* in "Green Finch and Linnet

Bird." The English translation of the words "Dies Irae" is "Days of Wrath"—essentially, the core premise of *Sweeney Todd.*[42]

The interwoven complexity of the score is staggering. Sondheim created a musical architecture so fully realized that passages from sixteen of its songs reemerge in the show's final thirteen minutes, a technique imported straight from Wagnerian opera. Throughout, unlikely emphases and tonal choices punctuating the songs undergird the show's powerful structure. Some are so subtle they're unlikely to be apparent to listeners, but they're all volitional. In "The Ballad of Sweeney Todd," the particular dissonance that concludes the phrase *the rosy skin/Of righteousness* makes righteousness itself seem hateful and horrifying. In the show's third song, Sweeney sings *There was a barber and his wife,/And she was beautiful;* Anthony Tommasini found in that brief phrase an example of Sondheim's careful intentions. The "spiky dissonance" of the unlikely chord behind *beautiful,* he wrote, "provides a haunting harmonic nudge to the mournful melody." The resulting sound—off-center, unsettled, strangled—was Sondheim's way, Tommasini wrote, of "mak[ing] the telling point that his wife's very beauty made her a victim." This is Sondheim the dramatist, expressing the character's agonizing feeling of loss. Chords so dense and convoluted they could confound a graduate seminar at a conservatory appear throughout *Sweeney,* each an expression of the menacing cloud that darkens the entire show. The agonized theme that accompanies the entrance of the Beggar Woman returns whenever she's on stage—but it also reappears when she's not present, an aural reminder of her centrality to the tale being told.[43]

Sondheim was convinced that even though audiences may not have been aware of these subtleties, he was certain they mattered. He used such motifs, he said, "to re-arouse audience feelings." There was "nothing in the [music] that isn't used at least twice." Like *Night Music*'s basis in three-quarter time, or the roots of his *Follies* songs in the work of specific songwriters from the

1930s, it wasn't necessary for audiences to know what Sondheim was up to. But it mattered enormously to him. Asked in 1990 to pick his "Desert Island Discs" for the well-known British radio program, he listed "The Ballad of Sweeney Todd" along with works by Ravel, Stravinsky, Bartok, and Brahms. The only other piece of his own that he included was "Poems," from *Pacific Overtures*. But he had approached that song, as remarkable as it was, as a problem to be solved; "The Ballad of Sweeney Todd" came from his gut.[44]

Maybe that's why he found the show so easy to write. He spent less time creating this score than he did on any other show. He said it was easy, that it was (mostly) fun, that he loved the chance to indulge his passion for horror movies. When rehearsals began for *A Little Night Music*, he'd only written ten of its eventual fifteen songs; when *Sweeney* rehearsals began, only one song was not yet finished. There were no out-of-town tryouts—just nineteen Broadway previews (the next Sondheim-Prince show, *Merrily We Roll Along*, required forty-four). He told Mark Horowitz, "It just wrote—as Barbra Streisand would say—'like buttah.'"[45]

Sondheim's score collected another Tony (one of eight for the show), but *Sweeney Todd* only returned 59 percent of its investors' money. The reviews were divided between lustrous praise and a few rabid assaults. But two reactions—from Leonard Bernstein and critic John Lahr—burrowed especially deep under Sondheim's skin.

Weeks before opening night, he had erupted in rage at Burt Shevelove and two other friends at the Broadway hangout Joe Allen's during a late dinner following the show's first preview. They were surrounded by the restaurant's trademark: the advertising posters for failed shows, most of them instantly forgotten, that hung on every wall. On most nights, it was a theme diners could laugh at. But on this night Shevelove, who was Sondheim's closest male friend, prefaced his comments on *Sweeney* by asking if Sondheim wanted the good news first, or the bad news. Sondheim blew up. "There is no bad news, Burt!" As he continued, his rage did not abate. Diners at nearby tables were stunned by its sustained vehemence. Shevelove was reduced to tears. For Sondheim, the raw edges of anxiety could become blade-sharp when the first paying audiences saw one of his shows. The rage that emerged from what one of his favorite actors called the "furnace" inside him could be terrifying. New colleagues who were subjected to these toxic outbursts were convinced that their relationships with Sondheim were over. But, as it happened with Shevelove, Mary Rodgers, Mandy Patinkin, and various others, the rages passed, and relationships endured.[46]

Not always, or at least not always in the same fashion. Leonard Bernstein's friendship with Sondheim did not end because of Bernstein's reaction to *Sweeney Todd*, but it was permanently altered. They had always been competitive with each other, but in the years when Sondheim's recognition as a composer was rising and Bernstein's was waning, the ground had shifted. "As Steve got more famous," John Guare said, "Lenny became more hostile." Bernstein didn't exactly assault Sondheim's music, but he did belittle it, even if mostly in private. His high regard for his former collaborator's lyrics was clear, but few things nettled Sondheim so much as being dismissed or diminished as a composer. Praising Sondheim's lyrics after a preview of *Company*, Bernstein had never said a word about the music. When an anxious Sondheim repeatedly asked him what he thought about the music, Bernstein continued to talk only about the lyrics.[47]

Bernstein's final Broadway show, in 1976, was *1600 Pennsylvania Avenue*, an expensive calamity that opened on a Tuesday and closed the following Saturday. Two years later, his wife died, sending him into an emotional nosedive. Less than one year after that, when *Sweeney* opened, Bernstein wasn't happy for his friend. *Sweeney Todd*, he told Mary Rodgers, was so "disgusting" that it was "enough to make you want to throw up in your galoshes." Then: "Steve finally got to write a musical that suits his temperament perfectly."[48]

Bernstein's daughter Jamie thought her father's damning reaction had to do with his mood at the time, and perhaps his growing dependence on amphetamines, but it was also aggravated by simple jealousy. Sondheim agreed, attributing Bernstein's response to *Sweeney*, which he had learned about indirectly, to a pervasive, flailing insecurity now drowned in envy. Sondheim's insight could have been a sign of his own relative contentment, his settling into himself. It might also have been a declaration of victory.[49]

Bernstein lived for another eleven years, and the strain that had entered their relationship expanded. They continued to execute the rituals of friendship, but Sondheim rejected Bernstein's dinner invitations, "because I really couldn't deal with the ego inflation that would happen when other people were around." They saw each other one on one, but only two or three times a year.[50]

After Bernstein's death at seventy-two in 1990, Sondheim was more direct in his criticisms of his old friend. He said that apart from Bernstein's work in *West Side Story* and *Candide*, he couldn't write a ballad; when one of Sondheim's mentees mentioned Bernstein's "Some Other Time" (from *On the Town*), he dismissed it with a wave of his hand and withering praise: He said he liked the sighing sound behind the words "Oh well . . ." Sondheim felt Bernstein tried so hard, and so unsuccessfully, to be current with the culture that he could have been called "Rip van Withit." By way of evidence, Sondheim described the rock music in Bernstein's *Mass* as "actively embarrassing." In 1995, he said Bernstein's self-aggrandizement had been "a form of self-importance that I found both embarrassing and silly."[51]

In a *Newsweek* interview back in 1973, Bernstein had said Sondheim's life was "a massive inhibition." One could define "antithesis" by positioning that comment next to a description of Bernstein's personality. In a way, it was remarkable they remained friends for as long as they did.[52]

Bernstein was involved, even if involuntarily and peripherally, in a *Sweeney Todd* incident that Sondheim would not forget. In *Harper's* magazine, John Lahr used the occasion of the show's opening to write a lengthy piece about how Sondheim's career, in Lahr's view, made "a cult of blasted joys and jubilant despairs." He acknowledged Sondheim's talent but called him "a laureate of disillusion" and a "connoisseur of chaos." He said "words of passion fail him, those for rage come easily," and that Sondheim's work betrays "disgust with family." Near the end of the piece, he finally addressed *Sweeney* in four sentences. The show was "shallow camp," Lahr wrote, and "boulevard nihilism."[53]

Problem was, he hadn't seen it. In 1979, lead times for printing and distribution compelled monthly magazines to lock in the text several weeks before the on-sale date, and nearly two months before the cover date. To make the piece timely, the magazine's editors had determined that it should be available shortly after the show's March 1 opening, even though Lahr's article addressed the show only briefly. Relying solely on the text of the show, which had been provided to him in advance, he strafed it.

Sondheim frequently tried (with infrequent success) to avoid reading reviews. He was unable to adopt Noël Coward's attitude toward criticism, even though he cited it: "It's perfectly simple. They're wrong." Instead he steamed and fumed and on occasion exploded. He variously called critics "apes" and "assholes." They were "merciless" and "vicious" and "waiting for a chance to shoot me through the heart."

His initial reaction to Lahr's piece was strikingly mild. He was angry, of course, strongly objected to a few of Lahr's judgments, and said he resented his interpretation of a comment he'd once made. But his "Dear John" letter was calm in temperament, polite in tone, and even somewhat sanguine: "I hope you'll get a chance to see the show," he wrote. But the fact that Lahr hadn't done so before writing the article was its entirely justified gist, and the brevity of Lahr's "Dear Steve" reply—just the four words "I guess you're right"—burned. What grew into a thirty-year grudge was likely exceeded in length only by Sondheim's terminal distaste for Robert Brustein. Fifteen years after the *Harper's* piece was published, Sondheim fulminated about Lahr in a television interview. Another fifteen years after that, he resurrected the story in *Finishing the Hat*.[54]

Twin ironies framed the Sondheim-Lahr confrontation. In his letter, Sondheim suggested that Lahr "might have asked . . . Leonard Bernstein what he thinks of the score." Sondheim should have been glad he didn't, as "throw up in your galoshes"—a comment Bernstein didn't make until after the show opened—probably wouldn't have helped his case. And when Lahr finally saw *Sweeney*, he loved it. It was, he wrote in the *New Yorker* in 2004, "by far the greatest" of all of Sondheim's shows. "I don't think a critic will ever admit he's wrong," Sondheim once said. At least one did, even if it took him twenty-five years to say so.[55]

On March 27, 1979, Sondheim had a heart attack, barely three weeks after *Sweeney Todd* opened. It almost certainly had nothing to do with his squabbles with Lahr, his differences with Bernstein, or anything else extrinsic; creating Sweeney had been an entirely pleasurable experience. He'd always been reasonably active physically; he liked to swim, and it was not uncommon in those years to see him bicycling from East Forty-ninth Street to the theater district. But years of drinking, smoking, and drugs had aggravated whatever genetic predisposition to heart disease he might have had. His continuing war with Foxy couldn't have helped. When he'd received The Letter, he said, he responded with that scalding four-pager of his own, unloading years of hurt and grievance, and when Foxy later sought to make amends, he maintained, he sent a copy of The Letter back to her. He continued to support her (at the cost of $80,000 a year), but had little to do with her. She sent congratulatory telegrams on opening nights, but they did not speak. She was oblivious. He seethed.[56]

The heart attack took him by surprise. He'd had no intimations of mortality beforehand, but now they couldn't be avoided. He began to watch his diet, and he cut down—for a while—on his drinking. He bought an exercise bike. Friends noticed that he was, said one, "bright-eyed and bushy tailed," no longer as sallow and pale as parchment. With the guidance of one friend, the men's wear designer Lee Wright, he even began to care about his appearance. The heart problems never really went away—he had at least one more heart attack, which he chose to keep private—but Sondheim managed to view the state of his health from an ironic remove. One night in 2004, he was dining with Richard Avedon, Mike Nichols, and Barry Diller (and the journalist Patricia Marx) at Orso, his favorite theater district restaurant, after a performance of *Assassins.* The men jointly—and jovially—whistled past the graveyard, trying to top one another as they argued who among them was going to be the first to die of heart disease.[57]

In March of 1980, almost exactly a year after the heart attack, Sondheim turned fifty. The determination to exercise continued, even if a post-attack pledge to confine his drinking to wine soon evaporated. What he called his "constant series" of short-lived relationships persisted. Some were more rewarding than others, but none approached even the fringes of commitment. Like Bobby in *Company,* he was surrounded by loyal and loving friends, and he was alone. His birthday party in the Belasco Theater glittered with an expansive incarnation of The Blob. His stepmother and both of his half-brothers were there as well. Foxy wasn't on the invitation list, but Dr. Milton Horowitz, Sondheim's psychiatrist, was.[58]

With *Sweeney Todd* behind them, Prince and Sondheim looked for their next project. Prince wanted Sondheim to accept a commission to write an opera based on Billy Wilder's *Sunset Boulevard.* Hugh Wheeler would write the book, Prince would direct, Angela Lansbury would star as Norma Desmond. Years earlier Sondheim and Burt Shevelove had discussed the possibility of a musical based on the movie, but whatever interest Sondheim had once had could not attach itself to an operatic version. "If I wanted to do an opera," he told Prince, "then this is something I would consider. But I don't want to do an opera, therefore I won't consider it." Though he professed to hate opera, he in fact knew the repertoire intimately. He thought Giacomo Puccini was a harmonic genius, and especially cherished the last quartet in the third act of *La Bohème.* He loved Alban Berg's *Wozzeck* and Benjamin Britten's *Peter Grimes.* When Beverly Sills headed the New York City Opera, she invited Sondheim to write one for the company, presumably based on whatever story he wished to tell. "I asked if she would give me two weeks of uninterrupted performances with the same cast," he remembered. "There was silence." But his resistance wasn't solely a matter of wanting to replicate Broadway production standards. It went deeper: like the singer-songwriter pop music of the 1970s, opera was about the singer, he said, and musicals were about the song.[59]

It was Judy Prince who suggested that her husband should create a musical about young people, and when Hal proposed using the 1934 George S. Kaufman–Moss Hart play *Merrily We Roll Along* as their source material, Sondheim immediately said yes. Their choice was either daring or foolish: a show business narrative running backward in time was the sort of challenge both men were drawn to, but it could possibly challenge the

Judy Prince, the woman Sondheim called his muse, 1974. It was her idea that he and her husband create a musical about young people.

audience even more. A year before its first performance, George Furth, whom they brought in to write the book—another Judy suggestion—told a friend that Sondheim was convinced it would be a failure.[60]

Furth also recounted the "suffering" and "agonizing" that Sondheim endured during the early stages of the show's creation. This may have been because the inverted structure of the work disrupted Sondheim's usual process of building a score chronologically, laying out elements early that can reappear later in modified form without disrupting either narrative or musical logic. The story focuses on Franklin Shepard, who is encountered at its beginning as a vain, shallow, and completely dislikable film producer in his forties; at the show's end, he is an idealistic young composer imagining a meaningful and emotionally gratifying future. Chronology excepted, it was, Sondheim said, "nothing more nor less than an updated version of *Allegro*," the Rodgers and Hammerstein failure he had witnessed up close in 1947, the show whose theme Oscar had described as "losing sight of your goals." This time, though, Sondheim considered the subject of *Merrily We Roll Along* to be closer to home, or at least to the world he saw around him: the theme, he told George Furth, was "First you compromise your art, then you lose it." Fairly early in the show (but not the chronology), the audience encounters the show's most dramatic song, "Not a Day Goes By," as an expression of rage and hurt; much earlier in the chronology (but deep into the second act), the song reappears as an expression of ardent young love. In effect, the backward-running clock placed the reprise before its original statement.[61]

Sondheim's slow progress on the show also arose from his admitted uneasiness with Prince's determination to cast inexperienced young performers. Prince believed the cast's youth and freshness would win over the audience despite what Sondheim considered its "very depressing" plot. Prince certainly persuaded himself: "Some people think that Steve and I do cold, intellectual shows," Prince said early on. "This is the show where we're going to show them that that's not who we are at all. This show is full of heart, warmth, humanity, humor, and musical comedy." Then they got to work on a show about three young people who start out glowing with optimism but end up emotionally disfigured, or creatively thwarted, or drunk. Backwards.[62]

One song Sondheim sketched out would have taken the

inverted chronology of the show to convoluted extremes: it chronicled the pregnancy of the main character's wife from end to beginning. The song, he explained, would "start with the scream of birth and end with the scream of orgasm." He was talked out of it.[63]

The number in *Merrily We Roll Along* that Sondheim often said was the only fully autobiographical song he ever wrote was "Opening Doors," the invigorating, playful, and upbeat recollection of the years when he, Prince, and Mary Rodgers were themselves starting out, brightly trying to make it in show business. Of course, the three main characters in *Merrily We Roll Along* were not the surrogate son of musical theater's most successful lyricist, the daughter of its most successful composer, or a young man whose pluck and ambition had him working at the side of Broadway's leading director at twenty-two. They'd had to open doors when they started, but they really hadn't had to push on them terribly hard.

Most of the show recalled Sondheim's early discontents more than the collegial joys. The repeated trope in "Old Friends"—*Here's to us!/Who's like us?/Damn few!*—is a barbed reprise of the Robert Burns aphorism he had learned at Williams. In one section of "Opening Doors," the coarse producer who rejects Frank's music is an unsubtle (if amusing) caricature of the producers and critics who had once called Sondheim's music unhummable: *Why can't you throw 'em a crumb?/What's wrong with letting 'em tap/Their toes a bit?/I'll let you know when Stravinsky has a hit—/Give me some melodee-dee-dee . . . !*" The moment in the show that was even closer to Sondheim's lived experience than "Opening Doors" isn't a song; it's a critical scene when the young Frank is asked, even begged, to play a song at a Blob-ish party and then the crowd starts "talking while you're playing, and drinking and completely ignoring you, having stuck you there at the piano. And that's autobiographical." The rawness of those painful experiences was real. What was equally real, and implicitly expressed, was his unabating resentment of those who had dismissed him as a composer.[64]

While Prince tried to figure out what the show would look like, Sondheim labored on the music. Prince had imagined making the young actors look old at the opening scene—graying hair, age-appropriate clothing—then having them grow younger and younger through makeup magic and true-to-the-times costumes. He basically ended up with no costumes or sets at all, just T-shirts for the actors, bleachers for the sets. Sondheim had his own distinctive idea: Determined to represent the musical tastes of the period the show spanned (roughly 1955–1980), he decided to lean heavily on the AABA or ABAB structures of the era's conventional pop songs. This was so far removed from his long-line mode, or from various other extended forms he had mastered, that *Merrily* turned out to be, he said, the most difficult score he would ever write. For Sondheim, composing *Sweeney*'s grim and brooding score had been stress-free. By contrast, writing its successor—largely conventional in musical form, tuneful in expression, as "hummable" as any he would produce—was torture.[65]

This was partly because he was determined to tie the various pieces of the show together through the repeated use of musical motifs, subtly applied. The outstanding example of this, as it happens, was launched in the original production by a song that was eventually dropped from the score. "The Hills of Tomorrow" both raised the curtain on Act 1 and brought it down at the end of Act 2. It's a typical graduation song, sonorous and stately, that is first sung while the older, corrupted Frank, by now a famous film producer, addresses his high school class's twenty-fifth reunion. It reappears two and a half hours later in the show (which is to say, twenty-five years earlier in the characters' lives) when the young, idealistic Frank speaks to his class as valedictorian. Along the way, its opening notes (*Behold the hills . . .*) appear and reappear. The phrase introduces the first measures of "Good Thing Going." It shows up throughout "Bobby and Jackie and Jack," supporting the words *We're bringing back style to the White House* and many other phrases. It's all but omnipresent in "Opening Doors," as punctuation, italics, asides, declarations, running through the song's "B" section (*They're always popping their cork/. . . The cops the cabbies the salesgirls . . . /You gotta have a real taste for maniacs . . .*"). When Frank is auditioning singers for his cabaret act it shows up as *Who wants to live in New York?* And when the cynical producer fails to see Frank's genius, it underlies *There's not a tune you can hum* and *Why can't you throw 'em a crumb?* Throughout the song Frank is at the piano, engaged in a version of Sondheim's own laborious process, running through thirty-two different harmonizations of the theme as he searches for the right key for "Good Thing Going." "Everything in that number is me," Sondheim told Mark Horowitz. Frank, he explained, was "trying out everything until he gets it."[66]

Sondheim also found many other ways to knit the score together, the introduction to one showing up in the bridge of another, the accompaniment to a third forming the melody of a fourth. He once likened this interlocking compositional technique, which he had learned while studying Beethoven with Milton Babbitt, to the rearrangement of "modular furniture." That was a modest way of explaining how he turned a series of songs based on pop forms into an ingeniously integrated whole.[67]

But when compositional complexity threatened to overtake the talents of the young performers, Sondheim managed to adjust. Frank's collaborator and best friend, Charley Kringas, sings "Franklin Shepard, Inc.," an account of the collapse of their partnership and their friendship—a rapid-fire, word-filled, five-minute number that must play as both critically dramatic and bitterly comic. Prince and Sondheim placed this weight on the shoulders of Lonny Price, a twenty-two-year-old actor of limited vocal ability who had barely two years of professional experience. "Franklin Shepard, Inc.," with its devilishly complex lyrics, was one of the last songs Sondheim had completed, just days before previews began. "I had only three good notes," Price recalled, so Sondheim "kept putting them in the song. It was like the greatest tailor in the world making you a suit." In every production since, every Charley has worn the brilliant garment Sondheim fashioned from those same three notes.[68]

Not everyone in the cast was so lucky. When Sondheim asked the then-unknown Jason Alexander, who played the producer Joe Jacobson, if there was anything he wanted to tell him about his voice, Alexander said he had trouble hearing chromatic scales. When Sondheim came back with Alexander's material in "Opening Doors" (*Why don't you throw 'em a crumb? . . .*), it was entirely chromatic. "It's time you learn," he said.[69]

By the end of rehearsals, the show seemed to be in good shape. By the time the curtain came down at the end of the first preview just days later, the principals sensed a catastrophe at hand. Audiences hated it, right from the start. Actor David Loud was distracted by what he thought was a flickering light until he realized that its unsteady glow was caused by audience members walking past an exit sign as they departed the theater, sometimes in the middle of a number. The absence of costumes and scenery was at best puzzling, at worst an insult to people who had paid for a night in a Broadway theater, not in a high school gym. Many in the young cast revealed their youth more than their talent. Choreographer Ron Field appraised the cast's dance skills bluntly: "I'm not saying that there were two or three kids that I had to bury behind the good ones. If I buried the bad ones, you'd have been looking at the set." Franklin begins the show as an egregious cad, which made anything resembling empathy for the main character a challenge for the audience. Even firing the lead actor during previews and replacing him with the relatively experienced Jim Walton didn't help.[70]

Nothing could save *Merrily We Roll Along*. Its six weeks of previews formed a marathon the actors had to run with heavy weights on their shoulders. Sondheim chose to remember it as an exhilarating time—fixing that scene, adjusting that song, otherwise calling upon the most inventive aspects of the Prince-Sondheim partnership—but it was nonetheless unproductive. The two postponements of its announced opening night were perceived by many as precisely what they were: the death rattle of an ailing show. Three weeks into previews, despite the rewriting and restaging, Sondheim found himself thinking that it was "one of the worst shows I ever saw." Word of mouth was terrible, and after its grim opening night many of the reviews ("shambles," "blunder," "dud") were even worse. The biggest surprise might have been that the show lasted sixteen performances. Assessing their partnership thirty years later, Sondheim said, "Hal's function was to keep the truck moving, mine to see it didn't fall off the cliff." This time, the metaphor hadn't worked. What George Furth had sensed five months earlier—Sondheim's belief that *Merrily* would be a failure—concluded in a bleak form of wish fulfillment.[71]

Over the next four decades, a series of directors improved it brick by brick. Songs cut from the original were reinstated, others were moved from one place in the book to another. Hoping to make Frank more sympathetic, Furth and Sondheim bestowed a son on the troubled Shepard family. The graduation song that underlay so much of the score was finally dropped, leaving behind only a series of shadows in the music that had been based on it: variations without a theme.

The show itself left behind not a shadow, but a chasm. The usual publisher of scripts from Sondheim shows stopped publication; in 2023, a single proof copy of the unpublished book was available for sale for $4,500. *Merrily* had managed to make it through seven more performances than *Anyone Can Whistle*, but this was worse. The earlier show had been a thirty-four-year-old's failed experiment; this one was the work of two men who had earned endless acclaim as they went about remaking the American musical theater. In his late eighties, Sondheim insisted that, except for "Opening Doors," *Merrily We Roll Along* "isn't about my life," but he also said, "I identify with the show intimately." Looking backward—appropriately—to his fifties, it was clear that its violent crash left behind the deepest wounds he would ever suffer in his professional life. And, it turned out, he believed they were inflicted by envy.[72]

6

Reaching the Summit

In 1964, Stephen Sondheim found himself in a he-said/ he-said dispute with lyricist Alan Jay Lerner. The subject of their spat was inconsequential, but Sondheim felt he had to address it—even though, he wrote, "I am well past the stage of losing sleep over small malices and theater bitchiness."[1]

Hardly. Over the following years, he'd grumble and gripe and sometimes rant about "the professional bitches" in New York who see a show early so they can "tell all their friends how terrible it is." Before *Sweeney Todd*, out-of-town tryouts had protected his shows, he said, "from the vultures" who started to badmouth his work before it settled into its final form. "They're out to destroy you," he said. They were moved by "viciousness." His popularity in the New York theater world was certainly not enhanced by what he'd said to Clive Hirschhorn when *Pacific Overtures* was about to open, comments he'd never disavowed—among them, "there's very little I admire" on Broadway.[2]

The morning after *Merrily We Roll Along* opened in 1981, his response to a congratulatory message from Patti LuPone revealed at least a semblance of serenity: "Thanks for the good wishes," he wrote. "I wish they had worked." But by the time the show closed two weeks later, serenity had been replaced by peevishness, which over time curdled into rage. He reported that he'd overheard a conversation in the lobby: "'It's the end of Prince and Sondheim,' and someone else said, 'And about time.'" The reviewers, he said, "thought it would be fun to chop us up in public and they had a great time." Even three decades later, he thought the entire experience had been soiled by Broadway people who resented that he and Prince "had done eccentric shows and yet were not living in garrets." Simply put, the theater community "hated me and Hal."[3]

Sondheim hated right back. Seven months after the *Merrily* disaster, he described the world of producers and backers and agents and various other Broadway types as "stupid" and "useless." He had started his career motivated by "the idealistic notion, when I was 20, that I was going into the theater. I wasn't. I was going into show business and I was a fool to think otherwise." After *Merrily We Roll Along*, he thought about stepping away from Broadway altogether. "At this moment in my life," he said in the summer of 1983, "I really am considering not writing anymore."[4]

It wasn't a ruse. His two decades of festering distaste for Broadway had ripened into an incapacitating funk. He said he wanted to "find something to satisfy myself that does not involve Broadway and dealing with all those people" who had assaulted his show out of what he perceived as dishonorable motives. "I don't want to be in this profession," he said. "It's just too hostile and mean-spirited."[5]

There's a song in *The Frogs* called "It's Only a Play" that suggested an alternate reaction to criticism. The title reappears five times in the lyrics, each time following a stanza of advice

Sondheim might have invoked in the wake of *Merrily We Roll Along*. At one point, the character sings *It really doesn't matter/What somebody writes;* at another, the performer declares that *words are merely chatter,/And easy to say/It doesn't really matter/It's only a play*. But Sondheim was unable to follow his own advice. He was in his early fifties. His health wasn't great. All three of his most recent shows—*Pacific Overtures, Sweeney Todd, Merrily We Roll Along*—had been financial flops, and the critical response had been deeply divided. He could (and did) blame Prince for *Merrily*'s ill-conceived staging. He could (and did) blame critics for their stupidity, and the Broadway community for its mean-spirited envy. But he couldn't not worry. He couldn't relax. *Merrily* wasn't "only a play"; like all of his work from the moment he decided to write lyrics solely for his own music, it was a part of him.

So he pondered alternatives. He was going to invent video games. He was going to write a mystery novel. He didn't want to conduct; he had soured on that years earlier when, he believed, Bernstein persuaded him to conduct a piece in order to embarrass him. Remembering the difficulty he'd had with the task, Sondheim told an interviewer in 1982 that Bernstein "liked it that I'd fall on my ass." He did not want to direct: "I don't like dealing with people," he explained in 1982. "The fun's not dealing with them."[6]

Some of his closest friends believed him when he said he was done with Broadway. But when he told his agent, Flora Roberts, that he was going to stop writing for the stage, she asked him who would care and then answered the question herself: "Nobody but you and me." That rang true. He began to reconsider, and was drawn back from his disabling despair by someone he did not know, and who came from a theatrical world far removed from Broadway. In the last five words of the first volume of the Hat Box, which takes the reader up through *Merrily*

We Roll Along, Sondheim explained the onset of his creative reawakening: "Then I met James Lapine."[7]

The widely held belief that the *Merrily* disaster led to a rupture in Sondheim's personal relationship with Prince isn't accurate. Although Prince thought it was time for them to take a break from each other professionally, they remained close friends. Less than four months after the show closed, they visited Venice together, living large in the Gritti Palace. The fact that Prince went on to direct six shows (including *The Phantom of the Opera*) in the next six years with six different collaborators was beside the point; in the same crowded decade that had seen five Sondheim-Prince shows, he had directed seven Prince-with-Someone-Else shows (including *Evita*). But Prince's belief that his professional partnership with Sondheim had "run out of steam" was accurate. It was another two decades before the next—and only—time they would work together again.[8]

James Lapine did not necessarily bring a new burst of steam into Sondheim's life, but he brought something deeper: a collaboration that, over a period of thirteen years, yielded three musicals more firmly rooted in Sondheim's own psyche than any that preceded them. There had been a lot of Sondheim in *Company*, a veiled piece of him in *Sweeney*, and a vivid chunk of his life in *Merrily*. But *Sunday in the Park with George* was about the way an artist's inner life is expressed in the process of artistic creation. *Into the Woods* addressed loneliness, connection, learning from mistakes. *Passion* was informed by a discovery that Sondheim finally made in his seventh decade: the redemptive power of love.

Lapine was laconic where Prince was excitable, deliberate where Prince was impulsive. Prince had his mind set on Broadway when he was a child; Lapine was a graphic designer who drifted into the theater by accident, when he was teaching advertising design at the Yale Drama School. He wrote and directed three off-Broadway plays between 1977 and 1981; Sondheim had seen and admired his *Twelve Dreams*, a play rooted in Jungian psychoanalysis. A mutual friend introduced them.

Lapine's first impression of Sondheim was established when he came, at Sondheim's invitation, to Forty-ninth Street. Sondheim lit a joint, handed it to him, and then they talked, and talked, and talked. It was, on its surface, an improbable pairing: Sondheim was fifty-two, Lapine thirty-three. Sondheim, who had never lived south of Forty-ninth Street, was a creature of an elegant part of uptown Manhattan. Lapine, who came from a middle-class family in a small industrial city in north-central Ohio, couldn't have been more downtown, living at the time in a rat-ridden loft on Ann Street. Lapine knew very little about musicals; recalling the origin of their collaboration forty years later, he said, "that's what Steve liked about me." The only musical he had ever worked on was the one-act, off-Broadway *March of the Falsettos*, and *Sweeney Todd* was the only Sondheim show he'd ever seen.[9]

In one of his mid-1990s interviews with Meryle Secrest, Sondheim said, "As I've told you repeatedly, I think writing is from the unconscious." Lapine helped him find his way there—or at least partway there, down the intricate pathways leading to the hidden laboratory of Sondheim's creative self. Answering a query about the origins of *Sunday in the Park with George*, Sondheim wrote, "The idea grew from both of us and was, if anything, executed more by [Lapine] than by me. The show is his more than mine—or at least equally his." One was the explorer; the other was the island to be explored.[10]

After that first, marijuana-fueled marathon in the darkened den, Lapine and Sondheim pushed further. Subsequent meetings led eventually to a decision to create a work of art based on a work of art: *Sunday Afternoon on the Island of La Grande Jatte*, painted by Georges Seurat in 1886. When Sondheim's friend

Cynthia O'Neal asked him what he was working on early in the show's development, he answered, "You want to see the cast? You want to see the set?"—and then handed her a postcard of Seurat's masterpiece.[11]

Two things about the painting provided Sondheim with both motivation and context: None of the forty-eight anonymous people who inhabit it are looking at one another, and—crucially—Lapine noted that one person was absent, namely the artist himself. That so little was known about Seurat's life was a gift. It gave Sondheim room to extrapolate from his own experience: "I'm able to get into Seurat's head," he told Secrest, "because there's a part of me that knows something about this."[12]

In fact, many parts of the inner Sondheim emerge throughout the show, particularly in the life and actions of George, the Seurat stand-in: the artist alone with his art ("Color and Light"); the precedence of art over human relationships ("Finishing the Hat"); the corruptions of commerce ("Putting It Together"); the impossibility, or maybe even irrelevance, of love in the life of an artist ("I am what I do," George tells his peeved lover, Dot, in "We Do Not Belong Together"). Most of all, running beneath the entire show is the aching sentiment expressed throughout his career, here embodied in three words the protagonist utters to himself: "Connect, George. Connect."

"As for what I'm working on now," Sondheim wrote to a fan in the spring of 1983 as the show was taking shape, "it's a small and peculiar musical [that] goes into rehearsal in two weeks for a workshop production. . . . The piece is designed for Off-Broadway, as I really don't want to write anything for Broadway ever again." It may not have been entirely his choice. The dismal financial performance of his recent shows couldn't have been encouraging to prospective backers, and his decision to collaborate with the very un-Broadway Lapine could hardly have helped.[13]

But Lapine had connections to André Bishop and the theater

he led, Playwrights Horizons, one of the not-for-profit pioneers of Theater Row. This small group of former pornography shops and burlesque houses on West Forty-second Street that had been converted into theaters were a midtown avatar of the downtown Off-Broadway ethos. Even more distant from Sondheim's experience was the idea of developing a show through a workshop process in a 135-seat theater, where sets would be minimal or non-existent, the orchestra would have only four pieces, and audiences—first invited, then paying—would effectively see the show in utero. At the first performance, there wasn't even a second act yet, and during its two months (including rehearsals) at Playwrights Horizons, Sondheim conjured eight songs that hadn't existed when rehearsals began. For Sondheim, it all worked just fine. He and Lapine would share a joint upstairs in Bishop's office before the show, waiting for the audience to arrive. Then Lapine would say, "It's magic time," and they'd descend to the theater. In 1976, Sondheim had disparaged not-for-profit producers, some of them government subsidized—even, and specifically, Joseph Papp's Public Theatre—for lacking the courage of those who put their own money on the line. Now Sondheim thought, "This is the way I want to work the rest of my life."[14]

Early in the workshop process (which was partly underwritten by Dorothy Hammerstein, Oscar's widow) Sondheim's agent issued a sort of warning to André Bishop. Sondheim was "a follower, not a leader," Roberts told him. "But if no one else is leading, he'll happily take over. You shouldn't let him." He didn't. Sondheim's relationship with Lapine mirrored his experience with Prince.[15]

Despite Sondheim's earlier protestations, *Sunday in the Park with George* did find its way to Broadway, courtesy of the Shubert Organization. Co-producer Emanuel Azenberg attributed the Shuberts' interest to "Sondheim intimidation." This was a version of the sometimes-acute fever that infects even the most commercial of producers: they like to be involved in prestige productions. But as opening night approached, it seemed the show might be a replay of *Merrily We Roll Along*. In the first preview, Act 1 ran an hour and forty-five minutes. Frantic adjustments could barely keep pace with the speed of preview audiences walking out of the theater. One of the producers took to holding the lobby door open to accommodate people leaving mid-show; it squeaked if he didn't. At the beginning of Act 2, the second line of "It's Hot Up Here"—*It's hot and it's monotonous*—prompted one audience member to shout, "It sure is!," which in turn provoked a burst of sympathetic laughter. With the deadline for Tony Award eligibility approaching, late changes (including the addition of the sublime "Children and Art" just seventy-two hours before the critics arrived) delayed the show's opening for nine fretful days. Expecting to be soon out of work, crew members gave the show a nickname: "Sunday in the Dark and Bored."[16]

Among the complications that cast, orchestra, and audience faced as *Sunday in the Park with George* made its awkward passage to opening night was its musical intricacy, which was as ambitious as the interwoven scores for *Sweeney Todd* and *Merrily We Roll Along*, and in some ways more complex. Several musicians turned down offers to play in the show's orchestra because the score was so challenging. "The opening sequence is a son of a bitch," said music director Paul Gemignani, by way of example, "because the chords have to come on the movement of the trees" on stage. The piano arpeggios that open the show reappear at the end of "We Do Not Belong Together" and, slowed down and slightly altered, form nearly the entire accompaniment to "Children and Art." The stippling rhythm in "Color and Light" (a direct counterpart to George's pointillistic painting technique) introduces a rhythmically intense motif that recurs throughout both acts. In fact, most of the songs in Act 1 have musical counterparts in Act 2—for instance, the angular title song, which opens the first act, is echoed in "It's Hot Up Here," which opens the second. Few in the audience might ever have realized it,* but the melodic hook of the show's signature song, "Finishing the Hat," comes back nearly intact in the second act as "Putting It Together." The melody that carries the title phrases of both songs is identical, save for the addition of the note behind *geth* in its second incarnation. But the dramatic tone of this fragment is so different in the two songs—even though the tune is not—that even Mandy Patinkin, who as George sang both for more than three hundred performances, never knew they were the same.[17]

For years, extreme Sondheim devotees have been able to identify one another with a question that is also an acknowledgment: "'Someone in a Tree' or 'Finishing the Hat'?" The question is which of the two songs is the greater work; the acknowledgment simply demonstrates that both asker and asked are members of the Cult of Sondheim—Sondheads—and both know these two emblematic songs are at the core of his accomplishment. Behind the narrative deftness of "Someone in a Tree" (the song that made Sondheim cry every time he heard it) is the effort of a young boy trying to connect. Beneath the pyrotechnic virtuosity of "Finishing the Hat" (the song he chose as the title for volume 1 of his complete lyrics) is the effort of a mature artist trying to create.

The inspiration for the song came as so many of Sondheim's best ideas did, from his librettist's words. Lapine's original book for the show included a scene in which George, sitting in the park with his sketch pad, ponders what he believes others—particularly his lover, Dot—simply do not understand. Lapine wrote, "I have to finish the hat," and a creative dam was swept away. The song "poured out" of Sondheim, Lapine remembered.[18]

* Including, I should acknowledge, me.

The melding of music and lyrics in "Finishing the Hat" show Sondheim at his most inspired. A series of repetitive phrases sets up the song: *Let her look for me to tell me why she left me—/As I always knew she would./I had thought she understood./They have never understood,/And no reason that they should,/But if anybody could* . . . Both the music and the lyrics of the five rhyming lines, so repetitive as to be nearly identical, establish a brooding, almost sullen mood. The rhythmic punctuation in the accompaniment to *Finishing the hat,/How you have to finish the hat,* already established in "Color and Light," signals the return of the show's essential subject matter. But the technical aspects of artistic creation move toward the personal in the song's bridge, which starts with a mighty *sforzando* supporting a soaring leap of an octave (*And how you're always turning back too late* . . .). Some musicians refer to a song's bridge as its "release," a usage that is particularly appropriate here. This moment in the song is an emotional release as well as a musical one—intense, emphatic, and for the character, necessary. Throughout the entire song, the lyrics are a pileup of subordinate clauses looking for resolution, which they finally locate in the last two lines. Those final lines form the only complete sentence in the entire song, and also the satisfaction George had been seeking: *Look, I made a hat/Where there never was a hat.* Sondheim considered it the only song he ever wrote that expressed his interior creative experience.[19]

The night he completed the song, Sondheim called John Weidman in a state of ecstatic agitation. Weidman, who had written the libretto for *Pacific Overtures*, had nothing to do with the new show, but Sondheim couldn't keep his excitement hidden; he needed to tell someone. Writing the song had solved a narrative problem, but he had also accomplished something larger than that. He didn't sing or play "Finishing the Hat" for Weidman, or even recite the lyrics—he only wanted to say that he had achieved something important. For all Weidman knew, he was the fifth person Sondheim had called that night, and he happened to be the only one to pick up the phone. Sondheim later said that the song reflected his experience of "trancing out" when he was writing or composing. But Weidman saw something more than that. "'Finishing the Hat,'" he said, "always felt to me as close to Steve looking in a mirror and writing down what he saw as anything he ever wrote." Weidman, and others, also invoked another visual metaphor in the lyric's key phrase: *How you watch the rest of the world/From a window/While you finish the hat.* There was the world, and there was the act of creation. George chose creation, and so did Sondheim.[20]

James Lapine believed that the deeper meanings of *Sunday in the Park with George* may have struck Sondheim at a subliminal level, but "it would not be like him to say, 'I want to write about an artist.'" In fact, Sondheim told Ryan Mekenian, an aspiring musical theater writer-director, that because "James and I were smoking pot the whole time," he couldn't recall how he'd arrived at certain decisions about the show. But he eventually agreed that the artist on stage, though initially conceived by Lapine, came to represent much of what he himself thought about making art. Discussing *Sunday* with author Martin Gottfried in the early 1990s, he said, "I believe all creative artists reveal themselves more in their work than in their conversations." Speaking through a show's characters enabled him to say things he wouldn't say out loud.[21]

In his *New York Times* review, Frank Rich compared George in *Sunday* to Franklin Shepard in *Merrily*. "Instead of a showbiz figure's self-martyrdom, we get an artist's self-revelation." He wrote that "this protagonist is possibly a double for Mr. Sondheim at his most self-doubting." He also called the show "audacious," "remarkable," "gorgeous," and "wondrous," and in the weeks following the opening Rich and his colleagues at the *Times* carried a torch that illuminated its road to success, publishing article after article about the show. In the parodic game Broadway types liked to play, "Sunday in the Dark and Bored" was discarded—the stage crew managed to keep their jobs for 604 performances—and was replaced by "Sunday in the *Times* with George."

Nearly a year into its run, *Sunday in the Park with George* won the 1985 Pulitzer Prize for drama. The Pulitzer committee has a formal nominating process, which was fulfilled in this case not by its creators or its producers but by a choral director Sondheim knew, acting on his own. The recognition consequently came as a complete surprise. What had come before it, however, was a complete shock. At the Tony Awards ceremony in 1984, *Sunday* won in only two categories, for design and lighting. *La Cage aux Folles* swept six, including best musical, best book of a musical (by Harvey Fierstein), best director of a musical (Arthur Laurents), and best score (Jerry Herman). Cynthia O'Neal, sitting next to Sondheim, said that when Herman's name was announced, Sondheim made "a sound that sounded like he'd been punched in the gut." He said he wanted to run up the aisle and leave immediately. O'Neal, knowing how the rest of the audience would react, persuaded him to stay.[22]

Still crueler indignity arrived moments later. In his acceptance speech, Herman said, "This award forever shatters the myth about the musical theater. There's been a rumor around for a couple of years that the simple hummable show tune was no longer welcome on Broadway. Well, that's alive and well at the Palace."

Herman later denied it was a dig at Sondheim. No one believed him.[23]

When Lapine and Sondheim learned that their show had won the Pulitzer, they were in California with George Furth, developing a revised version of *Merrily We Roll Along* for the La Jolla Playhouse. Prince's critical mistake—casting inexperienced young people—would not be repeated in La Jolla. For one preproduction workshop, Lapine had asked Kevin Kline and Jeff Goldblum to read the parts of Franklin Shepard and his songwriting collaborator Charley Kringas. Furth was shocked. Everything that had been awful about the original production was now, he said, "astonishingly wonderful." Sondheim explained it to him: "We just learned that when amateurs do it it's very amateurish, and when professionals do it it's wonderfully professional."[24]

Lapine conjured some radical changes in the show's arc, particularly in the way it starts and ends. "The Blob," one of the songs cut from the original production during previews and resuscitated in La Jolla, enabled Sondheim to apply a self-satirizing dagger to the crowd—very much his own crowd—that gathered around the Bernsteins back in the sixties. This version would become the stencil for subsequent revisions, and revisions of revisions, that producers would mount over the next three-plus decades. Few worked. The lead character, Frank, remained unsympathetic. The backward chronology threw audiences off balance. Authorized productions wandered from La Jolla to Leicester, England, and to Washington, London, and Cincinnati, with several stops in New York along the way. It took forty-two years from its original production to return, at last, to Broadway, where it was received by audiences both emotionally engaged and wildly enthusiastic.

It was neither Prince nor Lapine who was responsible for the revival of a different Sondheim musical in 1985, in a production that was in some ways more impactful than any production of any Sondheim show that had gone before it. If there was a specific moment when Sondheim fans turned into a cult, and Sondheim cultists became recognized cultural heralds, it occurred at the first of two benefit performances of *Follies* at Lincoln Center that September—the one that would lead James

Kirkwood to write in the liner notes for the subsequent album, "Where were you on the night of September 6?"

As the original *Follies* had receded into the past, it simultaneously attained epic status among Sondheim's most devoted fans. But a full-scale revival of *Follies* was unimaginable. It was too big a show, too lavish—the Ziegfeld-style costumes alone were budget-busters—too dependent on stars and sets and scale. The absence of new productions afforded its admirers the opportunity to speak of *Follies* the way an old soldier might recall the thrill of a long-forgotten battlefield victory. Their insistence on its virtues was intensified by the show's only palpable remnant, the badly botched original cast album from Capitol Records, which both enraged the show's devotees and, in turn, inspired their ardent advocacy for a new version. It was not a recording of *Follies*, but a *version* of *Follies*, poorly recorded and grievously abridged.

An opportunity presented itself once the glow from *Sunday in the Park with George* had burned away *Merrily We Roll Along*'s lingering fog. Ted Chapin, who had been Sondheim's gofer on the original production of *Follies*, was now the president of the Rodgers and Hammerstein Organization, the company that managed the rights to all the Rodgers and Hammerstein musicals worldwide. As such, the thirty-five-year-old Chapin was a powerful figure on Broadway, and a powerful advocate for the show that had launched his career. It was his idea to give the show the cast album it deserved, which in turn prompted the idea of recording it live, in concert.

A few months before the ensuing two-night stand at Lincoln Center (presented as a semi-staged charity benefit), George Furth told some friends that "becoming a legend has been good for [Sondheim], because he's risen to the title handsomely." That he had achieved the rank of legend was confirmed the day tickets for this new *Follies* went on sale. In that pre-internet age, when ticket buyers had to wait on telephone hold for ages or make a pilgrimage to the box office at Avery Fisher Hall, every ticket for the pair of performances—all 5,500 of them—was gone in two hours and 51 minutes. A few days before the first show, Samuel Freedman wrote in the *Times*, "All this activity suggests that both critics and audiences are catching up to Mr. Sondheim."[25]

He probably had no idea how accurate this would prove to be. Sondheim was able to recruit exactly the cast he wanted, including Mandy Patinkin, Elaine Stritch, Barbara Cook (who had last appeared in a Broadway musical fourteen years before), and Carol Burnett (twenty years). It had been even longer since Lee Remick had made her one short-lived appearance in a Broadway musical: *Anyone Can Whistle.* Despite Remick's weakness as a singer, Sondheim wanted her as Phyllis, arguably the most important role in the show.

Producer Thomas Z. Shepard, who had overseen the recording of several Sondheim shows (not including the Capitol Records fiasco), considered it "the first truly adult musical," its subtext similar, he said, to what Edward Albee had evoked in *Who's Afraid of Virginia Woolf?* As such he didn't want applause interrupting the plot's somewhat grim unfolding on the cast album. But midway through the opening song, "Beautiful Girls," as the women in the cast came on stage one by one to the rousing accompaniment of the New York Philharmonic, Shepard's intentions were obliterated. A wave of applause, shouting, whistling, and other varieties of audible rapture rose to the last row of the topmost balcony, then rose and rose again as each of the female stars appeared on stage. For more than a minute it continued, at full pitch. As the evening unrolled, many of the singers—especially Stritch and Burnett—induced a similar response after their big numbers, and at the concert's end, the cheering and screaming and stomping returned and redoubled, achieving its final summit when Sondheim joined the cast on stage. Mandy Patinkin noticed that the person Sondheim hugged was Remick. "I stood there," Patinkin recalled, "and thought, 'He loved her.'"[26]

Herb Ross, who directed this no-sets concert version of the show, considered it "a staged oratorio." But it was more than that: it was a confirmation, even a coronation. Sondheim's transcendent role in the universe of musical theater had been confirmed.

Asked about the event more than thirty years later, Sondheim said, "It was good."[27]

Sondheim turned fifty-five in 1985. The success of *Sunday in the Park with George* and the Lincoln Center *Follies* had minimized, if not quite eliminated, the pain induced by *Merrily We Roll Along*. The horrors of the AIDS scourge were omnipresent (he would lose many intimates to it, including Michael Bennett, whose choreography had so enriched *Company* and *Follies*, and Lou Vargas, his friend and house man of nearly twenty years), but Sondheim himself remained free of infection. He dated various men, but not in conscious search of a lasting relationship. His professional partnership with Lapine, so clearly successful, had them working on what would become *Into the Woods*. He bought a handsome clapboard farmhouse set on twenty acres of meadow and hills and elm trees in Roxbury, in northwestern Connecticut. He set up his friend Peter Wooster, a talented designer, in the adjacent carriage house, where he would manage the renovation and redesign of the main house's interior. It evolved into a permanent residency as Wooster supervised the installation of the pool and the formal gardens and the professional croquet court and imported an old barn that he converted into a guesthouse. When a visiting John Guare once marveled at the never ending series of improvements, Sondheim said, "John, you forget. I *am* made of money."[28]

But, as generally contented as he seemed to be, Sondheim was drinking heavily again. The wine-only pledge he self-imposed after his heart attack in 1979 had been discarded. Drugs returned as well; he believed they, like alcohol, made him productive and happy, and if anyone ever heard him express deep regret over his devotion to them, they've kept it a secret. One evening in the mid-1980s, as Sondheim, Lapine, and George Furth prepared to see the first licensed production of *Merrily We Roll Along* at a small theater in Metuchen, New Jersey, he urged a tab of ecstasy on Lapine, took a hit himself, and told him not to mention it to the stridently abstemious Furth (whose only addiction was Alcoholics Anonymous). Lou Vargas drove as Sondheim and Lapine rolled to Metuchen together, their oblivious colleague sandwiched between his two merrily tripping colleagues.[29]

In 1985, after the revised *Merrily* opened in La Jolla, the two men immersed themselves in *Into the Woods.* Lapine said that as much as *Sunday* had been created in clouds of marijuana smoke, *Into the Woods* was fueled by cocaine—"mounds" of it, he said, the best anyone could buy. (Sondheim once gave Mary Rodgers an antique pocket watch for her birthday; only years later did she discover a lump of cocaine nestled inside it.) Worried about his own health, Lapine stopped using along the way. Sondheim persisted. A few years later he said he knew that coke was habit-forming, and not the best idea for someone who'd had a heart attack. He also said that it energized him.[30]

However concerned he may have been about his collaborator's cocaine and alcohol use, Lapine said working with Sondheim was always a fulfilling and joyous experience. Once Richard Rodgers and *Do I Hear a Waltz?* were a distant memory, this was true for all of Sondheim's collaborators, who marveled at his verbal quickness, his nonpareil wit, his ability to put a quarrel (or worse) behind him and then get back to work. But the Lapine partnership was an especially creative one. The shows with Prince had all been presented to him (*Company* by Furth and Prince, *Follies* by James Goldman, *Pacific Overtures* by John Weidman via Prince) or based on pre-existing material (*A Little Night Music, Sweeney Todd, Merrily We Roll Along*). The first two shows he created with Lapine arose entirely from ideas jointly generated and constructed from the ground up.

Unlike Prince, Lapine was a writer as well as a director. The shared process of invention began early, before a single word of dialogue (much less any lyrics or music) had been written. *Sunday in the Park with George* had emerged from several weeks of getting to know each other, circling around various subjects, discussing assorted forms and styles, and smoking a lot of pot before plunging into the mystery of the Seurat painting that provoked the show. By the time they began work on *Into the Woods*, Sondheim and Lapine knew each other intimately, and they found their way to their source material fairly quickly. Though Sondheim had never read fairy tales as a child, immersing himself in such plot-driven material appealed to his notion of being a playwright in song. Explaining his approach to his work, Sondheim often said "Content dictates form." Telling five separate stories ("Jack and the Beanstalk," "Little Red Riding Hood," "Rapunzel," "Cinderella," and one they invented about a baker and his wife) could have dictated the form of a mere anthology. But to Sondheim and Lapine, the psychological complexity of the fairy tales demanded that they unravel the tales and knit them back together into one intricate, propulsive, and psychologically complex story.[31]

The merger of Sondheim the puzzle maker and Lapine the Jungian psychological explorer made the emotional depth and resonance of *Into the Woods* seem inevitable. Sondheim's two decades of psychoanalysis and the approaching birth of Lapine's first child must have shaped their work on the show as well. Lapine believed that fairy tales arose from the collective unconscious. Sondheim said Lapine also believed that fairy tales can give children false expectations—in this case, the expectations that are shaken, shattered, and finally resolved at the end of the second act. Even though Lapine led the way on the project, Sondheim was his contented—and stimulated, and challenged, and thus inspired—running mate.

Into the Woods did not have a conventional overture, but all of its musical ideas are introduced at the opening curtain in the title song, a thirteen-minute tour de force that presents five stories, eleven characters, one cow, and the network of links (both situational and psychological) that connects them. One of the essential musical ideas takes the form of a short series of somewhat sinister notes subtly embedded in the accompaniment to the witch's "rap." This brief theme haunts the entire show.

When the Baker places the magic beans into Jack's hands one by one, the theme rings out, each of the first five beans accompanied by a single note. There is no note for the sixth bean, which the Baker keeps for himself; the theme is consequently harmonically unresolved, hanging in the air, teasing the listener. It's a technique Sondheim used throughout his career to suggest something unfinished, to make the listener lean forward, waiting for that final note. Unlike painting, music takes place over time and has a sense of expectation and arrival. Chop off the last word of the last line of "Twinkle, Twinkle Little Star" and you're left with a feeling of nervous incompletion: *How I wonder what you*—period. In *Into the Woods,* the bean theme's search for resolution propels the entire show. It appears and reappears more than twenty times, sometimes harmonically resolved, sometimes not. It becomes the haunting melody of Rapunzel's song; it makes four appearances in the accompaniment to "Giants in the Sky"; it takes the form of a flute solo just before Jack's mother is killed; it supports "My Fault" first as a jittery, almost crazed riff for solo violin, and then Jack turns it into part of his angry self-defense. Near the show's end, it reappears in the accompaniment to "No One Is Alone."

Sondheim often said he believed that "the heart of music is

harmony." The heart of his own innovative harmonies appears in the detailed accompaniment that he wrote for every song. In fact, he usually wrote the accompaniment first ("what's going on inside the music"), finding his way to the melody as it emerged from his harmonic impulses. For Sondheim, harmony was not simply a series of chord changes. He insisted that when the vocal-piano versions of his songs were published, no chord names appeared above the staff, no guitar tablature, no signifiers of any kind other than the specific notes, in specific voicings, that appear in the accompaniment, every one of them a deliberate choice. In *Woods*, the completed accompaniments that emerged from his extensive explorations, ruminations, and revisions (ninety-eight pages of notes for "Children Will Listen" alone) were what he turned over to Jonathan Tunick for orchestration—and to the amateur pianist in his or her living room as well. He even wrote out the accompaniment for birthday songs he'd present to his friends.[32]

By one vital measure, *Into the Woods* became Sondheim's most popular work. It didn't recoup its investment until the original production went on the road, but ever since it has spawned hundreds of licensed productions around the world, more than any other of his shows. Its familiar characters and stories have made it especially popular for high school productions, often in the benign version known as *Into the Woods Jr.*, which ends before the killings and terrors of the second act. In the full version of the show, whether or not adult audiences appreciate its psychological depth is rendered irrelevant by the presence of dim Jack, beautiful Rapunzel, brave Little Red, and the other engaging characters. The wry and genial Narrator also contributes to the warm atmosphere, even as the story decays into chaos and sorrow. That he doesn't survive to the show's very end—the most heartwarming and affirmative ending in Sondheim's entire body of work—only makes the Narrator that much more sympathetic. (The avuncular tone Lapine was looking for was evident in his first choice to play the Narrator: Walter Cronkite. Others he approached included the TV commentator Edwin O. Newman and House Speaker Tip O'Neill, who had recently concluded his thirty-four years in Congress when the show opened on Broadway.) By the final curtain, after the second act has traversed a chilling series of disappointments, shocks, and six violent deaths, sympathy turns into something even more potent: understanding.[33]

Sondheim never would have decided at the outset of a project to use it as a vehicle to express his innermost feelings. But Lapine believed that his partner's work on *Into the Woods* "came from a very deep place," and "touched a lot of emotional stuff that he had kept buried or chose not to mine." More than two decades later, Sondheim came close to acknowledging this. "Ah, the woods," he wrote in *Look, I Made a Hat*. "The all-purpose symbol of the unconscious, the womb, the past, the dark place where we face our trials and emerge wiser or destroyed."[34]

There's certainly a touch of irony in that comment, but judging by the final product, it's only a touch. When *Into the Woods* opened in the fall of 1987, those who believed that the malevolent giant who stalks the stage was a symbol for the AIDS plague (or who thought the brutal deaths of Jack's mother and the Baker's wife had something to do with Foxy) missed the show's central points, expressed so clearly in its last three songs. From the first of them, "No More": *Trouble is, son,/The farther you run,/The more you feel undefined.* The curtain number, "Children Will Listen," reveals the theme that shapes the second act narrative: that all the confusions and deceptions and mistakes we make as we wander through the woods have consequences, and we had better mind them.

But it's the penultimate song, "No One Is Alone"—its music and lyrics as tender as any that Sondheim ever wrote—that captures both the essence of *Into the Woods* and its creator's private longings. It also provides the bean theme, finally resolved, in the accompaniment behind the words *Sometimes people leave you/Halfway through the wood,/Others may deceive you./You decide what's good.* There were moments during the show's development that so troubled Sondheim, and cut so close, that he was calling friends to say that his work was no good, that he couldn't do it anymore. "No One Is Alone" was particularly vexing. "It was an extremely hard song for him to write and it was equally hard for him to play for us," Lapine told Craig Zadan. "It's very scary when you start getting close to what you really feel and put it on paper." Sondheim may have been unsettled by the act of writing "No One Is Alone," but he also believed, as he once told an interviewer, that "you can be very naked in a lyric, and say what you want to say."[35]

The poet Richard Wilbur, a great Sondheim admirer, once said that a song could "represent precisely that moment when our feelings are brought to the pitch of thought." After fifty years of being alone, Sondheim described the specific thought that shaped the song, defined the show, and informed his life: "We are all profoundly alone," he said. "But not when we are connected with each other."[36]

In 2010, the copy editor of *Look, I Made a Hat*, working on Sondheim's chapter about *Into the Woods*, noted an apparent syntactical error in the lyrics for "I Know Things Now." Grammarians would object to *Nice is different than good;* it should be "Nice is different *from* good." Asked if he'd like to fix it, Sondheim's reply was definitive: "No." He wrote "than" because that's how Little Red would have said it (just as he believed, with lifelong regret, that Maria in *West Side Story* would never have said *It's alarming how charming I feel*). He could spend an hour deciding whether to change a seemingly insignificant preposition, and he could excoriate himself for decades for a tiny mistake that only he perceived. Thirty years after he wrote "Finishing the Hat," he declared the song imperfect because of "the glaring flaw of the word 'wait's,' which should rhyme with 'late' but doesn't quite." (*And how you're always turning back too late/From the grass or the stick/Or the dog or the light,/How the kind of woman willing to wait's/Not the kind that you want to find waiting . . .*) He was similarly attuned to the smallest molecules of his music. Nonesuch Records president Robert Hurwitz, who worked with Sondheim for a decade, noted that when he was in a recording studio as the actors and a full orchestra were making the cast album, Sondheim would sit in the control room, seemingly not engaged, idly reading the *Times*, the *New Yorker*, even *MacWorld*. Then he'd look up and say, "The French horn just played an E instead of an E-flat."[37]

That focus, joined to an instinctive pursuit of perfection, informed his fervid devotion to usage and grammar, not just in his own work or that of the other lyricists he dissected in the Hat Box. When the Tony-winning projection designer Wendall Harrington, who had worked on two of his shows, wrote to Sondheim to suggest they collaborate on a book—his lyrics, her designs—he took pains in his reply to correct her punctuation. When a fan from Milwaukee wrote to request an autograph, he obliged—but in his reply, he wrote, "I won't tell your parents you don't know how to spell 'inconvenient.'" During an interview with Terry Gross for *Fresh Air*, he interrupted her to correct her grammar.[38]

When it came to language—in lyrics, in life—Sondheim would liken his rigorous devotion to something else he was passionate about: puzzles. "I love puzzles because they have a solution. I love rules. That's what a lyric is. Set up the rules and see what you can do with it." From another interview: "The fitting together of notes, the fitting together of words have by their very nature a puzzle aspect. It's the creation of form out of chaos." And in a third interview, he reached deep into his past to explain his attraction to puzzles, and their link to his work: After "my own world went into chaos, I spent the rest of my life trying to put the pieces together."[39]

When *Into the Woods* closed in the late summer of 1989 (with three Tonys, including Best Score, in hand), Sondheim was fifty-nine. His 1980s may not have been as astonishing as his '70s (when he added five shows to the standard musical theater repertoire, and collected three Tonys for Best Score and three more for Best Musical). But after the devastation of *Merrily We Roll Along*, his recovery with *Sunday in the Park with George* and *Into the Woods* and the resurrection of *Follies* had confirmed his preeminence in musical theater.

It also gave him room to stretch. He reconnected with Warren Beatty (for whom he had composed the "love theme" for Beatty's 1981 film *Reds*), this time for the score of *Dick Tracy*. Among the five songs he wrote for the film was the torchy "Sooner or Later," for the character played by Madonna. Sondheim discovered that the singer was "meticulous, extremely demanding, and only concerned with the work"—and, therefore, likable. He also hoped her popularity might make it his second hit; that didn't happen, but he did win the Oscar for Best Song. Barbra Streisand's *The Broadway Album*, with six Sondheim songs (plus two more with his lyrics from *West Side Story*), sold four million copies and established a friendship with a singer whose talent he admired, even if he hadn't always liked her performances ("movie-star narcissism," he'd sneered in 1968). Like Madonna, Streisand won his affection for "her meticulous attention to detail." An even larger success accrued to "Putting It Together," from *Sunday in the Park with George*. Licensed by Xerox for a six-year advertising campaign, it may well have been heard by more people than even "Send in the Clowns."[40]

By the end of the 1980s, Sondheim had reached his prime. The house in Connecticut was becoming more important to him, and the "found family" he had created over the years enabled him to believe that he was finished with the one he had been born into. Other than providing her with regular financial support, he said, he no longer had anything to do with Foxy. His success, evident in the scores of newspaper, magazine, and television interviews he gave, made him familiar to a world that stretched far beyond the village of Broadway. The lopsided smile, the cyst on the left side of his forehead (benign, prominent, and permanent), his habit of closing his eyes and rocking his head back when he spoke—he was everywhere.

His friends cherished him. He had no small talk, but he was a fabulously witty conversationalist. Flora Roberts noted that "all his friends wanted to make him smile." They all were abashed or thrilled or moved by his generosity—with career help, with birthday presents, with much of the credit for his own success that he in turn attributed to his collaborators. A repeating motif in interviews, Tony acceptance speeches, and other venues was his insistence that his librettists (to whom he dedicated *Finishing the Hat*) were those "who made something out of nothing." Lapine, for one, thought he was a bit embarrassed from getting all the credit for work that didn't originate with him. But there's no question that his appreciation of his librettists was genuine. Back in 1976, when *Pacific Overtures* was about to begin its tryout in Boston, Prince asked John Weidman to go to the theater with him. Sondheim and Prince, who between them had already won thirteen Tonys, had addressed the billing for themselves and their twenty-nine-year-old rookie librettist. There, on the theater's marquee, Weidman saw their solution: "The new Prince-Sondheim-Weidman musical."[41]

Sondheim sometimes placed barriers between himself and his closest friends and collaborators, often arising from periodic sulks or, worse, spasmodic bursts of rage. The sudden gusts of temper would arrive in a flash, then subside nearly as quickly. It was a phenomenon that would recur throughout his career. At the first performance of *Assassins* in 1990, Mandy Patinkin sat in the front row taking notes in full view of the performers, because he was planning a one-man show that might include a few of the songs; Sondheim was incensed, and sent what Patinkin described as "a vicious note" that "just cut my nuts off." When Patinkin called to apologize, Sondheim said, "No big deal. Maybe I just needed to write the letter; now I'm fine." Ted Chapin, who had produced the Lincoln Center *Follies*, recalled him exploding at Mary Rodgers over a misunderstanding about some lyrics of his that she was planning to use in her 1997 show *Hey, Love;* "he wrote her a letter that really, really hurt her," Chapin said. Lapine saw his pent-up fury dissipate over time, but some of those who experienced it first-hand say it continued well into his eighties. Jack Viertel, who produced three Sondheim revivals for the *Encores!* series at City Center, said that in 2016, when they had a brief contretemps—again, over a misunderstanding—he learned an essential lesson about Sondheim: "Don't piss the guy off." In this instance, involving a book Viertel had recently published, there was probative evidence of that lesson in the scorching letter Sondheim sent him. It was clearly written in a frothing rage, its intensity apparent in the four typos it contained in just fourteen lines. The next time they met, Sondheim was perfectly cordial and never brought up the issue again.[42]

Another aspect of Sondheim's relations with friends and others was a sort of force field he erected to secure his desire for distance. Elaine Stritch called it "a dangerous quietness." At parties at his house, few would dare approach Sondheim before he approached them. Mary Rodgers said, "If you walk into a room he'll ignore you. And if you ignore him, *then* he'll come over and say hello. It's like some goddam cat!" Rodgers believed that he felt anyone approaching him must want something from him, even old friends like her. Her advice: "The best way is to leave him alone, say hi, and just go gliding along and talk to somebody else." Remembering the weeks when she was working with Sondheim and Lapine in La Jolla, Wendall Harrington said if she saw Sondheim standing alone, she wouldn't dream of approaching him. Jamie Bernstein, who was playing Cutthroat Anagrams (a particularly ferocious version of the game) with Sondheim nearly to the end of his life, said she would never call him, believing if he wanted to play, he'd call her. It was a pattern of reluctant engagement that Sondheim confessed to Cynthia O'Neal, who knew him for more than sixty years. She once asked why she hadn't heard from him for a while. "You forget," he replied. "I'm not the caller. I'm the call-ee."[43]

He didn't invite emotional intimacy. Stritch told a friend, "When you say something personal to Steve, he says 'Taxi!' " Ted Chapin's professional and personal relationship with Sondheim stretched over decades, but when he wanted to talk to him, he would first call Sondheim's assistant, Steve Clar. Clar would tell Chapin whether to come right over, or to call an hour later or the next morning. "It allowed me to adjust my mood to his mood," Chapin said.[44]

But there was another way to accommodate Sondheim's mood: get him to work. Viertel noted Sondheim's "outsized, sometimes very nasty personality." But "put him in a rehearsal room, or sitting in a theater during tech," he said, and Sondheim's diffidence and distancing vanished. Lapine saw the same thing. He felt that because Sondheim had no children and no mate, familial love was beyond his imagining. He had to find that with his collaborators.[45]

One of the obvious problems with *Merrily We Roll Along* was its central character: Franklin Shepard was hard to love, or even to like. Audiences could not connect with him until deep into the second act when they encountered the much younger, worthier Frank at the onset of his career. Even then, it demanded a leap of faith; if you've spent ninety minutes disliking someone, it isn't easy to expel that feeling from your mind. In a different fashion, *Pacific Overtures* also lacked the sympathetic characters a musical generally needs. There are moments when Manjiro (the fisherman-turned-samurai) and Kayama (the ex-samurai who welcomes westernization) might have seduced the audience, but the show's extreme stylization makes that impossible. Both characters are representations, not individuals.

But neither of those shows posed nearly the empathy challenge of *Assassins*, the next Sondheim show after *Into the Woods.* The narrative was an exploration of the personalities and motivations of people who wanted to kill a president. Collaborating with Weidman for the first time since *Pacific Overtures*, Sondheim was writing about people who were deranged, violent, and possessed by demons. While developing the show with Weidman, Sondheim told a friend that "it's calculated to make *Anyone Can Whistle* seem like the smash of the century." It was, he said, intended "strictly for off-Broadway."[46]

Of course, audience identification was never on the to-do list for Sondheim and Weidman. They sought instead to present a dark side of the American Dream, one that made this unsavory group believe the pursuit of happiness was not enough—they felt *entitled* to happiness, and if they didn't attain it then someone else had to bear the blame and accept the consequences.

Just as Lapine provided pathways deep into Sondheim's psyche, Weidman took him outside of himself. *Assassins* is by far the most political of Sondheim's shows, even though the expression of the politics was Weidman's, as had been the case with *Pacific Overtures.* They spent several weeks discussing their ideas for the show, but Sondheim didn't write any music or lyrics for *Assassins* until Weidman finished an entire draft of the libretto; it was the first time he'd done that since *Saturday Night.* At the end of *Merrily We Roll Along*, as the three main characters search for Sputnik in the skies above, Frank says that musicals "are a great way to state important ideas." In the show's 2023 revival, twenty-first century audiences that had endured two decades of jukebox musicals and celebrity-bio shows could chuckle at the irony of Frank's earnest naïveté. The ironies in *Assassins* were likelier to bring gasps than chuckles.[47]

Weidman's virtuosic interweaving of the stories of nine assassins (or wannabe assassins) brings them all together near the end of the one-act show, when they persuade Lee Harvey Oswald to go ahead with his own appalling idea. Audiences and critics may have admired Weidman's work, but they didn't embrace it. Even if critics could accept the show's dark premise, Sondheim's artfully American songs, rooted in sources as novel (for him) as Stephen Foster, John Philip Sousa, and even the Carpenters ("Unworthy of Your Love"), led few critics to anything like the rapture many had expressed about the scores for *Sunday in the Park* or *Into the Woods*. Maybe they took the Carpenters pastiche seriously; though it has its fans, it's a pretty limp song. Maybe they were put off by the unexpected musical arrangements by Michael Starobin (who'd also done *Into the Woods*), which he had had to shoehorn into an off-Broadway budget: the entire band consisted of a pianist, a percussionist, and Starobin himself playing a synthesizer. That Sondheim, so dedicated to complex harmonies and varied musical textures, found this acceptable suggests the extent to which he was moving away—psychologically, at least—from Broadway.

After critics beat up the show on its January 1991 opening at Playwrights Horizons (where *Sunday* had been launched), the faint but hopeful images of a Broadway transfer that Sondheim had been harboring (despite his disclaimers) vanished. Some reviewers found some things to like in *Assassins*, but not many things, and those they did find they didn't like enough. Such was Sondheim's stature at this point (and such was the size of the 135-seat theater) that every ticket for the planned two-month run had been sold in advance, so the reviews couldn't kill the show. But they unquestionably shaped the audience response, as negative reviews so often will. The abundant humor in Weidman's book got laughs, but as audiences perceived the gravity beneath the surface the laughs quickly decayed into unease. And by the time George H. W. Bush launched Operation Desert Storm midway through the run, patriotic feeling was running so high in the national consciousness that every television anchor or reporter was wearing a flag pin, and some were so enthusiastic about the war they seemed to be growing epaulets on their shoulders. What could be more unpatriotic at a time like that than a show that seemed to want to "understand" these homicidal orphans of history, and that ended with the entire cast pointing guns at the audience?

It would take fourteen years for *Assassins* to receive its due. A Broadway production scheduled for late fall in 2001 was canceled immediately after the horrors of 9/11, but three years later a limited 101-performance run at Studio 54 played to near-capacity houses. Directed by Joe Mantello, it was, Sondheim said, "as good a production of anything I have been connected with." As a revival it was ineligible for Best Score and Best Book, but it won five other Tonys in a year in which no other musical, original or revival, won more than three. More and more productions, both amateur and professional, demonstrated the show's arrival in the musical theater canon. The last *Assassins* that Sondheim himself saw was John Doyle's superb off-Broadway production in 2021, just weeks before his death. "The whole audience was stunned—just gasping," his friend Donna Rosen said. "All of us were seeing it through the lens of what had occurred at the Capitol on January 6." Sondheim turned to Rosen—tears pouring down his face, his hand clutching hers—and asked, "What has happened to our country? What has happened?"[48]

Perhaps the powerful emotion it provoked in Sondheim was one of the reasons he often declared *Assassins* "perfect," insisting that it came closer to realizing his intentions than any of his other shows. Only a hundred minutes long, born in a tiny off-Broadway theater, buffeted by horrified audiences and unpleasant reviews, absent anything close to a hit song in its score . . . if he were asked to do it again, he said, he wouldn't change a thing. During his angry scuffle with Jack Viertel—who was himself an *Assassins* fan—Sondheim said, "I am as proud of that show as any I've been connected with. And I'm right."[49]

Two days after encountering Sondheim at the Lincoln Center *Follies*, Larry Kramer wrote him a letter. Kramer, who had known Sondheim for years, was a playwright, a novelist, and a gay activist. In his most celebrated play, *The Normal Heart*, Kramer was likely thinking about himself when he had one of the characters say, "That's how I want to be defined: as one of the men who fought the war."[50]

Kramer's war was the battle against the lethal AIDS epidemic and particularly against governmental indifference to it, which led him to become a co-founder of ACT-UP, the most passionate and most disruptive of the groups agitating against wider indifference to the disease. As AIDS raced through New York's creative arts community after its arrival in the city in 1981, Kramer's sense of urgency was coupled with a long-held concern about the way gay people were perceived in the larger culture. Obituaries of men killed by the disease euphemized the cause of death, calling it pneumonia, or "an infection," or some other term that would deflect the reality that the person who had died was homosexual. This was twenty-five years before gay people could openly serve in the military, nearly thirty before the Supreme Court legalized same-sex marriage. Kramer felt there was a story about gay life that needed to be told, and he asked Sondheim if he would be interested in collaborating on a show that would deal with "the sheer joy, elegance, pain, complications of being a gay man," and "letting it all out, honestly. (Not that either of us has been dishonest.)"[51]

Sondheim declined both honestly and politely. He had never

written "from an idea," he told Kramer. "That is, from having something to say about a particular subject." That was undeniable; in all of his work, he was motivated by plot and character and storytelling. When some people described *Into the Woods* as "a metaphor for the AIDS crisis," or even "originally written in 1987 in response to the AIDS crisis," he demurred: "The trouble with fables," he said, "is that everybody looks for symbolism." But it was also true that declarations about the issues of the day were simply alien to the publicly diffident Sondheim. His political views, as he would later say about Israel and Zionism, conformed in most matters to those expressed by the *New York Times* editorial board. They were generally liberal, generally careful, and in the world he lived in, perfectly respectable.[52]

His only known political expressions from the years of his early success were not meant for public display. First was the assertion in an off-the-record interview in 1963 that "I'm very anti-union" because "the [theatrical] unions, as they are in every other business in the United States, are way out of hand and are crippling the whole economy." Seven years later, as one of many Blobbists present at the Bernsteins' fund-raising party for the Black Panthers, he was mentioned by Tom Wolfe in his brutal takedown, in *New York* magazine, of what Wolfe famously called "Radical Chic." Political themes in his work were unstated or understated. He came to believe *Follies* was about "the collapse of the American dream," but he hadn't entered into the project with anything like that in mind. Hal Prince was determined to turn *Sweeney Todd* into a tale of the unfairness of *those below serving those up above* (from the lyrics to "A Little Priest"). But Sondheim said he "couldn't care less about the social aspects" of the plot; he'd been attracted to the story only because of his appetite for melodrama. *Pacific Overtures* had a strong political viewpoint, as did *Assassins,* but these views were ineluctably embedded in John Weidman's original visions for both shows. When Barbra Streisand asked him to write new lyrics for the *Follies* anthem "I'm Still Here" to express her view of Hollywood sexism, he gave her these, in the voices of producers and others whom she felt had belittled her: *Talent she's got but those speeches—/Why can't she shut up and sing?* and *Songwriting, acting, producing—/What does she think, she's a man?* Though Sondheim was pleased with what he'd written, he later took pains to say, "the militant feminism is hers, not mine." The modifier "militant" suggests the inelastic nature of his political consciousness.[53]

Sondheim offered his most direct political statement in 1992, when he was awarded the National Medal of Arts, to be presented in a White House ceremony by President George H. W. Bush. The director of the National Endowment for the Arts had recently been fired by Bush, who did not approve of some of the NEA's recent grantees. It was a cause that had been taken up by culture warriors in the Republican Party's right wing who targeted artists they deemed blasphemous or otherwise transgressive. Sondheim, who in the 1970s had been involved in selecting NEA grantees in music and theater, could not abide these interventions. The endowment, he said in a rare public statement, "is rapidly being transformed into a conduit, and a symbol, of censorship and repression rather than encouragement and support." It would therefore be "an act of the utmost hypocrisy" to accept the award.[54]

The support and encouragement of artists was in fact Sondheim's chosen cause. He occasionally contributed to Democratic candidates but did not actively campaign with or for them. Yet his support of the arts was public, and it was steadfast. "Art is as close to a religion as I have," he said in 2005. It was the center of his politics as well.[55]

The realm of art that most engaged him was, of course, the theater, and its advancement became a cause he embraced for six decades. This was evident, first, in his assumption of the presidency of the Dramatists Guild in 1973. As they are the owners of their own work, playwrights, composers, lyricists, and librettists cannot belong to a union, but the guild devised and effectively enforced an approved contract that became the standard agreement between Broadway (and other) producers, and the writers and composers whose interests the guild represented.

The guild presidency was not just an honorary position. Sondheim led its governing board, lobbied members of Congress to keep the guild free from producer-promoted antitrust legislation, and generally used his eminence to protect its members. He did that on a smaller scale, too, responding instantly to emergency calls from writers enraged at (or intimidated by) producers who were trying to squirm their way around a guild member's protections and guarantees. He was motivated, he said, by his concern for "the artist's plight in the contemporary world," where "it's just very hard to make a living"—not for him, obviously, but very much so for the rising generation of theater artists he felt obliged to protect.[56]

When Sondheim stepped down from the guild presidency in 1981 (he did remain on its governing council), he founded the Young Playwrights Festival. The YPF solicited submissions from teenage playwrights from all over the country, the winners to be professionally produced, with professional actors. Modeled on a program Sondheim had encountered in London, the YPF soon turned into a passion and he became its most devoted supporter. Playwright Jonathan Marc Sherman, who began submitting plays when he was sixteen and won twice before he was twenty, said Sondheim "willed the YPF into being" and kept it going through his intense commitment and "bottomless" generosity. In a moment in his professional life when he was strenuously avoiding the public eye—it was the year of *Merrily We Roll Along*—Sondheim nonetheless appeared on commercial television because, he said, "there was a point" to it: promoting the festival. Half of the proceeds from the Lincoln Center *Follies* went to YPF, and he participated in every YPF fund-raising event; one year, he even donated his cherished silver Jaguar XJ6 to the organization's fund-raising auction.[57]

In 1982 Sondheim told a reporter, "We want this to be a continuing festival, not only annually, but in other cities all over the country." In time, localized versions of the festival blossomed across the map, from Los Angeles to Pittsburgh and from Seattle to Sarasota, and even to the Blue Ridge town of Abingdon, Virginia, population 8,300. Abingdon's YPF was specifically designed to discover and nurture teenage playwrights in Appalachia, and by 2018 it was receiving more than 600 entries a year.[58]

Sondheim's initial devotion to the YPF, as generous as it was, also provided him with a form of emotional ballast at a time when he was unmoored. His post-*Merrily* comments about Broadway for the Columbia Oral History archive in 1982 hissed and sizzled with a range of freely expressed emotion that ran from distaste to fury. But the YPF enabled him to redirect his energy toward a portion of the theater world free of critics or commercial producers, where he wouldn't deploy the churlish resistance that could sometimes stain his interactions with Broadway.

His role in YPF was also, inescapably, a reflection of his deepest desire: the wish to have children. When he was nearly eighty he told an interviewer, "If I had to live my life over again, I would have children. That's the greatest mistake I made." He explained that "being a homosexual and raising children" was "just not acceptable" when he was younger. One of Sondheim's finest songs, "Children and Art," from *Sunday in the Park with George*, aches with yearning just as it affirms what matters in life. In Sondheim's own life, he managed the art, but he repeatedly expressed his rue over the absence of children. It was, he said, "a great regret."[59]

Except: Jonathan Marc Sherman, who had progressed from

precocious YPF winner to successful professional to close friend, once told him, "You have more children than anyone I have ever met." Director Lonny Price, who as an actor had played Charley Kringas in the original, misbegotten *Merrily We Roll Along*, echoed Sherman. "He didn't have biological children," Price said. "But there are so many of us that are his kids." After Sondheim's death, political satirist Randy Rainbow (whom Sondheim considered "brilliant," his lyrics "as good as anyone writing today") said, "He practically raised some of us. It never occurred to me that he could possibly feel anything but overwhelmingly paternal."[60]

Sondheim's immediate family, as it were, was made up of the young men and women whose theater careers he had helped nurture. These included Howard Ashman, Jason Robert Brown, Stephen Flaherty and Lynn Ahrens, Adam Guettel, Jonathan Larson, Lin-Manuel Miranda, Jeanine Tesori, and the authors of *The Book of Mormon*, Trey Parker and Matt Stone—together, winners of thirty-three Tony Awards. He gave Larson detailed comments on nearly every scene and song in *Rent* and did much the same for Miranda when he was developing *Hamilton*. He showed up at early workshops of *Mormon* to encourage Parker and Stone, who had never written for the theater. When Guettel—Mary Rodgers's son—was just fourteen, he asked Sondheim to critique some music he had written; after receiving his comments, Guettel said that he found them "not very encouraging." Sondheim gently corrected the son of his oldest friend: "For me," he wrote, "true encouragement consists not so much of burbling as of detailed attention."[61]

He spread his encouragement widely. When John Guare brought his best playwriting students at the Yale Drama School to New York, Sondheim invited them to his house for dinner. (One of them, Michael Mitnick, said Sondheim particularly relished telling a story about the time his neighbor Katharine Hepburn—with whom his relations were always chilly—"tiptoed barefoot through the snow to tell him to shut up after he'd been playing the same four bars of 'The Ladies Who Lunch' for three days.") He wrote letters of recommendation—to schools, to employers, to whomever—for young writers, some of whom, like Jonathan Marc Sherman, weren't interested in the school or the job, only in the thrill of owning a letter of praise signed by Stephen Sondheim. Hopeful theater artists from all over the country wrote to him, asked for his advice, sent him tapes of their work. His responses were almost unfailingly polite, and at times so encouraging that he would ask the writer to send more, or to visit him when in New York; many did. (He might not be so polite, however, when a correspondent had suggestions about how Sondheim might improve his own work. At least once, his reply was, "Nothing is more obnoxious than un-asked-for criticism. Yours takes the cake.")[62]

Shortly after Sondheim's death, an article in the *New York Times* about his relationship with those he mentored bore the headline, "Cherished Words from Theater's Encourager in Chief." A year later, at Sondheim's memorial service in the theater named after him, Lin-Manuel Miranda said, "There is no repaying this kind of mentorship." Perhaps not for its beneficiaries—but Miranda also noted that Sondheim sent him an email just a week before he died, saying, "I feel like I've repaid, partially at least, what I owe Oscar."

Still, there were moments when exasperation—or more profound forms of displeasure—colored Sondheim's engagement with supplicants. In 1983, he invited the twenty-seven-year-old Ricky Ian Gordon (who went on to substantial success as an opera composer) to his house for drinks. First wine, then pot, then Gordon asked, "So what happened with *Merrily We Roll Along*?," which was only two years in the past. When Gordon said his own view was based on seeing the first preview, Sondheim stiffened. He told Gordon he thought it was presumptuous to form an opinion based on an early preview. As Gordon described it, Sondheim then abruptly left the terrace where they'd been sitting, and moments later rushed back in "like a tsunami, and amid a mass of angry half sentences I couldn't decipher because I was scared, devastated, and completely freaked out that Stephen Sondheim was yelling at me [and] looking like he want[ed] to kill me, I heard him say, 'People like you are why I am leaving the theater!'" When Gordon protested, the volume of Sondheim's bellowing ratcheted up to 11. They ended up screaming at each other out on Forty-ninth Street, Gordon on the sidewalk ("YOU . . . ARE . . . NOT . . . MY . . . FATHER!"), Sondheim standing, enraged, in his doorway. For nearly thirty years, even as Gordon rose in eminence as an opera composer, and even as he won the Richard Rodgers Award in a year when Sondheim himself was one of the judges, the chill remained. Sondheim was cordial, but nothing more. Not until 2012, when they met at a party, did he indicate that he had gotten past the anger that gripped him thirty-nine years before.[63]

Gordon was not alone. After the disastrous first preview of *Merrily*, the aspiring songwriter Alex Rybeck, who was working as an apprentice on the show, made the mistake of offering Hal Prince detailed notes in front of the other principals—notes about casting, about some of the arrangements, and much more. Sondheim, who was present at the meeting, had known Rybeck since he was an undergraduate at Oberlin; after Rybeck arrived in New York, Sondheim had given him thorough notes on the songs he'd been writing. Now, the twenty-four-year-old apprentice was unreeling the sort of criticism that can only be fueled by the temerity of youth and intensified by the thrill of his very presence in the same room as his sometime mentor.

The next day, Prince told Rybeck to stop coming to the theater in the daytime, when the cast, crew, and creators were in rehearsal—because, Prince said, "my artist" would be upset by his presence. Rybeck, riven with both guilt and shame, later pleaded with Prince: "I would do anything to make it up to [Sondheim]." Prince could only say that Rybeck wasn't the first one to go through something like this.[64]

Years before, to Corby Kummer—another aspiring protégé who had presumed too much—Sondheim had simply said, "You want me to be your Oscar. I can't be."[65]

At work with his collaborators, Sondheim absolutely welcomed ideas, criticisms, even the merciless suggestion that a song he'd long labored on should be cut from the show; he might nod in agreement, say "No big deal," and move on. When he'd call people in the middle of the night to read a line of lyrics, he'd listen to their criticism and dive back into the work. He'd give a few samples of a lyric to his librettists, then pull their opinions out of them: "Which of these do you like best? Why do you like it best?" And then, James Lapine said, "he'd go off and write another one." Sondheim said that he needed to be around people who would question his work. George Furth's "uncomprehending" reactions to his songs frustrated him while they were developing *Company*. He partly attributed the failure of *Anyone Can Whistle* (for which Arthur Laurents was both librettist and director) to the absence of internal criticism: "There was nobody making us question our own work except our own intelligence, and that just isn't enough." When director Jerry Zaks first discussed *Assassins* with Sondheim and Weidman, Sondheim—whom Zaks had never worked with—"kept insisting that I not feel inhibited about expressing ideas." At some point, he made it easier, installing a second telephone line in his house, with a number he revealed to his collaborators, and no one else.[66]

People outside the collaboration, like Gordon and Rybeck, learned not to offer unsolicited opinions. But sometimes, even an *un*offered opinion would set him off. Four years before the composer-lyricist Jason Robert Brown's first show (*Parade*) opened

With Arthur Laurents, in one of their good moments, 2008.
In one of the bad ones, Sondheim told Laurents
"you're just good enough to know you're mediocre."

on Broadway, he and a friend had dinner with Sondheim after he'd given them tickets to *Putting It Together*, a revue of his work in the mode of *Side by Side by Sondheim.* The two young men talked about everything *but* the show, their silence making it clear to Sondheim that they had been disappointed by it.

Brown, who had noticed Sondheim's discomfort, called the next day to apologize. By then, discomfort had given way to anger. Two decades later, Brown paraphrased Sondheim's seething response: "Once a creation has been put into the world, you have only one responsibility to its creator: be supportive. . . . If you come to my show and you see me afterwards, say only this: 'I loved it.' It doesn't matter if that's what you really felt. What I need at that moment is to know that you care enough about me and the work I do to tell me that you loved it, not 'in spite of its flaws,' not 'even though everyone else seems to have a problem with it,' but simply, plainly, 'I loved it.' "

"If you can't say that, don't come backstage, don't find me in the lobby, don't lean over the pit to see me. Just go home, and either write me a nice email or don't." And finally, "If I beg you, plead with you to tell me what you really thought, what you actually, honestly, totally believed, then you must tell me, 'I loved it.' "

Brown was abashed, but he was also grateful. "That evening of dreadful mistakes gave me one more reason to be thankful for Stephen Sondheim," he said. "I could have spent an entire life worshiping at his altar and never understanding that such great art as he creates can only be born of deep vulnerability."[67]

In 1988, Leonard Bernstein celebrated his seventieth birthday at Tanglewood in western Massachusetts, the summer home of the Boston Symphony Orchestra. He had been conducting there for a half a century. A series of concerts to honor him concluded with a fifteen-minute standing, shouting, and singing ovation. Earlier, at the invitation-only gala birthday event, Lauren Bacall sang Sondheim's lyrics for "The Saga of Lenny," built on the frame of Kurt Weill's "The Saga of Jenny," from *Lady in the Dark*. It was funny, it was clever (Sondheim found a way to work into the lyric references not just to Hammerstein, but also Wittgenstein, Rubinstein, and Gertrude Stein), and it was affectionate. But it was also in part a remonstration: *Poor Lenny/Ten gifts too many*—Sondheim's way of saying, "Why didn't you *focus?*"

The two men were still friends at this point but not remotely close as they had once been. Somewhere along the way, their career arcs had reversed. Sondheim's work rose in both professional and public esteem, while Bernstein's skill and reputation as a composer, which had reached its peak a few decades earlier, declined. The ravages of drugs and alcohol accelerated until Bernstein's death in the summer of 1990. For the rest of his life, Sondheim remained friendly with Bernstein's grown children, and—to them—always spoke lovingly about their father.

In *Finishing the Hat*, Sondheim explained that he never said anything hurtful about living people, whereas "speaking ill exclusively of the dead seems to me the gentlemanly thing to do. The subject cannot be personally hurt, and his reputation is unlikely to be affected by anything you say." (There were, of course, a few rare exceptions to this, such as Robert Brustein, John Lahr, and various other critics. He also tried not to make *positive* comments on the living—at least not in public—because, he said, "it hurts other people's feelings that they weren't mentioned.") In the book, he did take shots, vociferously, at lyricists whose work he did not like—Lorenz Hart, Noël Coward, various other notables—largely having to do with twisted syntax or grandstanding or insincerity. These comments were analytical, and though sometimes harsh, they were neither spiteful nor tainted by resentment. But in his interviews with Meryle Secrest five years after Bernstein's death, an unpleasant edge emerged. Discussing Bernstein's repeated assertion that no one had followed his own innovations in musical theater, Sondheim would have none of it. Bernstein "wasn't leading the pack at all," he said. "He was just blowing his own trumpet and it always pissed me off." He also explained that he wouldn't have said this while Bernstein was alive, as "it would have hurt his feelings." Then he added, "But it's bullshit. He just wanted to say he'd written a great musical"—*West Side Story*—"and nobody else could do it."[68]

This was obviously something that had been vexing him for decades, all the way back to their collaboration on *West Side Story*. It was not until after Sondheim had achieved his eminence that the various revivals of that show gave him substantial credit for its stature. If you'd stopped a civilian in the theater district in, say, 1980, and asked who'd written *West Side Story*, the answer would almost certainly have been "Leonard Bernstein."

Even in 1998, three years after Sondheim unleashed himself for Secrest, the burr still irritated him. In an essay about the art of biography, Secrest herself wrote about "what Leonard Bernstein thought . . . he was doing for musical theater when he wrote *West Side Story*, his ground-breaking musical of 1957."

Sondheim quoted those phrases in a chilly letter to Secrest, then followed them with a single word, underscored and tagged with a question mark: "*His?*"[69]

In 1991, Lee Remick died of kidney cancer at fifty-five. She and Sondheim had not seen much of each other in recent years, but his feeling for her remained undiluted. Two years after her death, he still referred to her in the present tense.[70]

Then in 1992 came the death of someone who occupied an infinitely more consequential place in his mind, however much he continued to deny it. Janet Fox Sondheim Leshin died in a nursing home in New Jersey, at ninety-four. She may have read her son's elaboration on one of the lessons of *Gypsy* in the second edition of Craig Zadan's *Sondheim & Co.*, published in 1989: "every child has to become responsible for his parents, that you outgrow your parents and eventually they become your responsibility." A few years after her death, he described his connection to Foxy as "a business relationship." He had continued to pay for her care, just as he had earlier paid her basic living expenses following her second husband's death. They talked occasionally, and he traveled to New Jersey to see her a couple of times a year. But he relied on his personal assistant to carry out necessary tasks relating to her. He did not attend her funeral. She was buried in her second husband's family plot in a Jewish cemetery in Queens. In 1995, three years after Foxy's death, he told Secrest he thought she had died in 1990.[71]

Sondheim's one notable reaction to his mother's death was his insistence that he had no reaction. The day she died, he was in England for a new production of *Merrily We Roll Along* and mentioned her death to the show's director as nothing more than an afterthought. James Lapine remembered him saying, "'Oh, yeah, my mother died last week.'" Arthur Laurents said, "Somebody asked him about his mother and he said, 'Oh, she's the same. Oh, I forgot. She died.'" Playwright Alan Ayckbourn quoted Sondheim: "Please don't sympathize. I don't want any sympathy."[72]

But his nonchalance was deceptive. In the years that followed, when he was asked to characterize her, Sondheim let loose with "monster" and "compulsive liar" and all the other imprecations he had accumulated over the decades. He told the story of The Letter at will. He accused her of stealing money from him. He might admit that she was smart and talented, but would go no further than that. Director John Doyle, who had a problematic mother of his own, said Sondheim felt the need to make it clear his mother was worse than Doyle's. Cynthia O'Neal said he insisted Foxy "hated him, and that was it." At Sondheim's memorial service in 2022, one of the speakers said, "He spoke fondly about his father. He spoke often about his mother." And the audience laughed the laugh of those who get the joke.[73]

Five years earlier, when Sondheim was eighty-seven, he'd said this to D. T. Max, who included it in his book, *Finale:* "I don't think about her. She was completely exorcised."[74]

In truth, she was with him until the end of his life.

7

After

Stephen Sondheim often said that no one over sixty-five ever wrote a successful musical, except when he said the same thing about people over sixty. It's difficult to find an exception apart from *The Sound of Music*, which opened on Broadway when Oscar Hammerstein was sixty-four (Richard Rodgers was a mere fifty-seven). Musical theater fans could debate whether *The Sound of Music* was good, but not whether it was successful.

Something slightly different could be said about Sondheim's last Broadway show, *Passion*, which began previews three days after his sixty-fourth birthday in March 1994. Whether it's good was, and remains, open to debate, even among devoted Sondheads. But it could not have been called successful. It took 52 often agonizing previews to get it into shape, and it played for only 280 performances. Relative to *Anyone Can Whistle* or *Merrily We Roll Along*, that run may seem like a success. But Sondheim's two previous collaborations with Lapine *(Sunday in the*

Park with George and *Into the Woods*) had each exceeded 600 performances. Including *West Side Story* and *Gypsy*, he had already had eleven shows on Broadway, had collected nine Tonys, and had become widely recognized as the man who had saved the musical, or had revolutionized it, or had turned it from entertainment into art. (Some, longing for a distant golden age, thought he had destroyed it.) His renown beyond the theater industry had attained a new peak. It would be hard to imagine, at that point in his career, that *Passion* could have run for anything *less* than 280 performances.

What at some interior, unspoken, perhaps even unconscious level had provoked him to write *Passion* was an experience he had never before achieved: He fell in love. He had long believed he never would; then, in 1991, Peter Jones showed up. Jones, a young songwriter at the beginning of a career that never really went anywhere, was one of the scores of young people who wrote to Sondheim and received an if-you're-ever-in-New-York invitation. For Jones, "if you're ever" seemed to mean "now." Within weeks he was on a train from Denver to the city, and eight days later he met Sondheim. On the ninth day, as the two men walked an icy path at his Roxbury home, Sondheim fell and broke his ankle; realizing he would be immobilized and in need of help, he asked Jones to stay.[1]

Jones, called "P.J.," was two generations younger, a vegan, non-drinking, non–New Yorker, and Sondheim was in a swoon. He burbled about him to all his friends, and took obvious pleasure in introducing him around. John Weidman thought he was "like a teenager in love." Sondheim himself, undone by his own self-discovery, consulted his psychiatrist. Dr. Horowitz asked if he'd told Jones that he loved him. He hadn't, so he told him immediately, in a phone call. In 1994, they exchanged rings. But by the end of the decade the intensity had abated, and they were no longer a couple. That they worked in the same field, but in galaxies far apart, hadn't helped, despite Sondheim's efforts to promote Jones's work. Planning a seventieth birthday concert in 2000, the Library of Congress asked Sondheim to provide a list of "Songs I Wish I'd Written"; there, along with work by Harold Arlen and George Gershwin and Cole Porter, and John Kander and Cy Coleman and Adam Guettel and many other notables, was Jones's "Bluellow," from a never produced musicalization of *Peyton Place.** After their romantic relationship ended, Sondheim employed Jones as an archivist and curator, and in 2012 he said they remained "very close friends."[2]

The pop lyricist Sammy Cahn ("Three Coins in a Fountain," "All the Way," "The Second Time Around," and dozens of others) once said Sondheim is "scared to say I love you" in his songs. Alan Jay Lerner admired Sondheim's gifts but felt that he "doesn't reach out and touch." At least for a time, that was by design: "I don't write unhappy or bitter songs deliberately," he told an interviewer in 1976. "I write love songs in which characters lie to themselves." Leonard Bernstein simply noted "the avoidance of the direct subjective 'I love you'" in his lyrics. After Sondheim had finally said it in his telephone call to Jones, he was soon able to say it on stage, in *Passion.* It was twenty-four years after Bobby, in *Company*, asked for someone *to hold me too close.*[3]

Falling in love had not been the conscious motivation for writing *Passion*, but Sondheim did say there was "a correlation," which James Lapine, once again his collaborator, confirmed. Hammerstein once said to Sondheim when he was starting out, "You've never fallen in love, so why write about falling in love?" Nearly half a century later, *Passion* was, in a way, Sondheim's reply.[4]

* Another oddity on Sondheim's "Wish I'd Written" list was "Bambalélé," an improbably joyful *coca* from northern Brazil, only eighty seconds long, that he had once identified as his favorite song. He discovered it on a recording from 1941 by Elsie Houston, sung in untranslatable Portuguese argot. Two years after the Library of Congress event, Audra McDonald recorded it for her album *Happy Songs.*

As it had been for *Sweeney Todd*, the idea for the show was Sondheim's alone, and also like *Sweeney* it was based on someone else's original material. In this case Sondheim used as his template the Italian film *Passione d'Amore* from 1981 (which was itself based on *Fosca*, a nineteenth-century novel by Iginio Ugo Tarchetti)—"a story worth singing," Sondheim said. Both critics and admirers often said any new Sondheim show was unlike any of his previous work. In the case of *Passion*, that was a gross understatement. The story centered on Fosca, an ugly, unhappy woman who falls in obsessive love with Giorgio, a happy and attractive man—a love requited only on her deathbed, near the end of *Passion*'s single, very long act. Lapine and Sondheim made the conscious decision to tell the story without wit or wordplay or even very many rhymes in the lyrics. It was "the world's first humorless musical," Sondheim said, winking only slightly. Even more apparent, the entire show was absent that sturdiest of Sondheim devices: irony. He once said of *Company* that it was the first "completely ironic" show on Broadway; a quarter of a century later, he referred to *Passion* as a "straight, non-ironic love story." He said it was about "unconditional love" —a subject new in his work and his life. Near the end of the show, Giorgio sings, *What's love unless it's unconditional?* What it was, Sondheim told an interviewer, was "the force of somebody's feelings for you [that] can crack you open." When a negative critique of the first London production ran in *The Sondheim Review* (not the first time a writer for the quarterly had disapproved of one of his shows), he called editor Paul Salsini, with whom he had always been cooperative, in a blistering fury, his whirling tirade unstoppable and unappeasable—as if he had been cracked open.[5]

Two primary musical themes run through *Passion*, and very little of the score is even discernible as separate songs. In an essay that Sondheim once cited with approval, the music critic

Francis Davis wrote that it was "a score that circled back on itself endlessly," its various elements virtual anagrams of one another. On the original cast album, only seven of the show's twenty-five musical pieces have titles, and in *Look, I Made a Hat* Sondheim even removed the titles from those, simply dividing the lyrics into numbered scenes. It was the same on stage: one song bled into the next, or into a new scene, without providing a moment where applause would have been appropriate. "I wanted [the audience] to experience one long, hour-and-forty-minute song," Sondheim said in 2004. "For those for whom the show works, that's exactly what happens." For those for whom it doesn't, that's one of the reasons. Sondheim specialist Rick Pender wrote that the absence of an intermission "made Fosca's pursuit of Giorgio oppressive and inescapable."[6]

The seven painful weeks of previews for *Passion* exceeded even the excruciating gestation of *Merrily*. Dumbstruck by a plot centered on an obviously deranged and unattractive main character, preview audiences found their voice in outbursts of inappropriate laughter or pained groans. During the preview ordeal, the authors found some twenty instances in the show that the audience—audibly—didn't buy, and they tried to correct them. Lapine spent several of those preview weeks all but hiding in his house, seared by some of the more volatile audience reactions. Sondheim, though, remained calm. The show, he said, was about "a desire to open up, to be more like Giorgio," and he was willing to pour as much of himself into its making as it required. The song known to fans (if not to Sondheim) as "Loving You"—Fosca's most ardent declaration of her ardor—was especially difficult for him to write, just as the spoken expression of love had been for Sondheim. It's also the most memorable piece in the entire score.[7]

After *Passion* opened in May 1994, both word of mouth and early reviews had prepared Sondheim's audience for something different and challenging. The critics were mostly positive, but even so their comments contained red flags. In the *New York Times*, Vincent Canby praised the show but also called it "embarrassingly blunt." In the *Atlantic*, Francis Davis praised the integrity and harmonic complexity of *Passion* but also said that both times he had seen it, the audience was so hostile that the producer could add to the theater marquee, "THE NEW HIT MUSICAL NOBODY LIKES!" No one who bought tickets for it was likely to be unaware of the difficult heroine, the leaky plot, the aura of gloom and pain they were about to encounter. Yet the most zealous of its adherents would have agreed with one particular reviewer, who admitted to experiencing "excessive feeling," that it "held me in its grip," and "had me sobbing uncontrollably at the end." He congratulated Sondheim and Lapine on their "triumph," particularly for "bringing dignity, profundity and passion to the impoverished commercial stage." That these words were written by Robert Brustein, the critic Sondheim loathed the most, suggests the show's impact on some of those who had opened themselves to it.[8]

It took a while for that cohort to expand. In various revivals, particularly one directed by Jamie Lloyd in London in 2010 and another by John Doyle in New York three years later, *Passion* finally jelled. Was it the passage of time that had finally invited the show into the standard repertory? Was it the fact that both of these productions were staged in small theaters (250 seats in London, 199 in New York) that suited its searing intimacy? Or was it because audiences finally realized that Sondheim had at last dropped the shield of irony and stripped himself bare? Doyle, who directed several other Sondheim revivals, said, "That's [Sondheim's] greatness—the complex human who can put so much of himself into the work."

He added, "That's the essence of the artist, isn't it?"[9]

While *Passion* was in development, Sondheim received a letter from Hal Prince, who was in London directing John Kander and Fred Ebb's *Kiss of the Spider Woman*. Their friendship had not evaporated in the wake of the *Merrily* debacle; Prince continued to consider Sondheim his best friend, and Sondheim returned the compliment. The reinvigorating arrival of Lapine into Sondheim's life and work appeared to have washed away the remnants of any lingering ill feeling he might have harbored. In 2009, as a revival of *A Little Night Music* directed by Trevor Nunn was about to open, Sondheim sent Prince a note: "To quote Fredrika at the end of the first act, I miss us."[10]

Prince's letter, though, made it clear that all was not right in their relationship. Thinking of what he might do next after *Spider Woman*, he made a clumsy effort to reunite professionally with his old friend. They had discussed some possibilities over the preceding decade, but none culminated in anything more than conversation. Now Prince told Sondheim it was time to work with someone who could produce shows that would begin at a distance from Broadway, which had been his *Spider Woman* strategy. Who that person might be was obvious, he wrote: "your erstwhile collaborator and best friend." Then Prince continued: "Steve, you know you're the best. Well, I know that. I also know that I'm the best. So it thoroughly confuses me that you choose to work" with anyone else, even though "I have made countless overtures—many shyly, I suppose, but some overtly." Groping for reasons why Sondheim had rebuffed his ideas, Prince prefaced the kicker by writing, "hold on now, don't get angry," which almost guaranteed the opposite. He believed Sondheim had not agreed to work with him, he wrote, because "You don't want the old Sondheim-Prince imprimatur, you don't want to share the glory."[11]

Sondheim took two weeks—and two and a half pissed-off pages—to respond. He pointed out that he had indeed turned down Prince's entreaty to produce *Assassins*, and recalled Prince's "furious response," which included accusations that Sondheim was "a coward" and "childish." "But the fact is," Sondheim's letter continued, "if I had said yes, *Assassins* wouldn't have been done at all." And the "countless overtures"? Sondheim noted that he had suggested ideas for two new shows but Prince had demurred. Most of all, Sondheim resented Prince's imputations about credit. "Have you ever known me to be concerned about such things? . . . Who is it who insists on printed directorial credit for all subsequent productions . . . , even though those productions may have absolutely nothing to do with the original?" And so on.[12]

There was a final page to the letter. The typhoon had spent itself. Sondheim asked after Prince's son, brought up some news of the Dramatists Guild, and suggested that he might be able to meet the Princes in Positano, where the two of them might come up with something to work on. Finally, he wrote, "Thanks for being so honest. Even if you are insane." He signed it, "Love, Steve."

How could he not? Nineteen years earlier, at the Shubert Theatre tribute concert that confirmed his place in the Broadway firmament, Sondheim had thanked Burt Shevelove, the evening's director, "without whom tonight would have not possible," and Prince—"without whom I would not have been possible."[13]

What James Lapine called "the whole Hal-Steve thing" did not extend into their later careers. Over the thirty-eight years from *Merrily We Roll Along* until Prince's death in 2019, they worked together only once, when Sondheim and John Weidman accepted Prince's offer in 2002 to direct *Bounce*, a new, retitled version of their problematic *Wise Guys*, three years after it had fizzled in a brief tryout at the tiny New York Theatre Workshop on the Lower East Side. From the moment the final curtain came down on *Spider Woman* in 1995 until his death in 2019, Prince directed three new musicals and one new play on Broadway, all of them failures. Sondheim's decline was different: From the day *Passion* closed in January 1995—just weeks before his sixty-fifth birthday—until his own death in 2021, no new Sondheim musical appeared on Broadway at all. Apart from revivals, his final Broadway success was *Into the Woods*, in 1989. Later, as jukebox musicals and Disney shows and productions featuring Hollywood celebrities annexed the theater business in New York, Sondheim could not get a new show on Broadway. He kept working, and working some more. But his work was no longer good enough.

In 1993, Sondheim had asked John Weidman to read *The Legendary Mizners*, a forty-year-old book by the journalist Alva Johnston. It was a lively (if risibly inaccurate) account of the roguish lives of the brothers Addison and Wilson Mizner in the late nineteenth and early twentieth centuries. (Addison was a high society architect; Wilson was many things—among them gold miner, playwright, boxing manager, restaurateur, and professional gambler—but mainly a hustler.) Sondheim believed the history-minded Weidman would spark to the idea, and he did. Originally commissioned by the Kennedy Center—the first time Sondheim had ever accepted a commission—the Mizner story became *Wise Guys*. And *Bounce*. And *Road Show*, eventually (and nearly fruitlessly) complicating seventeen years of its writers' professional lives. Frank Rich, with whom Sondheim developed a close friendship after Rich stopped reviewing, said that, for years, Sondheim "was constantly rewriting *Wise Guys*."[14]

Sondheim first thought of turning the Mizners' vivid adventures into a musical when he encountered Johnston's book as a twenty-three-year-old. He of course raised the notion with Oscar, who thought it was a good idea. But Irving Berlin, George S. Kaufman, and S. N. Behrman thought so too; even though Sondheim had already written an opening number, he dropped the idea, recognizing that he was a minnow trying to compete with three whales. The Berlin-Kaufman-Behrman show never happened, and four decades later Sondheim picked up the Mizner notion again, as work was winding down on what he called "the romantic gloom of *Passion.*" He also declined Prince's invitation to write the score for *Parade*, a historical piece embedded in the racism and anti-Semitism of 1915 Georgia. It was time, he wrote, to try "something jazzy and edgy."[15]

But: Readings, workshops, brief runs in small theaters; reassessing, rethinking, rewriting; changing producers, changing directors, changing titles—no musical could possibly have emerged victorious after so arduous a process. The Mizner story eventually went through each of its different versions with three different directors. After the initial fumbled attempt under the director Sam Mendes appeared in 1999, Prince stepped forward to ask if he could try to shape Version #2, now called *Bounce.* First staged in 2002, Prince's solution (which Weidman years later characterized as "more girls") turned out to be no solution at all. Weidman believed that one of the reasons Prince volunteered to do the show was to prove that only he could solve the problems that Sondheim had with any of his shows. But he couldn't.[16]

At one point, Weidman and Sondheim were summoned to the Princes' house in the ski resort town of Megève, in alpine France. "The Hal-Steve thing" now expanded to "the Hal-Steve-Judy thing." Weidman saw that "the tension among the three of them as they were finding each other again, after having been artistically divorced for so long"—twenty-one years, to be exact—"did not bring out the best behavior in any of them. But particularly not in Steve." Sondheim resented being there. He had possibly come to doubt Hal's true interest in the show. He was sulky and moody, and very little productive work came of the effort. After returning to New York he called Weidman to report that "Judy told me I behaved like a petulant child while I was over there. Was that your experience?" Weidman said, "Yeah, it pretty much was." Sondheim replied, "Okay, okay, thank you for confirming that."[17]

Version #3 of the musical, called *Road Show*, appeared in a production directed by John Doyle in 2008, and it, too, failed to ignite. As early as 2000, Sondheim had already said he had wasted most of a decade on the Mizner show. In *Look, I Made a Hat*, his lyrics and commentary about the various versions consumed 122 pages—fully a quarter of the entire book. Unlike *Assassins*, which Sondheim thought was his most nearly perfect show, no one could ever figure out how to save this one. The Mizners' lives were colorful enough; Weidman's various books were lively and funny and at times moving; and some of Broadway's finest performers, including Nathan Lane, Victor Garber, and Michael Cerveris, had appeared in its various incarnations. The otherwise overfamiliar score, replete with echoes of Sondheim's earlier work, did include at least one superior piece, the exquisite love song "The Best Thing That Ever Has Happened," which later became a standard at many gay weddings. Although it didn't survive the show's development, "A Little House for Mama," a sweet and sentimental song Addison Mizner sings to his mother, provided at least one intense emotional moment. The first time he heard it, *Wise Guys* director Sam Mendes found himself in tears. "The song was so effortless, so simple, yet seemed to speak to the heart of those who struggled (as Steve did) with a lifelong need to heal a relationship that can never be healed," Mendes wrote many years later. "I looked over to him and he was crying, too. 'Mothers,' he said."[18]

But the show just didn't work; the last line of the last version—Wilson says to Addison, "Sooner or later we're bound to get it right"—never came true. Maybe the picaresque material overwhelmed it. Maybe the music was simply too derivative of Sondheim's earlier work. He even resuscitated "Flag Song," which he'd originally written for *Assassins*, writing new lyrics under a new title, "It's in Your Hands Now"—the one time he ever reached into his trunk to find an old composition he could place in a new theatrical context. Maybe it was the absence of any informing musical idea, something that tied the score together the way

1930s pastiche had for *Follies*, or three-quarter time for *A Little Night Music*, or Japanese scales for *Pacific Overtures*, or American folk music for *Assassins*.

Or maybe it was simply because during most of the show's development, Sondheim was way past sixty-five.

Throughout the long and fitful life of the Mizner show, Sondheim continued to work on other projects. He wrote a few songs for *The Birdcage*, Mike Nichols's movie version (minus Jerry Herman's original music) of *La Cage aux Folles*, but only one survived intact in the final film. With George Furth, he wrote *Getting Away with Murder*, a limp mystery with no music and no future: it died after seventeen underwhelming Broadway performances. He set Shakespeare's Sonnet 43 to music for James Lapine's production of *King Lear* in Central Park. In London, he performed a duet with Andrew Lloyd Webber at a tribute to his friend the producer Cameron Mackintosh, singing parodies of their best-known songs: "Send in the Crowds" and "The Man Who Flogs the Music of the Night."* In 2005, while he was still trying to untie the knots that entangled *Road Show*, he wrote to Trey Parker, the co-creator of *South Park*, which Sondheim had long admired. He had loved Parker's film *Team America* (written with Matt Stone and Pam Brady), and asked, "Would you ever be interested in writing a stage musical with an old traditionalist, namely me?" Parker and Stone, working with composer Robert Lopez, were deep into *The Book of Mormon*, but a relationship was struck. In 2009, after sitting in on a workshop for *The Book of Mormon*, Sondheim told Parker,

* In addition to their mutual fondness for Mackintosh, Lloyd Webber and Sondheim shared a birthday, but not necessarily much more than that. One evening in the theater district, after encountering three members of the volunteer anti-crime group the Guardian Angels, a British friend asked Sondheim, "What do they do?" He replied, "They stop people going to see *Phantom of the Opera*."

"Don't change anything." After that, Parker recalled, "Whenever we saw him, he'd say, 'Let's do it, let's do a show.' He was great."[19]

One project that Sondheim stuck with for decades led him to look in the direction of new collaborators with Broadway experience. He engaged to various degrees with Alan Ayckbourn, Terence McNally, Craig Lucas, and David Ives (not to mention James Lapine and John Weidman) for *All Together Now*, an idea Sondheim had first discussed with Hal Prince back in 1992 (and began to develop with his *Forum* collaborator Larry Gelbart the year before that). It wasn't clear what the show actually was: McNally's version was a two-hander probing a couple's shared past, while Ives described his as "a musical that exploded a single moment in the lives of two people meeting for the first time." Sondheim didn't stop working on the project until 2020. In 2012, he'd told a British reporter, "I'm not a retiring type. I'm not a golf player. I can't imagine sitting in front of the television. Painful as it is, writing is still fun, and I don't have anything else to do." So he kept writing.[20]

Sondheim wasn't home that night in 1995 when a powerful fire swept through the house on Forty-ninth Street; he was out with Mike Nichols that evening, taking in a drag act. Most of his prized collection of antique games and puzzles was lost in the fire. So was a treasured letter of praise that one of his heroes, composer-lyricist Frank Loesser, had sent him when Sondheim was snubbed at the Tony Awards by his collaborators on *A Funny Thing Happened on the Way to the Forum*. But by some miracle, singed boxes containing his sketches and ideas and revisions and annotated scores, stored in a closet adjacent to his office, survived. (So did the records that he later shipped to the Library of Congress.) "I save everything," Sondheim once said. "Everything is in boxes, everything I've ever written. Every sketch, every idea." This was the material that ended up underpinning the two volumes of the Hat Box, and that eventually found a permanent home in the Library of Congress.[21]

He knew that was dumb luck, and during a year's worth of renovation and repair he made sure to have a cinderblock vault built in the basement. He had lived in the elegant house for thirty-five years at that point and was still living there (and in Roxbury) when he died, twenty-six years later. He cherished the house itself, but also its nearly transcendent meaning to him. When asked by the Library of Congress to name the songs he wished he'd written, one was the achingly sentimental "Home," from Kander and Ebb's *70 Girls 70* (*with friends that will need me/And love that will feed me/All paths seem to lead me/Home*). He also admired a song with the same title written by Charlie Smalls for *The Wiz* (*Maybe there's a chance for me to go back there/Now that I have some direction/It sure would be nice to be back home/Where there's love and affection*).* "Home must mean something to me," he said to Mark Horowitz. He was more expansive with John Kander, whom he'd known since they were both starting out in the 1950s. At Sondheim's memorial service in 2022, Kander recalled a conversation they'd once had about what makes a home; they agreed that it probably requires someone to be there with you. Kander said Sondheim "looked into his wine glass and said, 'I think that's something that I'm never going to have.' "[22]

Then, Kander said, "He met Jeff."

When they met, Jeff Romley was twenty-three. Sondheim, whose romantic relationship with Peter Jones had become platonic by then, was fifty years older. If it wasn't love at first sight, it didn't take long to get there. They were a couple within a year. Soon after, Romley walked into the office of his employer,

* *The Wiz* was one of his favorite musicals. He saw it six times during its first Broadway run, in 1975. He also told Jamie Bernstein to see it, but "leave your brain in the lobby."

With Jeff Romley, 2013

Richard Frankel, who was co-producing a revival of *Company*. Romley, who thought it better if Frankel learned about the relationship directly from him rather than from random Broadway chit-chat, told him "I moved into Steve's house" over the weekend. Frankel asked, "Steve who?" He was floored when Romley told him.[23]

The well-kept secret soon became widely public. The two men ended up staying together the rest of Sondheim's life (they married in 2017, when Sondheim was eighty-seven). It was a relationship strengthened by their differences. "P.J. was a songwriter," John Weidman said. "Jeff went to Rangers games." Romley was also a triathlete, which was about as un-Sondheimian as one could get, and he was very much a product of his GenX/millennial era, which was perhaps even more un-Sondheimian. For a time, Sondheim's Oscar statuette for "Sooner or Later" sat atop Romley's Xbox in the top-floor bedroom in the Forty-ninth Street house (it did later service as a doorstop). "I live with a guy who goes to bed with his iPhone," Sondheim told D. T. Max in 2017, partly in good humor and maybe partly not. "He's looking at Facebook, Face-fucking-Book!"[24]

But that was trivial. Cynthia O'Neal, who had known Sondheim since the 1950s, said "the relationship with Jeff [gave him] more than anything he had ever expected." What he had longed for since he was a teenager but never saw coming was cemented with Romley: connection. Even as he reached the years of diminishing talent, declining production, and the associated discouragement—"I've hung up my boots," he told John Doyle after the *Bounce* failure—his friends saw a warmer Steve, a contented Steve. Jamie Bernstein, who had known him since she was a toddler, said, "Trading in the output for the happiness was a grand trade." James Lapine saw "the reservoir of anger inside of him dissipate." His playful side had never gone into hiding for terribly long, but by the early 2010s it began a nearly uninterrupted run. He took great joy in Willie and Addie, the two ill-trained poodles he had named after the Mizner brothers. He continued his puzzle-making, staging diabolically elaborate treasure hunts for various charities and to entertain his friends, and he continued to take on as many competitors as he could for Cutthroat Anagrams (Liev Schreiber, who came with Naomi Watts, was especially good at it).[25]

At the same time, the public Sondheim had entered what Ted Chapin called "the God Years." Back in April 1994, as *Passion* was about to open, *New York* magazine published a piece by James Kaplan titled "Is Stephen Sondheim God?," and now the zeal and devotion of his fans suggested they believed he just might be. With Frank Rich, Sondheim went on an unlikely multi-city, sixteen-event road tour, where packed, paying audiences leaned into his every word (especially as Rich vainly tried to get Sondheim to own up to the autobiographical elements in his work). He continued to give his blessing and extend his cooperation to the editors of *The Sondheim Review*, despite his earlier rage over their *Passion* article. The creator of *Desperate Housewives*, Marc Cherry, expressed his devotion by titling most of the show's 180 episodes with the names of Sondheim songs or excerpts from his lyrics; as the show concluded its eight years on network television, Cherry called the final episode "Finishing the Hat." A Sondheim character appeared on *South Park*, and again on *The Simpsons*, this time accompanied by a seven-second jingle he wrote for Buzz Cola. He played himself in a brief scene in the film *Camp*, where he's mobbed by a gang of teenage musical theater geeks ("Oh my God, it's him!"), and again, eighteen years later, in *Glass Onion*. Sondheim even wrote a self-spoofing lyric for the revue *Sondheim on Sondheim* (2010): *God/I mean the man's a god/Wrote the score to Sweeney Todd/With a nod/To de Sade—/Well, he's odd/Well, he's God.*[26]

It was much the same on Broadway. When Jerry Zaks, already a winner of three Tonys for Best Director, first met Sondheim, he recalled, "It was like meeting God." When Richard Frankel, whose producing credits included *The Producers*, *Hairspray*, and *Smokey Joe's Cafe*, first sat down with him to begin work on the 2005 revival of *Sweeney Todd*, Frankel thought, "How did I get here? Here I am with Stephen Sondheim, sitting on the couch, sharing a joint, and he's taking me seriously!" The show's director, John Doyle, said, "He did bring an aura with him."[27]

Elaborate staged tributes had been part of Sondheim's life since the gala at the Shubert Theatre in 1973. At his memorial service, his lawyer and friend Rick Pappas said Sondheim had made no formal funeral or memorial plans, then drew a knowing laugh when he invoked the previous Sondheim tributes by saying, "Steve often said he had the great good fortune to attend his own memorial on his 75th birthday. And on his 80th. And virtually, via Zoom, on his 90th." In the last twenty years of his life, he was on what seemed a never ending tour of lifetime achievement awards, special honors, and public salutes. He considered the medal he received from the American Academy of Arts and Letters in 2006 the greatest of his honors, partly because he was selected for the award by other eminent composers, and partly because previous winners included Milton Babbitt and Leonard Bernstein. That was topped nine years later, when Barack Obama placed the Presidential Medal of Freedom around his neck in a ceremony at the White House.[28]

Throughout his career, Sondheim had expressed a series of complaints about the people who ran the Tony Awards: their failure to honor music directors, conductors, and arrangers; their domination by commercial interests; their interest in publicity over art; and, not least, their decision to honor Jerry Herman in the year of *Sunday in the Park with George*. In 1981, speaking of the Tonys, he'd told Jerome Robbins, "I am *always* ashamed to take part in those ridiculous, meaningless, hypocritical ceremonies." But he approached his Tony for Lifetime Achievement in 2008 with a certain gravity. He was traveling, and couldn't attend the ceremony, but in his acceptance speech (delivered on his behalf by Mandy Patinkin), he said the award had "a faint whiff of 'you've outlived your usefulness.' And as you get older, you start to believe that some writers do, including me."[29]

More rewarding honors came on stage, in an ever growing flowering of anthology shows like *Sondheim on Sondheim* in 2010, in documentaries (*Six by Sondheim*, 2013), and in the quickening pace (and success) of revivals. Those in turn provoked new cast albums, including the previously unrecorded *Saturday Night;* he wept as he thanked the singers and musicians for what they had done with his first full score, which he called "my baby pictures." The outstanding Broadway version of *Assassins* directed by

When Sondheim received the Presidential Medal of Freedom in 2015, his fellow honorees included Barbra Streisand, Steven Spielberg, and Willie Mays

Joe Mantello in 2004 redeemed the effort Sondheim and Weidman had put into it, as John Doyle's *Passion* revealed the restrained power of that show in 2013. Filmed versions of his work (a plausible *Sweeney Todd* in 2007, a less plausible *Into the Woods* in 2014) spread his reputation nationally for a new generation.[30]

The victory lap seemed to have no end. He loved every revival, and he could be dismissive of friends and associates who might differ; when Peter Gethers, his editor for the Hat Box books, expressed some reservations about one revival, Sondheim was snippy and annoyed and a little bit contemptuous. Especially in his later years, Gethers said, "He never could think poorly of almost any production of one of his shows." The radical London production of *Company* directed by Marianne Elliott with a female "Bobbie" was, he said, "the greatest evening of musical theater I've ever seen." But as much as he loved them, one aspect of the revivals discouraged him: After the Kennedy Center staged a festival of six of his shows in 2002, he was asked if the celebration inspired new creativity. "Just the reverse," he replied. He worried he had little new to offer, except when he was discovering flaws in his earlier work he hadn't noticed before. He no longer had the energy for the fourteen- to seventeen-hour days he once could spend on a show. His late work was definitely Sondheim work, but he wasn't the same Sondheim. At eighty-one, he said to the *Times* of London, "If I play my favorite chord, am I repeating myself, or is that who I am?"[31]

Popular worship also had its downside. Coming upon Bernadette Peters in the milling crowd backstage after a concert at the Hollywood Bowl for his seventy-fifth birthday, he said, "Thank god I found you—they're passing me around this place like an hors d'oeuvres." Others wanted to show him off to their friends, as if he were a shiny piece of art. He said, "At my age, what I don't want to do is meet strangers, I don't want friends, I don't want to 'friend' anyone or be 'friended' by anyone." He warned Lin-Manuel Miranda, "Everybody will want a piece of you. You will always be in danger." Overheated fans haunted Forty-ninth Street. He was wary and nervous at most public events, where so many people approached him saying "I hate to interrupt you" that he suggested someone should write a book called *I Hate to Interrupt You But I'm Going to Do It Anyway.* A woman whose husband had been a passionate devotee buried his ashes in front of Sondheim's house. He had to fend off a stalker by reporting him to the New York Police Department. "As a 31-year-old virgin," the man wrote to Arthur Laurents (of all people), whom he hoped would intercede on his behalf, "my attraction to [Sondheim] became an obsession. I learned of his home address and I gave him my ring as a symbol of my commitment. I also sent personal pictures, and gifts for Christmas and Valentine's Day. Every thought I had was about Steve, I guess I tried too hard and eventually scared him away." The man told Laurents that he was "simply following his lyrics"—*Somebody crowd me with love,/ Somebody force me to care.*[32]

Even in the God Years, Sondheim's engagement with politics remained mostly private and somewhat distanced. In an interview with the *New York Times* in 2003, he called George W. Bush a fascist—but asked the reporter not to quote him. In 2014, he and Weidman called off a production of *Assassins* at Ford's Theatre in Washington because, Sondheim told the actor George Dalzell, they didn't want "to inflame the already dangerous hostility" directed at President Obama. He stayed away from the culture wars as well. Asked by a friendly interviewer what he'd like to see "LGBT-wise" in the coming years, he said, "I'd like to see the term LGBT disappear from the English language."[33]

He was still not beyond fits of anger and even wrath. Having agreed to be honored, along with John Kander, at a charity gala put on by his longtime friend Susan Burden, he erupted when the master of ceremonies asked the audience to sing along while the orchestra played a song by each of them. As they struck the opening notes of Kander's universally familiar "New York, New York," Sondheim's response was volcanic: he turned to Peter Gethers and said, "They're going to do a fucking sing-along with my fucking song after 'New York, New York'? Nobody's going to know one fucking word of my song!" He stormed out before he even knew which of his songs they intended to play. In 2011, Sondheim did what he had blamed John Lahr for doing forty years earlier, writing an enraged thousand-word letter to the editor (that the *New York Times* published in its entirety) excoriating the people behind a new production of *Porgy and Bess* that he had not yet seen. But he'd been infuriated by changes in the plot he had read about, and even thrashed the show's star, Audra McDonald—whom he liked personally and admired professionally—for comments about the show that had irked him. McDonald later said she "respect[ed] his passion," but didn't much appreciate being "slapped around by Sondheim in such a public place."[34]

But, as was almost always the case, the anger and dyspepsia didn't last. His personal fondness and professional esteem for McDonald were quickly renewed. Bridges once burned (in some cases more than once) were repaired, if not completely restored: these were the years in which he reconciled with Jason Robert Brown, Ricky Ian Gordon, even (to a degree) Clive Hirschhorn, who had so angered him with his piece in the *Times* about *Pacific Overtures*. But Sondheim took a pass with Arthur Laurents; as Laurents lay dying in 2011 and asked to see him, Sondheim declined. In recent years they had exchanged some very nasty letters ("Did not answer this sick letter," Laurents wrote on one of Sondheim's). During a particularly bad patch in their relationship, Sondheim had told Laurents, "You're just good enough to know you're mediocre." When the *Encores!* revival series wanted to bring back *Do I Hear a Waltz?* in 2016, the Laurents estate objected to a change in the book. Sondheim said, "That's the thing about Arthur. He's just as much trouble dead as he was when he was alive."[35]

He did speak at Mary Rodgers's memorial service in 2014, and at Hal Prince's in 2019. But he didn't dwell on even these losses. When Jonathan Marc Sherman brought up Rodgers's death, Sondheim "just cut me off. 'Yeah, yeah, we're all falling off the perch. What are you drinking?' "[36]

In 2000, the *New York Times Magazine* had published "Conversations with Sondheim," a lengthy colloquy with Frank Rich. For the cover the editors picked a portrait by photographer Richard J. Burbridge that might have been stored in Dorian Gray's attic. Sondheim looked ravaged by time and by God knows what else. His familiar lopsided smile had sagged into a less familiar lopsided half-grimace. His rheumy eyes made him appear disconsolate, lost. David J. Nellis, who worked for the agency that licensed Sondheim's work, slapped a caption on it that soon zipped around the industry: "Will compose for food." Sondheim liked the joke and repeated it frequently.

But a portrait by his friend Richard Avedon in 2004 did not please him, and in time it would inflame Sondheim even past the elevated boiling point of his late years. In the Avedon photograph, the furrows in his forehead were four years deeper, the lopsided expression four years wearier. The caption on this one could have been, "A man in his seventies confronts his mortality." It's unclear what Sondheim's reaction to the photograph was at the time. Avedon died six months after the picture was taken.[37]

Eleven years later, though, it induced a late—and telling—rage, as well as evidence that posterity had begun to matter to him. His close friends Ben and Donna Rosen brought him downtown to the newly reopened Whitney Museum to reveal a surprise: they had purchased an original print of the Avedon portrait and donated it to the museum. "He was furious," Donna Rosen recalled. He said, " 'I hate that portrait. It's the ugliest portrait of me ever, and I don't ever want to see it again.' I said, 'but Steve, it shows so much emotion,' and he said, " 'I don't want people to see my emotions.' " Later, he told Ben Rosen, "You have to get that portrait out of the Whitney. I do not want that to be my lasting image."

The portrait by Richard Avedon from 2004 that enraged Sondheim and made him say, "I never want to see that portrait again"

Sondheim stopped speaking to Donna Rosen for weeks as his ire intensified. His communications with Ben consisted of a series of badgering phone calls: "Is it out? Is it out?" He demanded that the museum deaccession the photo, but museum rules made that impossible. The Whitney's lawyers eventually agreed with the Rosens to keep the photograph but not display it while Sondheim was still alive.

Three years after his death, it still had not appeared on the Whitney's walls.

The projects that kept Sondheim engaged in his late years were the two volumes of the Hat Box, and *Here We Are*, a show that was not produced until 2023, two years after his death. Writing the books was engrossing, invigorating, and creatively liberating. Writing the show was agony.

The Hat Box was Sondheim's most notable output in the last twenty-five years of his life. Together, the books provide a brilliant exegesis of the craft of lyric writing, vivid accounts of how his shows were put together, and acute critiques of the medium's most famous practitioners. (Irving Berlin, Cole Porter, Frank Loesser, Yip Harburg: good. Noël Coward, Lorenz Hart, Alan Jay Lerner: not so good. Oscar Hammerstein: problematic.)

He had signed a $100,000 contract to write a book for Knopf in the 1990s. But it wasn't until 2006, after "he had mostly run out of juice for the stage" (said director Sam Mendes), that Sondheim at last hurled himself into what became the first volume, *Finishing the Hat*. Thrilled that he was finally beginning to work on it, Knopf was prepared to rewrite the contract and give him a much larger advance. Sondheim declined, perhaps because he was not certain of his ability to pull off the task. But when he turned in the chapter on *Company* (which he addressed first because he thought it would be the most difficult one to write), Sondheim hedged: he told Peter Gethers that he feared it was dull and academic. On reading the chapter Gethers responded, "Are you crazy? Your prose is as good as your lyrics!"[38]

Even after his explosion over the Avedon portrait, Sondheim continued to maintain his long-held and often-expressed position that he had no interest in posterity. "Once you're dead," he had told Stephen Schiff for a *New Yorker* profile in 1993, "you can't enjoy the audience enjoying [the work]. So where's the pleasure?" Or, to Gethers, two decades later: "Who gives a shit? I'll be dead." But his devoted, focused, and years-long work on *Finishing the Hat* and *Look, I Made a Hat*, not to mention his anger about the Avedon portrait, suggest otherwise. Filled as they are with commentaries on the origins and development of every one of his shows, the books also constitute the closest he ever came to writing an autobiography. Of course, sticking to his professional life and dodging the personal meant that was not very close at all.[39]

His health began to catch up to his years. In 2009, speaking of his energy level in a conversation with Adam Guettel, Sondheim said "the balloon is collapsing." Six years later: "I don't even want to leave the couch to go to the next room." He had trouble climbing stairs, he was beset by macular degeneration. Surgery after a fall in London left him with "a hardware store inside my wrist." His balance became uncertain, his memory even more so. Atrial fibrillation, gastric reflux, too-frequent urination—the black clouds of age were gathering.[40]

None of this made the years he put into *Here We Are* any easier. (He'd first discussed the idea with Hal Prince in 1992.) A surreal fiction based on the Luis Buñuel films *The Discreet Charm of the Bourgeoisie* and *The Exterminating Angel*, the show was repeatedly slowed by a vast self-doubt that surpassed any that he had felt before. "You get less confident as you get older," he said. Peoples' expectations "make you very hesitant about doing anything else." At various times he told his collaborators, playwright David Ives and director Joe Mantello, that he simply couldn't do it. A frustrated Ives withdrew from the Buñuel project in 2019, then rejoined Sondheim six months later to take another crack at the long dormant *All Together Now* instead. "It looked like he was going to go back to work, but it just fizzled out," Ives recalled. They returned to the Buñuel project. In 2020,

Ives told Mantello, "I'm collaborating with someone who wants to seem to be writing a musical but actually doesn't want to write a musical." Mantello replied, "I just don't think his heart is in it." Looking back, John Weidman said "that was a large part of what his experience of himself was during the last part of his life—that he was supposed to be finishing this fucking show, and he wasn't getting it finished." Still, Sondheim worked because, he said, he didn't know what else to do. He was in "a slough of creative despond," he told an interviewer in 2017. He also said, "I'm fond of saying [George Bernard Shaw] kept writing plays until he was 94. Of course, the last 15 years they were terrible. But he did write them."[41]

Mantello eventually found what he thought was a dramaturgically plausible way to present the second act almost without music. Sondheim was open to it. Following a reading in early September 2021 with a cast that included Nathan Lane and Bernadette Peters, Sondheim appeared to have accepted the argument. "With any luck, we'll get it on next season," he said on *Late Night with Stephen Colbert.*

But there was no next season for Sondheim. He had managed to survive the Covid pandemic (he did tell a friend that "coronavirus" is an anagram of "carnivorous," and in the same note, written during the heart of the pandemic, he also noted that "Britney Spears" is an anagram of "Presbyterian"). He continued to respond to fans and others with gracious notes, but often the notes were left unsigned, as had never been the case before. Three weeks before he died, he told one supplicant, "I no longer have time for correspondence or autographs." The phrasing was almost premonitory. It wasn't that he was busy; "no longer" suggests that, at some level, he knew he was approaching the end.[42]

In the fall of 2021, twelve days before he died, Sondheim and Romley went to the opening night of John Doyle's new production of *Assassins.* The next day they were back on Broadway for a preview of Marianne Elliott's gender-reversed *Company*. A few days after that, a fan asked him to sign an old *Theater Week* cartoon of Sondheim arm wrestling with Andrew Lloyd Webber, a metaphor for their presumed rivalry. He declined; in his uncharacteristically abrupt response, he wrote, "I don't want to contribute to this kind of show business bullshit." Five days before he died, Sondheim offered an alternate (if rueful) title for his final show: *Fat Chance*.[43]

There was no memorial service for Stephen Sondheim until a year later. On November 14, 2022, nearly a thousand people filed into the Stephen Sondheim Theater on West Forty-third Street, which had been named for him on his eightieth birthday, twelve years earlier. It was an invitation-only event, arranged largely by James Lapine. Even though the theater was filled with people who had a personal or professional connection to Sondheim, one might also have considered it a version of something Sondheim himself had once said, and that Romley had posted on Facebook a week after his husband's death: "The theatre is a group of strangers coming together in a big dark room . . . and becoming a community."

There was no live music at the memorial, only recordings. "With So Little to Be Sure Of" from *Anyone Can Whistle* and "Someone in a Tree" from *Pacific Overtures* were the only songs from the Sondheim catalogue. Other pieces included a favored Chopin nocturne, the unlikely Brazilian folk piece "Bambalélé," and Maury Yeston's "New Words." In the Yeston song, the singer-narrator holds his child up to the night sky and teaches him to say "moon," and "stars," and finally "love." The song, one that Sondheim cherished, is a profound expression of a parent's love for a child.

Speakers included Leonard Bernstein's daughter Jamie, Hal Prince's daughter Daisy (Judy Prince had declined an invitation to speak, and did not attend), John Kander, and Sondheim collaborators Lapine, John Weidman, and Jonathan Tunick. Jeff Romley spoke, and so did Sondheim's half-brother Walter, with whom he'd remained close over the decades.[44]

It was writer Anna Quindlen, not widely known as a Sondheim friend, who quoted the afternoon's funniest Sondheim line, and also the most stirring. First, she said Sondheim had once told her, "If I were heterosexual and 20 years younger, and you were Jewish and unmarried, boy, could we have some good times." That got a laugh. And then she said something that induced a very different reaction, especially among those who knew him best: it was to Quindlen that he had once said, "I really do miss not having had a family." But, he'd added, "I suppose if I had one I wouldn't have had anything to write about."

Epilogue

I NEVER MET Stephen Sondheim. I sat near him in various theaters over the years, and—bizarrely—was mistaken for him a few times (two gray-haired Jewish men with ill-kempt facial hair wearing ancient sweaters). But I believe I came to know him during the three years I spent researching and writing this book.

But for most of that period, one puzzle remained unsolved. After I encountered the anecdote about *Sweeney Todd*, Judy Prince, and "the story of your life"—the puzzling scene I described in my prologue—I scoured the Meryle Secrest papers at the Beinecke Library at Yale University. Sondheim told Secrest he thought Prince's insight was on target, but he didn't explain what he meant, and neither did Secrest. I don't imagine he'd ever avenged himself with a murderous razor.

Over time, though, it became clear to me that Prince and Sondheim believed his life (at least up until the late 1970s) was, like Sweeney's, driven by revenge. Judy Prince doesn't give interviews, but in response to my request in 2023 I received a note from her daughter, the director Daisy Prince. "I asked my mother and she said it has to do with seeking revenge," she wrote. And: "Extrapolating from that I am sure you can fill in the contextual blanks."[1]

Extrapolation leads inevitably to Sondheim's relationship with his mother. Foxy was the subject of so many inflamed, enraged, and patently vengeful comments he made over the years that her malevolent (to her son) presence seemed to underscore his entire adult life. But extrapolation also leads to the critics who he believed had it in for him; the theater people who may have recognized his skill as a lyricist but dismissed him as a composer; the directors who'd distorted his work in regional revivals; the producers and corporations who had corrupted Broadway. Reflecting on the subject, it's impossible not to recall the two papers written by Sondheim's psychiatrist, Milton Horowitz, "On Revenge" and "Revenge and Masochism," in which Horowitz connected the revenge impulse to "deep loneliness" and "the need to connect." One also cannot ignore a postscript Sondheim appended to his angry letter to John Lahr, whose *Harper's* essay on *Sweeney Todd* in 1979 had so infuriated him. On the first day of the show's rehearsals, Sondheim told Lahr, Hal Prince had read aloud two quotations to the gathered cast, both from Lahr's biography of the playwright Joe Orton. The first was the book's opening sentence: "Life being what it is, one seeks revenge." The second was the book's epigraph, something Orton himself had written: "Cleanse my heart, give me the ability to rage correctly."[2]

I later encountered an interview with Sondheim in a 2011 issue of *American Theatre* magazine. Here Sondheim confirmed that revenge had been a potent force in his life. I asked the article's author, Rob Weinert-Kendt, if he could describe the moment in the midst of their generally upbeat conversation when Sondheim acknowledged this. "He seemed quiet, a little sheepish, not at all unwilling or defensive but a bit like I was asking him to pry open something that wasn't close to the surface," Weinert-Kendt said. "He searched for the words a bit more than at other points in the interview. It felt very much like a therapy moment." Weinert-Kendt also said, "It touched a chord, clearly. Another word I'd use for that moment was 'vulnerable.'" That Sondheim did not recognize his personal connection to *Sweeney Todd* until Judy Prince pointed it out suggests the extent to which his work had been invaded by the unconscious. That, too, had been a therapy moment.[3]

But Weinert-Kendt also believed that writing *Sweeney* was the culmination of one chapter in Sondheim's life, and to the degree that it embodied his hatred for Foxy, it was. Even in all the years that he continued to retail the story of The Letter ("Steve was a storyteller, and he knew Foxy was a good story," Peter Gethers said), even as he described her in the most brutal and spiteful language, there were moments when he revealed a softer set of feelings. He told Secrest he had occasionally sent her "letters that were friendly, warm, and loving." At various times, he said that she was intelligent, and amusing. Asked to name his favorite movies, he included *Torchy Blane in Chinatown*, an inconsequential late-1930s comic-mystery that shared a place on his list with *Citizen Kane*, *Smiles of a Summer Night*, *Pygmalion*, and other classics. The film's star was Foxy's close friend Glenda Farrell, who had made sure to have the screenwriters include in the film a party scene in which her character says to a departing guest, "Good night, Mrs. Sondheim."[4]

Only after he died could Sondheim's most devoted fans see this less charged, less complicated side of his relationship with his mother. When more than four hundred lots of his personal possessions were auctioned off in the summer of 2024 (for nearly

1.5 million acolyte-inflated dollars), a few stood out if you were searching for biographical detail, as I was: an engraved cigarette case that had belonged to Foxy; several pieces of her costume jewelry; and a handsome painting, by Foxy, of the Pennsylvania countryside. That he had troubled to save these artifacts of his problematic mother suggested, as The Letter did, another good story. But this one remained untold.[5]

Revenge is a powerful motivator; it's also taxing to sustain it.

But two other themes in Sondheim's ninety-one years resonated from his childhood to his death. Over time, he moved from alienation to connection, and from ambivalence to resolution. These were the parallel arcs that in fact defined him. The distancing alienation that plagued him, and that showed up so often in his work, was a dissonant chord that took him his entire life to harmonize successfully, to reach the point, he once said, "when you feel connected to the rest of the world." The need for resolution was provoked by his chronic, self-admitted ambivalence. "At least half my songs deal with ambivalence," he said, just as so much of his life was afflicted by it.[6]

Stephen Sondheim's universe changed when he met Jeff Romley; when he recognized, without demurrer, the breadth and depth of his accomplishments; and when he at last nodded toward posterity. Even as his creative capacities atrophied, his personal pleasures multiplied. His friends, most of whom had never imagined he would attain contentment, were all but unanimous in believing that the elderly Sondheim was the best Sondheim they had known. The Gold Medal from the American Academy, the Tony for Lifetime Achievement, the Presidential Medal of Freedom; a private life spent away from the limelight with his dearest friends; a deep and abiding partnership with the man he loved: He could not possibly have asked for more.

Still, after his death in his Roxbury home on November 26,

2021, more than he could have imagined came his way. Three days later, several hundred Broadway performers gathered in Times Square almost like a flash mob to sing "Sunday," from *Sunday in the Park with George*—the song he referred to as "the anthem." The gender-switched production of *Company*, which opened twelve days later, went on to win six Tony Awards. The producing director of the Pasadena Playhouse told a reporter that Sondheim shows, which had long been perceived as "too avant-garde" for regional theaters, had suddenly become "a sure bet." In 2023, a new *Sweeney Todd* commanded the third-highest average ticket price on Broadway. At the top of the list for several months of that year was the show that would have surely been, for Sondheim, the most gratifying of his revivals: a new *Merrily We Roll Along* directed by Maria Friedman that ran for 312 mostly sold-out performances before ecstatic, often handkerchief-clutching audiences, at a total gross just shy of $100 million. In many weeks, tickets for a show that had originally managed sixteen sour performances; that had been considered unfixable; and that had led to so much unhappiness and bitterness for Sondheim forty years earlier, sold for an average price of more than $250, and a top price of $649.[7]

It was a remarkable life, filled with remarkable accomplishment, and as the years continue to pass, recognition of his creative brilliance will only grow. David Ives, paraphrasing George Bernard Shaw, wrote, "you don't lose a man like that by his death. You only lose him by your own."[8]

It's appropriate, I think, to conclude this life of Stephen Sondheim with a comment he made while discussing his connection to Oscar Hammerstein. In 2017 Laurie Winer, Hammerstein's biographer, interviewed Sondheim about both Oscar's work and his own. When they got to *Sweeney Todd*, she asked him about his connection to the show's central character. His

Stephen Sondheim, 1999

reply could have summarized much of his work, and also nearly all of his textured, contradictory, troubling, and gratifying life: "The difference between Sweeney and me," he said, "is that I turned it into art."[9]

CHRONOLOGY OF SONDHEIM SHOWS

Saturday Night (created 1954; premiere, Bridewell Theatre, London, 1997)

West Side Story (lyrics only; music by Leonard Bernstein), Winter Garden Theatre, New York, 1957

Gypsy: A Musical Fable (lyrics only; music by Jule Styne), Broadway Theatre, New York, 1959

A Funny Thing Happened on the Way to the Forum, Alvin Theatre, New York, 1962

Anyone Can Whistle, Majestic Theatre, New York, 1964

Do I Hear a Waltz? (lyrics only; music by Richard Rodgers), Forty-sixth Street Theatre, New York, 1965

Company, Alvin Theatre, New York, 1970

Follies, Winter Garden Theatre, New York, 1971

A Little Night Music, Shubert Theatre, New York, 1973

The Frogs, Payne Whitney Gymnasium swimming pool, New Haven, 1974

Pacific Overtures, Winter Garden Theatre, New York, 1976

Sweeney Todd: The Demon Barber of Fleet Street, Uris Theatre, New York, 1979

Merrily We Roll Along, Alvin Theatre, New York, 1981

Sunday in the Park with George, Booth Theatre, New York, 1984

Into the Woods, Martin Beck Theatre, New York, 1987

Assassins, Playwrights Horizons, New York, 1990

Passion, Plymouth Theatre, New York, 1994

Road Show, Newman Theater at the Public Theater, New York, 2008

Here We Are, The Shed, New York, 2023

NOTES

Chapter 1. Before

1. *vindictive, graspingly, creepy:* Meryle Secrest interviews with Sondheim, various dates; *monster, celebrity:* Max, *Finale,* 20, 114.

2. *Lin-Manuel Miranda:* Sondheim memorial service, 2022.

3. *so genial:* Phyllis Battelle, International News Service, April 1, 1953.

4. *Barbara Billingsley:* Author interview with Robert Billingsley; *Aunt Foxy, husky voice:* Gould, *Mommie Dressing,* 153.

5. *whining little:* Harry Joe Brown Jr., conversation with the author, ca. 2003; *sarcasm:* Gottfried, *Sondheim,* 14.

6. *most damaging:* Meryle Secrest interview with Sondheim, May 9, 1995; *obedient:* www.nyma.org; *Emotional order:* Reminiscences of Stephen Sondheim, Columbia Center for Oral History Research, New York.

7. *nice:* Meryle Secrest interview with Sondheim, February 28, 1996.

8. *fiendish:* Trailer for film, www.imbd.com; *memorizing:* A

review of the film establishes that this would have been impossible (even for someone with as acute a mind as Sondheim's), as the score is only visible for a split second. More plausibly, the sound itself found a space in his mind, and he was able to recreate it later at the piano.

9. *Capehart:* Secrest, *Stephen Sondheim*, 33; *cookbooks:* Author interview with Peter Gethers; *exactly how:* Max, *Finale*, 15; *they stole, if you listened:* Author interview with Sherman.

10. *full of rage:* Susan Blanchard, in Gottfried, *Sondheim*, 13.

11. *acne:* Meryle Secrest interview with Sondheim, February 17, 1995; *competition:* Meryle Secrest interview with Alan Ayckbourn, n.d.

12. *Wet, nature, willow:* Sondheim in "The Art of Songwriting with Stephen Sondheim and Adam Guettel," 2009, youtube.com; *Apostrophe:* Kaplan, *Berlin*, 245; *urban irony:* Winer, *Oscar Hammerstein*, 317.

13. *hyper-critical:* Zadan, *Sondheim & Co.*, 161; *worst:* Zadan, *Sondheim & Co.*, 4; *writing like me:* "The Art of Songwriting with Stephen Sondheim and Adam Guettel," 2009, youtube.

14. *Do you still:* Gould, *Necessary Objects*, 101.

15. *Latin:* Meryle Secrest interview with Sondheim, February 3, 1995; *number theory:* Sondheim interviewed by Williams College professor Omar Sangare, 2020, "In conversation with Sondheim, Omar," youtube.

16. *Foxy:* Sondheim to Dorothy Hammerstein, June 1948, in Horowitz, *Letters of Oscar Hammerstein*, 445.

17. *addicted:* Secrest, *Stephen Sondheim*, 111.

18. *I'm told:* Andrew Heineman (Sondheim roommate), quoted in Steve Swayne, "Williams College Before, During, and After Sondheim," in Sheppard, ed., *Sondheim in Our Time*, 22; *didn't even know:* Meryle Secrest interview with Sondheim, January 29, 1995.

19. *oddballs:* Reminiscences of Stephen Sondheim; *a Jew to:* Heineman, quoted in Sheppard, ed., *Sondheim in Our Time*, 23.

20. *I don't know:* Meryle Secrest interview with Mary Rodgers, February 14, 1996; *sneers, Shakespeare:* Birmingham, *A Writer*, 96.

21. *slob:* Meryle Secrest interview with Sondheim, November

6, 1995; *ripe, genius:* Meryle Secrest interview with Dominick Dunne, November 30, 1995.

22. *groin:* Reminiscences of Stephen Sondheim; *taught geology:* Zadan, *Sondheim & Co.*, 6.

23. *very dry:* Reminiscences of Stephen Sondheim; *doctrinaire:* Robert Ceely, at www.ceelymusic.com/Biography.htm; *Anybody:* Horowitz, *Sondheim on Music*, 249.

24. *I fell, renowned composer:* Sondheim to Hammerstein, February 2, 1949, in Horowitz, *Letters of Oscar Hammerstein*, 446; *hummable:* Horowitz, *Letters of Oscar Hammerstein; drives:* Hart Perry interview for "Sondheim: A Musical Tribute," 1973; *an F-sharp:* Reminiscences of Stephen Sondheim.

25. *shards:* Ceely, www.ceelymusic.com/Biography.htm.

26. *horror, tyrant:* Meryle Secrest interview with Sondheim, May 31, 1995.

27. *losing sight:* Meryle Secrest interview with Sondheim, February 17, 1995.

28. *pointless:* quoted in "Babbitt: Transfigured Notes," https://fugueforthought.de/2017/11/06/.

29. *small musical:* quoted in Kapilow, *Listening*, 405; *cathedral:* "The Art of Songwriting with Stephen Sondheim and Adam Guettel," 2009, youtube.

30. *development:* Stephen Schiff, "Deconstructing Sondheim," *New Yorker*, March 8, 1993; *a song should:* Audio, CBS Orchestra, "The American Musical Theater," 1961. Show produced by WCBS-TV in cooperation with the NYPL Board of Education, Michael Mitnick Collection.

Chapter 2. Climbing High

1. *shallow:* Sondheim Papers, Wisconsin Historical Society, Hammerstein to Sondheim, August 6, 1953; *large wallets:* ms., "Climb High," Michael Mitnick Collection; *four-hour:* Prince, *Sense*, 249.

2. *lyrics:* Transcribed from *Sondheim Sings*, volume 2 (PS Classics, 2005). I've included these brief fragments from the lyrics under the copyright doctrine of fair use.

3. *learned about life:* Sondheim interviewed by Schuyler Chapin

for Irving S. Gilmore Award, Michael Mitnick Collection, probably 1989.

4. *sonnet:* Salsini, *Sondheim & Me*, loc 1110; *six thousand:* Meryle Secrest interview with Sondheim, February 18, 1995.

5. *Steve Sonheim: Variety*, January 21, 1953; *Bogart:* Meryle Secrest interview with Sondheim, February 18, 1995.

6. *me, writing:* Gottfried, *Sondheim*, 151.

7. *magical:* Meryle Secrest interview with Rodgers, February 14, 1996; *standards, infatuated:* Rodgers, *Shy*, 6, 7.

8. *monster, most awful, She doesn't:* Meryle Secrest interview with Sondheim, January 29, 1995.

9. *talk about forever:* Author interview with Jamie Bernstein.

10. *porcelain, thanks:* Rodgers, *Shy*, 145.

11. *clasping:* Rodgers, *Shy*, 84; *low flame:* "Stephen Sondheim, Academy Class of 2005, Full Interview," youtube; *writes in pencil:* Todd S. Purdum, "The Man Who Transformed Broadway," *Atlantic*, August 2019; *any relationship:* Author interview with Lapine.

12. *no longer be friends:* Sondheim to Prince, June 16, 1971, Prince Papers (LoC), B109F19; *treasured:* Sondheim to Laurents, October 17, 2008, Laurents Papers, B109F19; *vicious:* Laurents to Sondheim, August 3, 2008, Laurents Papers, B91F6.

13. *young lyricist:* L. Bernstein, *Findings*, 144.

14. *causes:* Mel Gussow, "Flora Roberts, 77, Play Agent with Astute Eye for Talent," *New York Times*, August 15, 1998, B14; *one hundred dollars:* Sondheim, *Finishing the Hat*, 4; *zipper:* Leonard Lyons, *New York Post*, n.d., author's collection; *Bronx Zoo:* Reminiscences of Stephen Sondheim.

15. *very advanced:* Salsini, *Sondheim & Me*, 93; *treasure trove:* Sondheim, *Finishing the Hat*, 6.

16. *unprepossessing, indoor, droopy:* Laurents, *Original*, 334.

17. *I've never:* Zadan, *Sondheim & Co.*, 14.

18. *frightened, collaboration:* "The Musical Theatre: A Talk by Stephen Sondheim," *The Dramatist*, Autumn 1978.

19. *really mean:* In *Six by Sondheim; genius:* Meryle Secrest interview with Sondheim, May 16, 1995.

20. *charming:* Bernstein to David Diamond, May 25, 1996, in

Simeone, *Leonard Bernstein Letters*, 352; *generally terrific, argue:* Gottfried, *Sondheim*, 49; *couldn't abide:* Sondheim interviewed by Lapine for *Sondheim on Sondheim*, Lapine Papers, B73.

21. *Harnick:* Sondheim speech, "Lyrics and Lyricists," 92nd Street Y, May 2, 1971; *I plead:* Battelle, International News Service, March 24, 1958; *new lyrics:* Miranda, Sondheim memorial service.

22. *Before Steve wrote:* Laurents, *Original*, 350; *about the name:* Frank Rizzo, "Sunday on a Campus with Sondheim," *The Sondheim Review*, Spring 1997, 30.

23. *raiding:* Laurents, *Original*, 350.

24. *limited passion:* "The Art of Songwriting with Stephen Sondheim and Adam Guettel," 2009, youtube; *bloodless:* Sondheim interviewed by Susan Lacy for *American Masters*, 1998; *duress:* Sondheim interviewed by Lapine for *Sondheim on Sondheim*, Lapine Papers, B73; *fuck/Krup:* Sondheim, *Finishing the Hat*, 51.

25. *not a cent:* Dramatists Guild symposium moderated by Terence McNally, April 18, 1985, youtube; *ashen:* Sondheim interviewed by Lapine for *Sondheim on Sondheim*, Lapine Papers, B73.

26. *cancel:* Sondheim to Bernstein, October 23, 1957, in Simeone, *Leonard Bernstein Letters*, 385.

27. *no style:* unsigned, "From Stage to Screen," *The Sondheim Review*, Winter 1995, 6.

28. *Dear Lenny:* Sondheim to Bernstein, in Simeone, *Leonard Bernstein Letters*, 383.

29. *clever:* Salsini, *Sondheim & Me*, 50.

30. *East Eightieth:* Meryle Secrest interview with Sondheim, May 23, 1995.

31. *egg heads: Billboard*, January 19, 1957.

32. *encouraged by, Jameson, Gee, someday:* Meryle Secrest interview with Sondheim, February 28, 1996. In interview transcripts, Jameson's name is mistakenly spelled "Jamison" or "Jamieson."

33. *explode:* Meryle Secrest interview with Erskine, March 17, 1995.

34. *will do anything, cannot do:* Robbins to Heyward, June 4, 1958, in Vaill, *Jerome Robbins by Himself*, 216.

35. *Beautiful Music:* Michael Mitnick Collection; *emotionally,*

bloody: Clive Hirschhorn, "Will Sondheim Succeed in Being Genuinely Japanese?," *New York Times*, January 4, 1976, D1.

36. *as played by:* Meryle Secrest interview with Sondheim, May 16, 1995; *Quogue:* Laurents diary, June 13, 1958, Laurents Papers, B130F1.

37. *You'll Never:* Laurents, *Original*, 381. The song's title had originally been "I'm in Pursuit of Happiness"; *generation apart:* Sondheim, *Finishing the Hat*, 61.

38. *too hard:* Mark Eden Horowitz, "A Prickly Rorem Goes Over Familiar Material," *The Sondheim Review*, Summer 2000, 5; *never had:* Jowitt, *Jerome Robbins*, 305; *drew more:* Charles Michener, "Words and Music—By Sondheim," *Newsweek*, April 23, 1973; *great advantage:* Vaill, *Somewhere*, 301.

39. *the rise and fall:* "The Art of Songwriting with Stephen Sondheim and Adam Guettel," 2009, youtube; *sit on:* Sondheim interviewed by Frank Rich, "Camera Three: Anatomy of a Song," 1976, youtube.

40. *coming up Rose's what?:* Citron, *Sondheim and Lloyd-Webber*, 92.

41. *talking dog:* Laurents, *Original*, 378; *imagination and brain:* Jowitt, *Jerome Robbins*, 324; *loud, vulgar:* unidentified 1963 tape, Shawn Mulligan/Christopher Scott Collection.

42. *couldn't wait:* Gussow notes from Sondheim interview, February 28, 2003, Gussow Papers, B140F10.

43. *twice a day:* Guernsey, *Broadway Song and Story*, 74; *crushing:* Viertel, *Secret Life*, 32.

Chapter 3. On His Own

1. *lost something, self-pity:* Sondheim to Prince, n.d., Prince Papers (LoC), B6F63.

2. *I was not proud:* Reminiscences of Stephen Sondheim; *mess:* Sondheim, unidentified 1963 tape, Shawn Mulligan/Christopher Scott Collection; *$115,000:* Meryle Secrest interview with Sondheim, February 3, 1995.

3. *moderately serious:* Meryle Secrest interview with Rodgers, February 14, 1996.

4. *virtually:* Meryle Secrest interview with Sondheim, May 31, 1995.

5. *you didn't:* Meryle Secrest interview with Sondheim, May 31, 1995; *People need: London Gay News*, May 20, 1976.

6. *a lyricist who:* Meryle Secrest interview with Tunick, August 30, 1995; *just bowled:* Meryle Secrest interview with Shepard, May 11, 1995.

7. *funniest man, we would each open:* Sondheim interviewed by John Guare, *Lincoln Center Theater Review*, Summer 2004.

8. *Of all the people:* Meryle Secrest interview with Sondheim, February 18, 1995; *polishing:* Reminiscences of Stephen Sondheim.

9. *eleven times:* Sondheim, unidentified 1963 tape, Shawn Mulligan/Christopher Scott Collection; *Call in:* Sondheim, *Finishing the Hat*, 87.

10. *apparent talent*, Meryle Secrest interview with Sondheim, May 16, 1995; *explain jokes:* Meryle Secrest interview with Sondheim, February 17, 1995; *never cracked, Damned if:* Gelbart, *Laughing Matters*, 207.

11. *stick to the subject, procrastinator:* Robbins unpublished interview with Craig Zadan, F: "Stephen Sondheim 1972–1973," Robbins Papers, B116F3.

12. *vulgarity:* Gelbart, *Laughing Matters*, 207; *close attention:* "The Musical Theatre: A Talk by Stephen Sondheim," *The Dramatist*, Autumn 1978; *quirkiness:* Meryle Secrest interview with Shepard, May 11, 1995; *musician's score:* Sondheim to Leonard Gershe, July 10, 1962, sondheimletters.

13. *universally panned:* Reminiscences of Stephen Sondheim; *ignoramuses:* Sondheim, *Finishing the Hat*, 253.

14. *bungling, enormity:* Sondheim to Leonard Gershe, July 10, 1962, sondheimletters; *fucking:* Kurt Peterson, in *On the Steps of the Shubert*, James Williams Productions, 2023; *Yes:* Author interview with Gethers.

15. *apologize, rupture:* Meryle Secrest interview with Sondheim, May 16, 1995.

16. *bitterest:* Sondheim to Leonard Gershe, July 10, 1962, sondheimletters.

17. *savor, never savored:* Meryle Secrest interview with Sondheim, May 23, 1995.

18. *Princess, Bogarde:* Sondheim to Laurents, July 4, 1965, Laurents Papers, B109F15; *Madrid:* Burton, *Leonard Bernstein,* 330.

19. *That's exactly:* Meryle Secrest interview with Rodgers, February 14, 1996.

20. *madly:* Jamie Bernstein, *Famous,* 22; *Snark:* Author interview with Jamie Bernstein.

21. *pig, never:* Meryle Secrest interview with Rodgers, February 14, 1996; *slobs:* Meryle Secrest interview with Sondheim, November 6, 1995; *wasn't visual:* Author interview with Wendall Harrington; *neglected:* Meryle Secrest interview with John Simon, May 11, 1995; *dishevelment:* Meryle Secrest interview with Craig Zadan, October 3, 1995; *unsmart casual:* Simon Callow, "The View from Here," AirMail.com, December 4, 2021.

22. *wouldn't want, Don't touch:* Author interview with Jamie Bernstein.

23. *too bad:* Meryle Secrest interview with Sondheim, May 16, 1995; *Muse:* Sondheim, *Finishing the Hat,* 252; *very smart:* Meryle Secrest interview with Sondheim, May 16, 1995.

24. *could almost:* Meryle Secrest interview with Stone, May 5, 1995; *one known interview:* Gussow notes, February 19, 1970, Gussow Papers, B132F2; *I'm certain:* Meryle Secrest interview with Hal Prince, May 10, 1995.

25. *Wanted to live, roster of beaux:* Gross, *Model,* 142–145; *Sondheim dress: Vogue,* May 1959; *surrounded by:* Meryle Secrest interview with Rodgers, February 14, 1996; *weren't concealing:* Earl Wilson, "It Happened Last Night," *New York Post,* April 9, 1964; *quite mad:* Secrest, *Stephen Sondheim,* 222.

26. *it was a romance, Paul Solomon:* Meryle Secrest interview with Sondheim, May 31, 1995; *a couple:* Author interview with Cynthia O'Neal.

27. *holy grail:* Author interview with Jane Klain; *he hoped:* Meryle Secrest interview with Laurents, September 27, 1995.

28. *wanted to prove, That's when:* Reminiscences of Stephen Sondheim.

29. *Streisand description:* Sondheim to Laurents, January 25, 1968, Laurents Papers, B109F19.

30. *Uggams:* Sondheim to Laurents, January 25, 1968; *Pinter:* Sondheim to Laurents, July 4, 1965, Laurents Papers, B109F19.

31. *little shit:* Rodgers, *Shy*, 9; *mesh:* Reminiscences of Stephen Sondheim; *sick and tired:* Sondheim to Laurents, n.d., 1964, Laurents Papers, B109F19; *grumpiness:* Sondheim to Laurents, August 3, 1963, Secrest Papers; *love you:* Sondheim to Laurents, n.d., 1964, Laurents Papers, B109F19; *can't wait:* Sondheim to Prince, September 28, 196[3?], Prince Papers (LoC), B6F63; *Meredith Willson:* McHugh, *Big Parade*, 413, and Sondheim, "From the Reader: What's Entertainment?," *New York Herald Tribune*, n.d., ca. August 1963.

32. *horrendous, final:* Sondheim to Prince, June 16, 1961, Prince Papers (LoC), B6F63; *Laurents at workshop performance:* Author interview with Lapine.

33. *thirty backers' auditions:* Sondheim, *Finishing the Hat*, 111; *extreme satire:* Hart Perry interview for "Sondheim: A Musical Tribute," 1973; *pure complicated:* Chapin, *Everything*, 59; *two smartest:* "The Art of Songwriting with Stephen Sondheim and Adam Guettel," 2009, youtube.

34. *nuts, I remember screaming:* Shapiro, *Nothing Like*, 76; *asked to be left out:* Laurents, *Mainly*, 26.

35. *cabbages:* Sondheim to Prince, n.d., April 1964, Prince Papers (LoC), B6F63.

36. *Columbus Symphony:* "Columbus/New York drama critic Norman Nadel, R.I.P.," *Columbus Dispatch*, November 6, 2010.

37. *cult flop:* Rich, *Hot Seat*, 946; *All the songs:* "The Musical Theatre: A Talk by Stephen Sondheim," *The Dramatist*, Autumn 1978.

38. *Steve won't really:* Zadan, *Sondheim & Co.*, 95.

39. *bitterest, tsuris:* Sondheim to Leonard Gershe, July 10, 1962, sondheimletters; *Burrows:* unidentified 1963 tape, Shawn Mulligan/Christopher Scott Collection.

40. *I was never:* Meryle Secrest interview with Sondheim, February 28, 1996.

41. *hang around:* Meryle Secrest interview with Jonathan Tunick, August 8, 1995; *Uncle Miltie:* Author interview with Jamie Bernstein; *palled around:* Author interview with Lapine; *Horowitz-Sondheim Clinic:* nypsi.org; *I am happy:* Meryle Secrest interview with Sondheim, February 12, 1995; *Bernard Berkowitz:* Mark Harris, interview notes for *Mike Nichols: A Life.*

42. *"On Revenge":* courtesy of Stephen Leibow, M.D.; "Revenge and Masochism," *Institute for Psychoanalytic Training and Research,* June 2004.

43. *Stardom:* A complete mock-up of the game, including instructions, was sold by the Doyle Galleries at the estate auction of Sondheim possessions, June 18, 2024; *pillows:* Sondheim to Robbins, n.d., probably 1966, Robbins Papers, B116F1.

44. *old pro:* "Herbert Sondheim, 71, Dead; Founded Couture Dress House," obituary, *New York Times,* June 2, 1966; *It's going:* Secrest, *Stephen Sondheim,* 186.

45. *The project:* Sondheim to Prince, April 26, 1964, Prince Papers (LoC), B6F63.

46. *I wanted:* early draft of Sondheim, *Finishing the Hat,* Michael Mitnick Collection; *streetwalking:* Zadan, *Sondheim & Co.,* 99.

47. *I watched him:* Louis Calta, "Rodgers and Sondheim Preparing a Musical," *New York Times,* November 6, 1964, 29.

48. *Sondheim, Laurents, and Mary Rodgers:* Various details of this event were related by Mary Rodgers in *Shy,* by Sondheim in *Finishing the Hat,* and by Arthur Laurents in *Original Story By.*

49. *The more:* R. Rodgers, *Musical Stages,* 319; *personal vindictiveness:* Laurents to R. Rodgers, July 17, 1965, Laurents Papers, B17F2; *Godzilla:* Bricusse, *Pure Imagination,* 179; *deserved:* "Lunch with the FT: Stephen Sondheim," *Financial Times,* October 15, 2010.

50. *chance to work:* Streisand, *My Name Is Barbra,* 154; *brought up on:* Sondheim, *Look, I Made a Hat,* 147.

51. *no leading up:* Laurents, *The Rest,* 137; *hated Brecht's work:* Zadan, *Sondheim & Co.,* 115; *Both of us, The only thing:* Author interview with Guare.

Chapter 4. The Hal-Steve Thing, Part 1

1. *wilder:* Sondheim to Prince, July 16, 1969, "Sondheim, Stephen, 1969," Prince Papers (NYPL), B356F.

2. *always around:* Gussow notes, February 19, 2070, Gussow Papers, B132F2; *triumvirate:* Prince, *Sense*, 230; *hopeless:* Sondheim to Prince, September 28, 196[?], Prince Papers (LoC), B6F63; *guarantee:* Burton, *Leonard Bernstein*, 422.

3. *spinning:* Author interview with Weidman; *Hal-Steve, dominated:* Author interview with Lapine; *minute after:* Sondheim interviewed by Frank Rich, Kennedy Center, April 29, 2002; *The Enthusiasm:* Sondheim memorial service.

4. *tried to pressure, incoherence, pushing it:* Sondheim to Prince, July 16, 1969, "Sondheim, Stephen, 1969," Prince Papers (NYPL), B356F.

5. *dictated:* Prince to George Furth, August 7, 1969, "Furth, George, 1969–1983," Prince Papers (NYPL), Box 356F.

6. *I'm going to:* Author interview with Weidman.

7. *panic:* Sondheim to Prince, July 16, 1969, "Sondheim, Stephen, 1969," Prince Papers (NYPL), Box 356F; *I can't:* Furth to Prince, August 15, 1969, "Furth, George, 1969–1983," Prince Papers (NYPL), Box 356F; *ready to drop out:* Furth to Prince, August 4, 1969, enclosing Furth to Sondheim, August 1, 1969, "Furth, George, 1969–1983," Prince Papers (NYPL), Box 356F; *about to board:* Prince to Furth, August 7, 1969, "Furth, George, 1969–1983," Prince Papers (NYPL), Box 356F.

8. *a man:* Gussow notes from Hal Prince interview, February 19, 1970, Gussow Papers, B132F2.

9. *the wheels:* Sondheim to Robbins, June 30, [ca. 1963], Robbins Papers, B116F1; *finally reduced:* Sondheim to Prince, July 16, 1969, "Sondheim, Stephen, 1969," Prince Papers (NYPL), Box 356F; *didn't own:* Lapine, *Putting It Together*, 44.

10. *didn't write:* "The Musical Theatre: A Talk by Stephen Sondheim," *The Dramatist*, Autumn 1978.

11. *homosexual:* Jacobs, *Still Here*, 170; *Hollywood adaptation:* Sondheim to Larry Kramer, April 7, 1979, Kramer Papers, B59F2.

12. *Feinstein:* Joan Hamburg Show, November 20, 2022; *He just drank:* Author interview with Lapine; *addict:* Author interview with O'Neal.

13. *AA, lonely people:* Author interview with John Guare; *wandering:* Chapin, *Everything,* 169; *tension:* Meryle Secrest interview with Sondheim, April 13, 1995; *million martinis:* Meryle Secrest interview with André Bishop, May 12, 1995; *guzzle:* Robert Hurwitz personal journal, quoting Renaud Mechant letter to John Adams.

14. *mental censors:* Meryle Secrest interview with Sondheim, February 28, 1996; *sodden:* Author interview with Weidman.

15. *I never saw:* Author interview with Lapine; *vodka:* Feinstein on Joan Hamburg Show, November 20, 2022; *extreme:* Author interview with Moss.

16. *fetal position:* Author interview with Guare; *drunk highs:* Meryle Secrest interview with Rodgers, February 14, 1996; *helped down:* Author interview with Weidman.

17. *incredible gifts:* Author interview with Hurwitz.

18. *beige hole:* Moss, *Art of Work,* 92; *a bit:* Gussow notes from Hal Prince interview, February 19, 1970, Gussow Papers, B132F2; *constant series:* Sondheim to Prince, September 28, 1963, Prince Papers (LoC), B6F63; *Ambivalence:* Kapilow, *Listening,* 372; *To Rodgers:* Gottfried, *Sondheim,* 88; *a world that:* "The Art of Songwriting with Stephen Sondheim and Adam Guettel," 2009, youtube; *living room:* Gussow notes from Judy Prince interview, Spring 1970, Gussow Papers, B132F2.

19. *$175,000:* Gussow notes from Hal Prince interview, February 19, 1970, Gussow Papers, B132F2; *Nichols told:* Prince to "Dear Gang," April 26, 1970, Furth Papers, B1F1.

20. *acid:* Jacobs, *Still Here,* 169; *two hours:* Zadan, *Sondheim & Co.,* 119; *cynicism:* Rodgers to Sondheim and Prince, June 3, 1970, Rodgers Papers.

21. *My way:* Silverman, interview with Karen Lerner, *Sondheim,* 105.

22. *downer, perfectly fine:* Lapine interview for *Sondheim on Sondheim,* Lapine Papers, B73; *chills:* Secrest, *Stephen Sondheim,* 261.

23. *great joy:* Gussow notes from Sondheim interview, February 28, 2003, Gussow Papers, B140F10.

24. *appreciated:* Author interview with Tommasini, and Author interview with Wheeler; *no such thing:* Gussow notes from Hal Prince interview, February 19, 1970, Gussow Papers, B132F2.

25. *Beatles:* Bricusse, *Pure Imagination*, 162; *McCartney:* Hart Perry interview for "Sondheim: A Musical Tribute," 1973; *Newman:* Author interview with Robert Hurwitz; *Nyro, Lulu, Mitchell:* Hurwitz personal journal, 2005; *Radiohead:* Max, *Finale*, 95; *Dylan:* Hart Perry interview for "Sondheim: A Musical Tribute," 1973.

26. *"Drinking Song":* Sondheim, conversation with Frank Rich and Jonathan Tunick for *Original Cast Album*, Criterion Collection; *inspiration from Foxy, popped into my head:* Bob Colacello, "Here's to the Ladies Who," interview with Sondheim, *Vanity Fair*, February 2012, also Author interview with Susan Berns Rothchild.

27. *schnecken:* unpublished notes, Alexandra Jacobs interview with Sondheim; *I thought:* Bell, *Elaine Stritch*, 147.

28. *My mother: London Gay News*, May 20, 1976; *I never thought:* Sondheim, Tony Awards acceptance speech, 1971.

29. *Majorca:* Meryle Secrest interview with Sondheim, May 18, 1995; *keychain, flop:* Max, *Finale*, 112–113.

30. *handiest:* "The Musical Theatre: A Talk by Stephen Sondheim," *The Dramatist*, Autumn 1978.

31. *good guy:* Chapin, *Everything*, 314; *point of the show:* Pender, *Sondheim Encyclopedia*, 150; *dour:* Sondheim interviewed by Tim Teeman, *The Times* (London), March 3, 2012.

32. *Tunick told:* Sean Patrick Flahaven, "Tunick: An Artist and a Craftsman," *The Sondheim Review*, Summer 1996, 22.

33. *a chance:* Sondheim, *Finishing the Hat*, 200; *Arlen:* Sondheim, *Finishing the Hat*, 222.

34. *separated from fact, Somebody else:* Meryle Secrest interview with Sondheim, January 29, 1995.

35. *Etai Benson:* Author interview with Benson; *Rabbi Samantha Frank:* Author interview with Frank.

36. *Yom Kippur:* Pogrebin, *Stars of David*, 291; *seder:* Max, *Finale*, 56; *attitude:* Pogrebin, *Stars of David*, 290–291; *not a Jew:* Meryle

Secrest interview with Laurents, November 27, 1995; *very deep:* Pogrebin, *Stars of David*, 291.

37. *grew up thinking:* Pogrebin, *Stars of David*, 290–291; *Your father:* Sheppard, ed., *Sondheim in Our Time*, 22. The classmate was the writer Stephen Birmingham.

38. *goyische:* Sondheim to Feiffer, n.d., Feiffer Papers, B12F6.

39. *gentile musical, unlike most, It seemed:* Zadan, *Sondheim & Co.*, 191.

40. *original title:* Sondheim, *Finishing the Hat*, 252.

41. *$16,000:* Pender, *Sondheim Encyclopedia*, 286.

42. *whipped cream:* Zadan, *Sondheim & Co.*, 182.

43. *rhythm section:* Zadan, *Sondheim & Co.*, 159; *so bewildered:* unsigned interview, "John McMartin: From Ben to Cap'n Andy," *The Sondheim Review*, Fall 1996, 16.

44. *ice cream truck:* Sondheim memorial service.

45. *Horowitz understood:* Author interview with Tommasini; *most beautiful:* Salsini, *Sondheim & Me*, 110.

46. *I express:* Tommasini, email to author, January 8, 2023; *I'm a playwright:* Horowitz, *Sondheim on Music*, 79.

47. *most fundamental:* Hurwitz personal journal, 2011.

48. *I'm not asking:* Horowitz, *Sondheim on Music*, 25; *Westenberg:* quoted in unsigned, "A Sondheim Song Is Like a Good Script," *The Sondheim Review*, Fall 1997, 24.

49. *virtual orgy:* Viertel, *The Secret Life*, 168.

50. *the puzzle takes over:* A frequent Sondheim comment, repeated to Anthony Tommasini, Adam Moss, and various others.

51. *curious way:* Zadan, *Sondheim & Co.*, 104; *normal speech:* Hart Perry interview for "Sondheim: A Musical Tribute," 1973.

52. *I spent:* Max, *Finale*, 51; *I said to Steve:* Zadan, *Sondheim & Co.*, 311; *Put a gun:* Author interview with Lapine.

53. *Steve arrived:* Salsini, *Sondheim & Me*, 108.

54. *Probably one:* Zadan, *Sondheim & Co.*, 394.

55. *Written in a single:* Kapilow, *Listening*, 391.

56. *the 90th time:* "TimesTalks, The *New York Times* Speaker Series: Celebrating Sondheim," January 10, 2004.

57. *national treasure:* Charles Michener, "Words and Music—By Sondheim," *Newsweek*, April 23, 1973.

58. *All of Broadway:* "Sondheim Given Musical Tribute," *New York Times*, March 12, 1973, 39.

59. *ran for three hours:* Zadan, *Sondheim & Co.*, 206; *most exciting:* Author interview with Kummer; *Steve's genius:* Viertel, in *On the Steps of the Shubert.*

60. *first public:* quoted by Kurt Peterson, in *On the Steps of the Shubert; proud, ages:* Max, *Finale*, 112–113.

Chapter 5. The Hal-Steve Thing, Part 2

1. *foreign language:* Sondheim, *Look, I Made a Hat*, vii; *Musical harmony:* Horowitz, *Sondheim on Music*, 17; *the problem:* Tommasini email to author, January 8, 2023.

2. *genius:* Author interview with Tommasini; *Lyrics make:* Harburg speech, "Lyrics and Lyricists," 92nd Street Y, December 20, 1970.

3. *bristled:* Hart Perry interview for "Sondheim: A Musical Tribute," 1973; *greatest living:* "Stephen Sondheim, Theater's Greatest Lyricist," *New York Times*, October 22, 1917, *T Magazine*, 143.

4. *tiny little, pewter ashtrays:* "The Musical Theatre: A Talk by Stephen Sondheim," *The Dramatist*, Autumn 1978; *sweat:* John Wilson, "Sondheim: Lyricist and Composer," *New York Times*, March 6, 1960; *tongue:* Hart Perry interview for "Sondheim: A Musical Tribute," 1973.

5. *those goddamned, unbearably:* Reminiscences of Stephen Sondheim; *it's a job:* Sondheim interview, "The American Musical Theatre," WCBS-TV, 1961; *hell:* Horowitz, *Sondheim on Music*, 73.

6. *Wallace Stevens:* Sondheim speech, "Lyrics and Lyricists," 92nd Street Y, May 2, 1971; *E. B. White:* "Desert Island Discs" interview, 1990; *most boring: London Gay News*, May 20, 1976; *no cultural background:* Reminiscences of Stephen Sondheim.

7. *space-saving:* Author interview with Mark Eden Horowitz.

8. *just kills me:* "The Art of Songwriting with Stephen Sondheim and Adam Guettel," 2009, youtube; *disgusting, coy:* Sondheim

to Arthur Laurents, n.d., in Laurents files in Secrest Papers; *the sound:* Author interview with Guare.

9. *Really?:* Reminiscences of Stephen Sondheim.

10. *requires:* Zadan, *Sondheim & Co.*, 170; *horrific, talking about, my public, Mason:* Reminiscences of Stephen Sondheim.

11. *really happy, Not having:* Reminiscences of Stephen Sondheim; *Pure music:* Meryle Secrest interview with Sondheim, February 28, 1996.

12. *piece of trash:* Hellman to Prince and Wheeler, December 12, 1982, Prince Papers (LoC), B3F55.

13. *a lark:* Sondheim, *Finishing the Hat*, 286.

14. *it would of course:* Author interview with Mitnick; *urinal:* Sondheim interviewed by John Guare, *Lincoln Center Theater Review*, summer 2004.

15. *snappish:* Meryle Secrest interview with Sondheim, February 28, 1996; *moral certainty:* Weber, "Robert Brustein, Passionate Force in Nonprofit Theater, Dies at 96," *New York Times*, October 29, 2023, n.p.

16. *palpable:* Sondheim, *Finishing the Hat*, 286.

17. *asshole:* Meryle Secrest interview with Sondheim, May 16, 1995; *Brustein hated:* Max, *Finale*, 58.

18. *I'M MRS.:* Author interview with John Weidman.

19. *heart surgery, pacemaker, only regret:* Michiko Kakutani, "Sondheim's Passionate Passion," *New York Times*, March 20, 1994, sec. 2, 1.

20. *essentially:* Sondheim, *Finishing the Hat*, 311.

21. *never existed:* Silverman, *Sondheim*, 61.

22. *phrase he attributes to Foxy:* Sondheim to "Dear Mom," undated, enclosed in Sondheim to Mary Rodgers, November 20, 2013, Rodgers Papers, B16/F34.

23. *God only:* Sondheim interviewed by Terry Gross, *Fresh Air*, April 21, 2010.

24. *agreed to proceed:* John Weidman, in "I Collabor Him and He Collabors Me," *The Dramatist*, September/October 2022; *What's interesting:* "The Musical Theatre: A Talk by Stephen Sondheim," *The Dramatist*, Autumn 1978.

25. *essential artistic:* Author interview with Weidman; *imaginary:* Clive Hirschhorn, "Will Sondheim Succeed in Being Genuinely Japanese?," *New York Times*, January 4, 1976, D1; *Oh look:* Horowitz, *Sondheim on Music*, 69; *translator-ese:* "The Musical Theatre: A Talk by Stephen Sondheim," *The Dramatist*, Autumn 1978; *onomatopoeic:* Author interview with Anthony Tommasini.

26. *hotel room:* Author interview with Weidman.

27. *Steve will:* Weidman, in "I Collabor Him," 12.

28. *poetic Orientalism, its attempt, swing:* Sondheim, *Finishing the Hat*, 32.

29. *I was so:* unsigned, "Sondheim on 'Someone in a Tree,'" *The Sondheim Review*, Summer 1997, 28; *extraordinary, undone:* Author interview with Weidman.

30. *left me:* Sondheim to Shear, April 6, 1994, sondheimletters; *Gershwin's:* M. E. Horowitz, "Sondheim at the Library: A Friendship with 'Steve,'" November 29, 2021, https://blogs.loc.gov/music/2021/11/sondheim-at-the-library-a-friendship-with-steve/.

31. *that doesn't:* Author interview with Weidman.

32. *The article:* Clive Hirschhorn, "Will Sondheim Succeed in Being Genuinely Japanese?," *New York Times*, January 4, 1976, D1.

33. *direct quotation:* Hirschhorn, "Will Sondheim Succeed in Being Genuinely Japanese?"

34. *meant to damage:* Zadan, *Sondheim & Co.*, 221; *complained about:* letters, *New York Times*, January 11, 1976, 19; *Hirschhorn defended:* "Green Room," *Plays and Players*, July 1976, 34; *severely misquoted:* Reminiscences of Stephen Sondheim.

35. *very attractive: London Gay News*, May 20, 1976; *creepy atmosphere:* Mel Gussow, "Sweeney Todd': A Little Nightmare Music," *New York Times*, February 1, 1979, C15.

36. *I was introduced:* Streep email to author, May 17, 2023.

37. *lost their minds:* Zadan, *Sondheim & Co.*, 249; *Len Cariou could:* Winer, *Oscar Hammerstein*, 295.

38. *only part:* "The Musical Theatre: A Talk by Stephen Sondheim," *The Dramatist*, Autumn 1978; *I'd love to:* Sondheim interview, outtake, for *Broadway: The American Musical*, PBS 2004.

39. *more than enough:* Hugh Wheeler, "author's note" on published script of *Sweeney Todd.*

40. *backers' audition:* Audio recording, Michael Mitnick Collection; *first person to use:* Max, *Finale,* 167; *mature little boy:* Crespy, *Richard Barr,* 337; *placing an ad: New York Times,* March 19, 1978, 12. *Broadway record:* Zadan, *Sondheim & Co.,* 252.

41. *black box:* Leticia Kent, "On Broadway Spectacle's the Thing," *New York Times,* March 12, 1978, D1; *budget overrun:* Frank Shanbacker, "Taking a Risk on Broadway," *Playbill,* December 1979; *foundry:* Crespy, *Richard Barr,* 184; *Masterpiece Theatre:* annotation on copy of *Sweeney* script, catalog for benefit auction for PEN, Christie's, December 2, 2014.

42. *drowned, horror movie:* Reminiscences of Stephen Sondheim.

43. *spiky, telling point:* Anthony Tommasini, "Critic's Notebook," *New York Times,* January 24, 2000, E1.

44. *re-arouse, nothing:* Mel Gussow, "Sweeney Todd: A Little Nightmare Music," *New York Times,* February 1, 1979, C15.

45. *like buttah:* Horowitz, *Sondheim on Music,* 148.

46. *rage at Shevelove:* Secrest, *Stephen Sondheim,* 381; *furnace:* Charles Kimbrough, in Lapine, *Putting It Together,* 158–159.

47. *As Steve, never said a word:* Author interview with Guare.

48. *disgusting, galoshes:* M. Rodgers, *Shy,* 185–186.

49. *amphetamines, Sondheim agreed:* Author interview with Jamie Bernstein.

50. *ego inflation:* Sondheim interviewed by Susan Lacy for *American Masters,* 1998.

51. *couldn't write, Oh well:* Author interview with Michael Mitnick; *Rip van, actively embarrassing:* Sondheim interviewed by Rob Weinert-Kendt, *American Theater,* April, 2011; *self-importance:* Rowland, *Leonard Bernstein,* 1:86.

52. *massive:* Charles Michener, "Words and Music—By Sondheim," *Newsweek,* April 23, 1973.

53. *blasted joys:* John Lahr, "Sondheim's Little Deaths," *Harper's,* April 1979.

54. *I hope you'll get:* Sondheim to Lahr, February 14, 1979,

Lahr Papers; *I guess:* Sondheim, *Finishing the Hat*, 375; *Fifteen years:* "Charlie Rose Show," June 3, 1994.

55. *might have asked:* Sondheim to Lahr, February 14, 1979, Lahr Papers; *by far:* Lahr, "Playing Your Hunches," *New Yorker*, December 13, 2004; *admit he's wrong:* Max, *Finale*, 204.

56. *$80,000:* Secrest, *Stephen Sondheim*, 344.

57. *bright-eyed:* Author interview with Jamie Bernstein; *One night in 2004:* Author interview with Patricia Marx.

58. *invitation list:* Prince Papers (NYPL), B7F4.

59. *Sunset Boulevard:* Meryle Secrest interview with Sondheim, September 12, 1995; *If I wanted:* Reminiscences of Stephen Sondheim; *Puccini, Wozzeck:* Max, *Finale*, 93; *Peter Grimes:* Sondheim interviewed by Schuyler Chapin, WQXR radio, March 26, 1969, Gilmore Music Library, New Haven; *I asked:* Salsini, *Sondheim & Me*, 106.

60. *failure:* Furth to Jerry Roth, November 17, 1980, Furth Papers, B1F4.

61. *suffering:* Furth Papers, B1F4, Furth to his mother, January 12, 1981, Furth Papers, B1F4; *nothing more:* Sondheim, *Finishing the Hat*, 421; *First you:* quoted in Furth to "Betsy and Bob [Duerr?]," April 20, 1985, B2F1, Furth Papers.

62. *Some people:* Prince quoted in Alex Rybeck, personal journal.

63. *start with:* Reminiscences of Stephen Sondheim.

64. *talking while:* "The Art of Songwriting with Stephen Sondheim and Adam Guettel," 2009, youtube.

65. *most difficult:* Horowitz, *Sondheim on Music*, 71.

66. *Everything in:* Horowitz, *Sondheim on Music*, 42.

67. *modular:* Salsini, *Sondheim & Me*, 291.

68. *three good notes:* Tepper, *Untold Stories*, 557.

69. *Jason Alexander:* Paul Salsini, "Before *Seinfeld*, George Was in *Merrily*," *The Sondheim Review*, Fall 1999, 15.

70. *flickering light:* Tepper, *Untold Stories*, 551; *I'm not saying:* Zadan, *Sondheim & Co.*, 276.

71. *one of the worst:* Reminiscences of Stephen Sondheim; *Hal's function:* Sondheim, *Look, I Made a Hat*, 5.

72. *$4,500:* Between the Covers Rare Books, betweenthecovers .com, retrieved February 23, 2025; *isn't about, I identify:* Max, *Finale*, 192.

Chapter 6. Reaching the Summit

1. *small malices:* Sondheim to Lerner, January 23, 1964, Lerner Papers, B16F30.

2. *professional bitches, tell all:* Zadan, *Sondheim & Co.*, 255; *vultures, out to destroy:* Wayman Wong, "Sondheim Speaks About His *Passion*," *The Sondheim Review*, Summer 1994, 7; *viciousness:* Reminiscences of Stephen Sondheim; *there's very little:* Clive Hirschhorn, "Will Sondheim Succeed in Being Genuinely Japanese?," *New York Times*, January 4, 1976, D1.

3. *Thanks for:* Sondheim to Lupone, November 17, 1981, sondheimletters; *It's the end:* Stephen Schiff, "Deconstructing Sondheim," *New Yorker*, March 8, 1993; *living in garrets:* Sondheim, *Finishing the Hat*, 382; *hated me and Hal:* Meryle Secrest interview with Sondheim, March 13, 1995.

4. *stupid, useless:* Reminiscences of Stephen Sondheim; *idealistic:* Secrest, *Stephen Sondheim*, 116; *At this moment:* Reminiscences of Stephen Sondheim.

5. *don't want, hostile:* Lapine, *Putting It Together*, 16.

6. *video games:* Gottfried, *Sondheim*, 153; *mystery novel:* Zadan, *Sondheim & Co.*, 295; *Bernstein persuaded, I don't like:* Reminiscences of Stephen Sondheim.

7. *Nobody but:* Lapine, *Putting It Together*, 149–150.

8. *Venice:* Gritti hotel bill, March 29, 1982, Prince Papers (NYPL), B7F3; *run out of steam:* Meryle Secrest interview with Sondheim, February 28, 1996.

9. *lit a joint, that's what:* Author interview with Lapine.

10. *As I've told:* Meryle Secrest interview with Sondheim, September 12, 1995; *The idea grew:* Sondheim to Thomas Parisi, March 11, 1985, sondheimletters.

11. *You want to see:* Author interview with O'Neal.

12. *I'm able:* Secrest, *Stephen Sondheim*, 348.

13. *As for what:* Sondheim to Robert Burnett, May 17, 1983, sondheimletters.

14. *share a joint:* Lapine, *Putting It Together,* 129; *disparaged:* Clive Hirschhorn, "Will Sondheim Succeed in Being Genuinely Japanese?," *New York Times,* January 4, 1976, D1; *This is the way:* Lapine, *Putting It Together,* 109.

15. *a follower, shouldn't let him:* Meryle Secrest interview with André Bishop, May 12, 1995.

16. *intimidation:* Lapine, *Putting It Together,* 140; *lobby door:* Sondheim interviewed by Williams College professor Omar Sangare, "In conversation with Sondheim, Omar Sangare," 2020, youtube; *It sure is!:* Lapine, *Putting It Together,* 204; *Dark and Bored:* Salsini, *Sondheim & Me,* loc 20.

17. *son of a bitch:* Zadan, *Sondheim & Co.,* 310; *Patinkin:* Horowitz, *Sondheim on Music,* 99.

18. *poured out:* "I Collabor Him and He Collabors Me," *The Dramatist,* September/October 2022, 12.

19. *considered it:* Sondheim, *Finishing the Hat,* 408.

20. *The night he:* Author interview with Weidman; *trancing out:* Terry Gross interview, *Fresh Air,* April 21, 2010.

21. *it would not be:* Author interview with Lapine; *because James:* Sondheim to Mekenian, April 23, 2007, sondheimletters; *I believe all:* Gottfried, *Sondheim,* 161.

22. *a sound:* Author interview with O'Neal.

23. *later denied:* broadway.com, "Ask a Star," December 8, 2004.

24. *astonishingly, We just learned:* Furth to "Bobby," November 20, 1984, Furth Papers, B2F1.

25. *becoming a legend:* Furth to "Betsy & Bob [Duerr?]," April 20, 1985, Furth Papers, B2F1; *All this:* Samuel Freedman, "Sondheim's Follies Revisited," *New York Times,* September 1, 1985, sec. 2, 1.

26. *truly adult:* quoted in Freedman, "Sondheim's Follies Revisited"; *I stood there:* Secrest, *Stephen Sondheim,* 466.

27. *staged oratorio: Follies in Concert,* DVD, 2001; *it was good:* Jacobs, unpublished Sondheim interview notes for *Still Here.*

28. *John, you forget:* Author interview with Guare.

29. *ecstasy:* Author interview with Lapine.

30. *mounds, Worried:* Author interview with Lapine; *lump:* M. Rodgers, *Shy*, 265; *habit-forming, energized:* Meryle Secrest interview with Sondheim, February 28, 1996.

31. *never read:* Zadan, *Sondheim & Co.*, 338.

32. *what's going on inside:* Schiff, "Deconstructing Sondheim."

33. *The avuncular tone:* Author interview with Lapine.

34. *deep place, touched:* Author interview with Lapine; *Ah, the woods:* Sondheim, *Look, I Made a Hat*, 58.

35. *calling friends:* "I Collabor Him and He Collabors Me," *The Dramatist*, September/October 2022, 12; *extremely hard, very scary:* Zadan, *Sondheim & Co.*, 351; *very naked:* Lapine quoting Sondheim, to Lisa Kron, interview for *Dramatists Guild Legacy Project*, 2011.

36. *represent precisely:* Minkoff and McClatchy, *Poetry*, unpaginated; *profoundly alone:* "Into the Woods MTI Conversation Piece with Stephen Sondheim and James Lapine," youtube.

37. *reply was definitive:* Author interview with Peter Gethers; *glaring flaw:* Sondheim, *Look, I Made a Hat*, 30; *French horn:* Author interview with Hurwitz.

38. *correct her punctuation:* Author interview with Harrington; *I won't tell:* Meryle Secrest interview with Ted Chapin, March 13, 1995; *correct her grammar:* Terry Gross interview, *Fresh Air*, April 21, 2010.

39. *I love puzzles: Games* magazine, January 1983; *fitting together:* Schiff, "Deconstructing Sondheim"; *my own world:* Meryle Secrest interview with Sondheim, February 17, 1995.

40. *Madonna:* Zadan, *Sondheim & Co.*, 379; *Streisand:* Stephen Holden, "Barbra Streisand: This Is the Music I Love. It Is My Roots," *New York Times*, October 10, 1985, sec. 2, 1.

41. *all his friends:* Meryle Secrest interview with Flora Roberts, May 24, 1995; *who made something:* Sondheim, *Finishing the Hat*, 112; *new Prince-Sondheim-Weidman:* Author interview with Weidman.

42. *vicious note:* Meryle Secrest interview with Patinkin, May

16, 1985; *really hurt her:* Author interview with Chapin; *Don't piss the guy:* Author interview with Viertel.

43. *dangerous: The Sondheim Review*, Fall 1995, 10; *if you walk, gliding:* Meryle Secrest interview with M. Rodgers, February 14, 1996; *would never call:* Author interview with Jamie Bernstein; *call-ee:* Author interview with O'Neal.

44. *Taxi!:* Author interview with Corby Kummer; *Clar would, allowed me:* Author interview with Chapin.

45. *outsized:* Author interview with Viertel; *Lapine saw:* Author interview with Lapine.

46. *it's calculated, strictly:* Sondheim to Michael Granoff, October 26, 1988, sondheimletters.

47. *Sondheim didn't:* Author interview with Weidman.

48. *as good a production:* Unsigned interview, "Elaine Stritch: 'I think of it as a work of art,'" *The Sondheim Review*, Fall 2004, 16; *gasping, What has happened:* Author interview with Rosen.

49. *perfect:* Sondheim, *Look, I Made a Hat*, 143, also in a speech at Northwestern University, 1995; *as proud:* Author interview with Viertel.

50. *That's how:* Kramer to Sondheim, September 8, 1985, Kramer Papers, B68.

51. *sheer joy:* Kramer to Sondheim, September 8, 1985, Kramer Papers, B68.

52. *from an idea:* Sondheim to Kramer, September 8, 1985, Kramer Papers, B68; *fables:* Suffolk University "News and Features," March 30, 2010.

53. *very anti-union:* 1963, Mulligan Scott Collection; *collapse:* Freedman, "Sondheim's Follies Revisited"; *couldn't care less:* Meryle Secrest interview with Sondheim, May 23, 1995; *militant feminism:* Sondheim, *Finishing the Hat*, 223.

54. *rapidly, utmost: Los Angeles Times*, May 14, 1992.

55. *Art is:* Pogrebin, *Stars of David*, 291.

56. *emergency calls:* Author interview with John Weidman; *artist's plight:* Gottfried, *Sondheim*, 162.

57. *willed the YPF, bottomless:* Author interview with Sherman; *there was a point:* Reminiscences of Stephen Sondheim.

58. *Abingdon:* A. A. Cristi, "Young Playwrights Announced at Barter Theatre," BroadwayWorld.com, November 9, 2018.

59. *If I had to live, not acceptable, great regret:* Alan Franks, "Sondheim: My Ideal Collaborator Is Me," *The Times* (London), April 25, 2009.

60. *You have more:* Sherman, Sondheim memorial service; *so many of us:* Laura Collins-Hughes, "Cherished Words from Theater's Encourager-in-Chief," *New York Times*, December 1, 2021, sec. AR, 7; *as good as anyone:* Sondheim quoted in Margaret Engel, "Randy Rainbow's Witty World," *Washington Post Magazine*, May 28, 2019.

61. *gave Larson detailed comments:* Larson to Sondheim, December 8, 1994, Larson Papers, B14F7; *Book of Mormon:* Author interview with Trey Parker; *not very, For me:* Sondheim to Guettel, September 17, 1981, sondheimletters.

62. *tiptoed barefoot:* Author interview with Mitnick; *Nothing is more:* Clar, Sondheim memorial service.

63. *So what happened:* Ricky Ian Gordon, *Seeing Through*, unpaginated ms., Author interview with Gordon, and Katz, *Home Fires*, 496.

64. *later pleaded:* Rybeck to Prince, November 24, 1981, and Prince to Rybeck, December 12, 1981, "Merrily We Roll Along," Prince Papers (NYPL), Box 356F, and Rybeck email to author, May 10, 2023.

65. *You want:* Author interview with Corby Kummer.

66. *Which of these:* Author interview with Lapine; *There was nobody:* Sondheim speech, "Lyrics and Lyricists," 92nd Street Y, May 2, 1971; *kept insisting:* Author interview with Jerry Zaks.

67. *dreadful mistakes:* Jason Robert Brown, "How I Insulted Sondheim and the Wisdom Received Thereby," October 31, 2012, jasonrobertbrown.com, also emails from Brown to author, June 10, 2024, and December 20, 2024.

68. *it hurts other:* Max, *Finale*, 124; *wasn't leading:* Meryle Secrest interview with Sondheim, May 16, 1995.

69. *what Leonard Bernstein, His?:* Sondheim to Secrest, April 3, 1998, Secrest Papers, B3.

70. *present tense:* Gottfried, *Sondheim*, 69.

71. *every child:* Zadan, *Sondheim & Co.*, 52; *business relationship:* Meryle Secrest interview with Sondheim, February 3, 1995; *her funeral:* Frank Rich, "Conversations with Sondheim," *New York Times Magazine*, March 12, 2000; *three years after:* Meryle Secrest interview with Sondheim, May 16, 1995.

72. *afterthought:* Max, *Finale*, 112–113; *Oh, yeah:* Author interview with Lapine; *Somebody asked:* Meryle Secrest interview with Laurents, September 27, 1995; *Please don't:* Meryle Secrest interview with Ayckbourn, n.d., 1995.

73. *stealing:* Max, *Finale*, 112–113; *smart:* Meryle Secrest interview with Sondheim, February 18, 1995; *felt the need:* Author interview with Doyle; *hated him:* Author interview with O'Neal; *spoke fondly:* Jeff Romley, Sondheim memorial service.

74. *I don't:* Max, *Finale*, 113.

Chapter 7. After

1. *Peter Jones:* Secrest, *Stephen Sondheim*, 471–473, and Meryle Secrest interview with Jones, May 30, 1997.

2. *like a teenager:* Author interview with Weidman; *Horowitz asked:* Meryle Secrest interview with Jones, May 30, 1997; *very close:* Sondheim interviewed by Tim Teeman, *The Times* (London), March 3, 2012; *"Bambalélé":* Sondheim interviewed by Schuyler Chapin, WQXR radio, March 26, 1969, Gilmore Music Library, New Haven, call number OHV 284 a.

3. *scared, doesn't reach:* Steyn, *Broadway Babies*, 129; *unhappy or bitter: London Gay News*, May 20, 1976; *avoidance:* Zadan, *Sondheim & Co.*, 390.

4. *correlation:* Sondheim, interview, "Charlie Rose Show," June 3, 1994; *confirmed:* Author interview with Lapine; *You've never: London Gay News*, May 20, 1976.

5. *worth singing:* Sondheim, *Finishing the Hat*, 145; *first humorless:* Salsini, *Sondheim & Me*, 39; *completely ironic:* Author interview with Peter Gethers; *non-ironic, unconditional:* Sondheim interview, "Charlie Rose Show," June 3, 1994; *crack you open:* Michiko Kakutani, "Sondheim's Passionate *Passion*," *New York Times*, March 20, 1994, sec. 2, 1; *called Paul Salsini:* Salsini, *Sondheim & Me*, 67.

6. *once cited:* Meryle Secrest interview with Sondheim, May 31, 1995; *circled back:* Davis, "Infection," *Atlantic*, March 1995; *I wanted:* "TimesTalks, The *New York Times* Speaker Series: Celebrating Sondheim," January 10, 2004; *oppressive:* Pender, *Sondheim Encyclopedia*, 393.

7. *twenty instances:* Pender, *Sondheim Encyclopedia*, 397; *hiding:* Lapine, in "I Collabor Him and He Collabors Me," *The Dramatist*, September/October 2022; *a desire:* Michiko Kakutani, "Sondheim's Passionate *Passion*," *New York Times*, March 20, 1994, sec. 2, 1; *especially difficult:* Donna Murphy, "A Celebration of the Life and Work of Stephen Sondheim," Stella Adler Center for the Arts, February 2, 2022.

8. *new hit:* Davis, "Infection," *Atlantic*, March 1995; *excessive feeling:* Brustein, *New Republic*, August 1, 1994.

9. *complex human, essence:* in "Passion—Sondheim @ 90 Roundtable," January 20, 2021, youtube.

10. *I miss us:* Sondheim to Prince, December 10, 2009, sondheimletters.

11. *Prince's letter:* Prince to Sondheim, June 25, 1992, Prince Papers (LoC), B6F64.

12. *Sondheim took:* Sondheim to Prince, July 9, 1992, Prince Papers (LoC), B6F64.

13. *thanked:* "Sondheim Given Musical Tribute," *New York Times*, March 12, 1973, 39.

14. *constantly rewriting:* Author interview with Rich.

15. *Berlin, Kaufman, Behrman:* Kaplan, *Irving Berlin*, 293–294; *Parade:* Prince, *Sense*, 273; *romantic, jazzy:* Sondheim, *Finishing the Hat*, 181.

16. *more girls, reasons:* Author interview with Weidman.

17. *Megève:* Author interview with Weidman.

18. *so effortless:* Mendes, "He Was Passionate, Utterly Open, and Sharp as a Knife," *The Guardian*, November 29, 2021.

19. *Would you ever:* Sondheim to Parker, February 17, 2005, sondheimletters; *Don't change, Whenever:* Author interview with Parker; *Guardian Angels:* Bricusse, *Pure Imagination*, 460.

20. *Gelbart:* "Sondheim idea," November 3, 1991, B180F5, Gelbart Papers, UCLA Library Special Collections; *McNally's:* Raymond-Jean Frontain, "Mutual Admiration," *The Sondheim Review*, Spring 2011, 30; *a musical that exploded:* Frank Rich, "The Final Sondheim," *New York Magazine*, August 28, 2023; *retiring type:* Sondheim interviewed by Tim Teeman, *The Times* (London), March 3, 2012.

21. *I save everything:* Reminiscences of Stephen Sondheim.

22. *Library of Congress:* Horowitz, *Sondheim on Music*, 246–249; *Home must:* Mark Eden Horowitz, unpublished article about concert; *The Wiz:* Author interview with Jamie Bernstein.

23. *Romley, Frankel:* Author interview with Frankel.

24. *P.J. was:* Author interview with Weidman; *Xbox:* Author interview with Michael Mitnick; *goes to bed:* Max, *Finale*, 106.

25. *relationship with Jeff:* Author interview with O'Neal; *I've hung:* Author interview with Doyle; *Trading:* Author interview with Jamie Bernstein; *reservoir:* Author interview with Lapine; *Schreiber, Watts:* Author interview with Jamie Bernstein.

26. *God Years:* Author interview with Chapin.

27. *meeting God:* Author interview with Zaks; *How did I:* Author interview with Frankel; *He did bring:* Author interview with Doyle.

28. *considered the medal:* Author interview with Anthony Tommasini.

29. *I am always:* Sondheim to Robbins, October 14, 1981, Robbins Papers, B116F5.

30. *baby pictures:* Author interview with Robert Hurwitz.

31. *snippy and annoyed:* Author interview with Gethers; *greatest evening:* David Ives, "Amazing Afternoons: Writing with Sondheim," davidives.net; *reverse:* "The Art of Songwriting with Stephen Sondheim and Adam Guettel," 2009, youtube; *If I play:* Sondheim interviewed by Tim Teeman, *The Times* (London), March 3, 2012.

32. *Thank god:* George Dalzell email to author, July 7, 2024; *At my age:* Max, *Finale*, 106; *Everybody will:* Miranda, Sondheim memorial service; *someone should write:* Max, *Finale*, 73; *buried his*

ashes: Gail Levenstein email to author, August 4, 2022; *As a 31-year-old:* name withheld by author, letter to Arthur Laurents, February 13, 2006, Laurents Papers, B109F19.

33. *fascist:* Gussow notes from Sondheim interview, February 28, 2003, Gussow Papers, B140F10; *inflame:* Sondheim to Dalzell, March 26, 2014, sondheimletters; *LGBT:* Sondheim interviewed by Tim Teeman, *The Times* (London), March 3, 2012.

34. *fucking singalong:* Author interview with Gethers; *enraged letter:* "Arts Beat: Stephen Sondheim Takes Issue with Plan for Revamped 'Porgy and Bess,'" *New York Times*, www.nytimes.com, August 10, 2011; *his passion, slapped around:* McDonald interviewed by Terry Gross, *Fresh Air*, May 15, 2012.

35. *even Clive Hirschhorn:* By the 1990s, Sondheim was inscribing the published versions of his shows to Hirschhorn; many were offered for sale in the 2020s; *asked, declined:* Author interview with Donna Rosen; *Did not answer:* Sondheim to Laurents, September 29, 1999, Laurents Papers, B109F19; *You're just:* Author interview with John Weidman; *That's the thing:* Author interview with Jack Viertel.

36. *just cut:* Author interview with Sherman.

37. *Avedon portrait:* Author interview with Donna Rosen.

38. *run out:* Sam Mendes, "He Was Passionate, Utterly Open, and Sharp as a Knife," *The Guardian*, November 29, 2021; *prepared to rewrite, Are you crazy:* Author interview with Gethers.

39. *Once you're dead:* Stephen Schiff, "Deconstructing Sondheim," *New Yorker*, March 8, 1993; *Who gives:* Author interview with Gethers.

40. *balloon:* "The Art of Songwriting with Stephen Sondheim and Adam Guettel," 2009, youtube; *I don't even:* Sondheim interviewed by Tim Teeman, *The Times* (London), March 13, 2015; *hardware store: Sydney Morning Herald*, November 22, 2012.

41. *less confident:* "The Art of Songwriting with Stephen Sondheim and Adam Guettel," 2009, youtube; *Buñuel project:* Frank Rich, "The Final Sondheim," *New York Magazine*, August 28, 2023; *a large part:* Author interview with Weidman; *slough:* Max, *Finale*, 39; *I'm fond:* Max, *Finale*, 86.

42. *carnivorous:* Simon Callow, "The View from Here," AirMail .com, December 4, 2021; *I no longer:* Sondheim to Joseph Planta, November 3, 2021, sondheimletters.

43. *show business bullshit:* Sondheim to Scott Mikita, November 18, 2021, sondheimletters; *Fat Chance:* Michael Paulsen, "Days Before Dying, Stephen Sondheim Reflected: 'I've Been Lucky,'" *New York Times,* November 26, 2021, A1.

44. *Judy Prince:* Author interview with Lapine.

Epilogue

1. *seeking revenge:* Daisy Prince, email to author, April 27, 2023.

2. *deep loneliness, need to connect:* Horowitz quoted in Stephen Leibow, M.D., unpublished paper on Horowitz's "Revenge and Masochism," delivered to Toronto Psychoanalytic Society, 2004.

3. *He seemed quiet:* Rob Weinert-Kendt, email to author, March 13, 2023.

4. *storyteller:* Author interview with Gethers; *letters that were:* Meryle Secrest interview with Sondheim, May 9, 1995; *favorite movies:* list provided to author by Mark Eden Horowitz.

5. *auctioned off:* Doyle Galleries estate auction of Sondheim possessions, June 18, 2024.

6. *when you feel:* Zadan, *Sondheim & Co.,* 353; *ambivalence:* Gottfried, *Sondheim,* 112.

7. *too avant-garde, sure bet:* Ben Brantley, "Stephen Sondheim Doesn't Want to Be Your Savior," *New York Times,* November 25, 2023, SR 10.

8. *you don't:* David Ives, "Amazing Afternoons: Writing with Sondheim," davidives.net.

9. *The difference:* Laurie Winer, notes from Sondheim interview, Spring 2017.

BIBLIOGRAPHY

THE PRINTED RESOURCES on Stephen Sondheim's life and work are vast, and the amount that has accrued in digital media yet vaster. The collection of interviews Meryle Secrest conducted in 1995 and 1996 for her biography *Stephen Sondheim: A Life* are preserved on tape in the Beinecke Rare Book and Manuscript Library at Yale University in New Haven. Transcripts of "Reminiscences of Stephen Sondheim," a series of interviews conducted and transcribed by the Columbia Oral History Project, became available for citation and quotation only after his death in 2021.

I have not included citations for quotations from reviews identified in the text by the newspaper or magazine they appeared in; except as indicated, all of them were published in the days immediately following the specific show's opening night.

Archives

Leonard Bernstein Papers, Library of Congress
Jules Feiffer Papers, Library of Congress

George Furth Papers, New York Public Library
Mel Gussow Papers, Harry Ransom Center, Austin
Larry Kramer Papers, Beinecke Library, New Haven
John Lahr Papers, Mugar Library, Boston
James Lapine Papers, Beinecke Library, New Haven
Jonathan Larson Papers, Library of Congress
Arthur Laurents Papers, Library of Congress
Alan Jay Lerner Papers, Library of Congress
Harold Prince Papers, Library of Congress
Harold Prince Papers, New York Public Library
Jerome Robbins Papers, New York Public Library
Mary Rodgers Papers, Library of Congress
Richard Rodgers Papers, New York Public Library
Meryle Secrest Papers, Beinecke Library, New Haven
Stephen Sondheim Papers, Wisconsin Historical Society (a limited selection of documents donated by Sondheim very early in his career)
Reminiscences of Stephen Sondheim, Columbia Center for Oral History Research, New York

Books

Bell, John. *Elaine Stritch: The End of Pretend.* Page, 2019.
Bernstein, Jamie. *Famous Father Girl.* HarperCollins, 2018.
Bernstein, Leonard. *Findings.* Simon & Schuster, 1982.
Birmingham, Stephen. *A Writer Writes: A Memoir.* Lyons, 2022.
Bonanno, Margaret Wander. *Angela Lansbury: A Biography.* St. Martin's, 1987.
Bricusse, Leslie. *Pure Imagination: A Sorta-Biography.* Faber & Faber, 2016.
Brustein, Robert. *Making Scenes: A Personal History of the Turbulent Years at Yale, 1976–1979.* Random House, 1981.
Burton, Humphrey. *Leonard Bernstein.* Doubleday, 1994.
Chapin, Ted. *Everything Was Possible: The Birth of the Musical "Follies."* Knopf, 2003.
Citron, Stephen. *Sondheim and Lloyd-Webber: The New Musical.* Oxford University Press, 2001.

Crespy, David A. *Richard Barr: The Playwright's Producer.* Southern Illinois University Press, 2013.

Gelbart, Larry. *Laughing Matters.* Random House, 1998.

Goldman, William. *The Season.* Harcourt, 1969.

Gordon, Ricky Ian. *Seeing Through: A Chronicle of Sex, Drugs, and Opera.* Farrar, Straus and Giroux, 2024.

Gottfried, Martin. *Sondheim.* Abrams, 1993.

Gould, Lois. *Mommie Dressing.* Doubleday, 1998.

———. *Necessary Objects.* Dell, 1972.

Gross, Michael. *Model: The Ugly Business of Beautiful Women.* William Morrow, 1995.

Guernsey, Otis L., Jr., ed. *Broadway Song and Story: Playwrights/Lyricists/Composers Discuss Their Hits.* Dodd Mead, 1985.

Harris, Mark. *Mike Nichols: A Life.* Penguin Press, 2021.

Horowitz, Mark Eden. *Sondheim on Music: Minor Details and Major Decisions.* Rowman & Littlefield, 2019.

———. *The Letters of Oscar Hammerstein.* Oxford University Press, 2022.

Jacobs, Alexandra. *Still Here: The Madcap, Nervy, Singular Life of Elaine Stritch.* Farrar, Straus and Giroux, 2019.

Jowitt, Deborah. *Jerome Robbins: His Life, His Theater, His Dance.* Simon & Schuster, 2004.

Kander, John, and Fred Ebb. *Colored Lights: Forty Years of Words and Music, Show Biz, Collaboration, and All That Jazz.* Faber & Faber, 2003.

Kapilow, Rob. *Listening for America: Inside the Great American Songbook from Gershwin to Sondheim.* Liveright, 2019.

Kaplan, James. *Irving Berlin: New York Genius.* Yale University Press, 2019.

Katz, Donald. *Home Fires: An Intimate Portrait of One Middle-Class Family in Postwar America.* HarperCollins, 1992.

Kort, Michele. *Soul Picnic: The Music and Passion of Laura Nyro.* St. Martin's, 2002.

Lapine, James. *Putting It Together: How Stephen Sondheim and I Created "Sunday in the Park with George."* Farrar, Straus and Giroux, 2021.

Laurents, Arthur. *Mainly on Directing: Gypsy, West Side Story, and Other Musicals.* Knopf, 2009.

———. *Original Story By.* Knopf, 2000.

———. *The Rest of the Story: A Life Complete.* Applause, 2012.

Max, D. T. *Finale.* HarperCollins, 2022.

McHugh, Dominic. *The Big Parade: Meredith Willson's Musicals from* The Music Man *to* 1491. Oxford University Press, 2021.

Minkoff, George Robert, and J. D. McClatchy, eds. *The Poetry of Song.* Poetry Society of America, 1992.

Mordden, Ethan. *On Sondheim: An Opinionated Guide.* Oxford University Press, 2015.

Moss, Adam. *The Art of Work: How Something Comes from Nothing.* Penguin Press, 2024.

Pender, Rick. *The Sondheim Encyclopedia.* Rowman & Littlefield, 2021.

Pogrebin, Abigail. *Stars of David: Prominent Jews Talk About Being Jewish.* Broadway, 2005.

Prince, Harold. *Sense of Occasion.* Applause, 2017.

Rainbow, Randy. *Playing with Myself.* St. Martin's, 2022.

Rich, Frank. *Hot Seat: Theater Criticism for the New York Times, 1980–1993.* Random House, 1998.

Rivadue, Barry. *Lee Remick: A Bio-Bibliography.* Greenwood, 1995.

Rodgers, Mary, and Jesse Green. *Shy: The Alarmingly Outspoken Memoirs of Mary Rodgers.* Farrar, Straus and Giroux, 2022.

Rodgers, Richard. *Musical Stages.* Random House, 1975.

Rowland, Steve. *Leonard Bernstein: An Oral History,* volume 1. Time Out of Joint Press, 2021.

Salsini, Paul. *Sondheim & Me: Recalling a Musical Genius.* Bancroft Press, 2022.

Secrest, Meryle. *Shoot the Widow: Adventures of a Biographer in Search of Her Subject.* Knopf, 2007.

———. *Somewhere for Me: A Biography of Richard Rodgers.* Knopf, 2001.

———. *Stephen Sondheim: A Life.* Vintage, 2011.

Shapiro, Eddie. *Nothing Like a Dame: Conversations with the Great Women of Musical Theater.* Oxford University Press, 2014.

Shawn, Allen. *Leonard Bernstein: An American Musician.* Yale University Press, 2016.

Sheppard, W. Anthony, ed. *Sondheim in Our Time and His.* Oxford University Press, 2022.

Silverman, Stephen M. *Sondheim: His Life, His Shows, His Legacy.* Black Dog & Leventhal, 2024.

Simeone, Nigel. *The Leonard Bernstein Letters.* Yale University Press, 2013.

Sondheim, Stephen. *Finishing the Hat.* Knopf, 2010.

———. *Look, I Made a Hat.* Knopf, 2011.

Steyn, Marc. *Broadway Babies Say Goodnight: Musicals Then and Now.* Faber & Faber, 1997.

Streisand, Barbra. *My Name Is Barbra.* Viking, 2023.

Swayne, Steve. *How Sondheim Found His Sound.* University of Michigan Press, 2005.

Tepper, Jennifer Ashley. *The Untold Stories of Broadway*, volume 1. Dress Circle, 2013.

Vaill, Amanda. *Somewhere: The Life of Jerome Robbins.* Crown, 2008.

———, ed. *Jerome Robbins, by Himself: Selections from His Letters, Journals, Drawings, Photographs, and an Unfinished Memoir.* Knopf, 2019.

Viertel, Jack. *The Secret Life of the American Musical: How Broadway Shows Are Built.* Sarah Crichton/Farrar, Straus and Giroux, 2016.

Winer, Laurie. *Oscar Hammerstein II and the Invention of the American Musical.* Yale University Press, 2023.

Zadan, Craig. *Sondheim & Co.*, second edition, updated. Da Capo, 1994.

Instagram Sites

sondheimletters
sondheimphotos

Videos and Other Recordings

Audio recording, Stephen Sondheim Memorial Service, New York, November 14, 2022.

Raw footage from Stephen Sondheim interview in "Sondheim: A Musical Tribute," directed by Hart Perry, 1973, Michael Mitnick Collection.

Unlabeled audio recording; appears to be a recording of a class Sondheim visited in 1963, possibly at the request of conductor Lehman Engel. Shawn Mulligan/Christopher Scott Collection.

youtube.com: Throughout, citations for videos available on youtube include titles or keywords that can be used to locate them.

CREDITS

Frontispiece: Photograph by Richard Avedon, © The Richard Avedon Foundation
Foxy Sondheim: Courtesy Susan and Berns Rothchild
Oscar Hammerstein II: Pictorial Press Ltd./Alamy
Sondheim at Williams College: Jack Birchall/Courtesy Sawyer Library Special Collections, Williams College Library
Bernstein, Sondheim, and Laurents: Everett Collection Historical/Alamy
Mary Rodgers and George Abbott: Ben Martin/Getty Images
Nancy Berg: Friedman-Abeles/New York Public Library
Sondheim, Lee Remick, and Allen Ludden: CBS via Getty Images
Sondheim and Hal Prince: © Mark Chester 2025
The Ladies Who Lunch: Courtesy Susan and Berns Rothchild
Sondheim in the "Letter L" position: © 1991 Hans Namuth Estate, Courtesy Center for Creative Photography, University of Arizona
Judy Prince: Fairchild Archive/WWD/Penske Media via Getty Images

Sondheim and Arthur Laurents: Carolyn Contino/BEI/Shutterstock

Sondheim and Jeff Romley: J Grassi/Patrick McMullan via Getty Images

Receiving the Presidential Medal of Freedom: Alex Wong/Getty Images

Portrait by Richard Avedon from 2004: Photograph by Richard Avedon, © The Richard Avedon Foundation

Stephen Sondheim in 1999: Fred R. Conrad/*The New York Times*

Brief quotations of lyrics from "When I Get Famous" and "Where Do I Belong?" and other songs are included under the copyright doctrine of fair use.

"Together Wherever We Go"
from *Gypsy*
Words by Stephen Sondheim
Music by Jule Styne
© 1959 (Renewed) Rilting Music, Inc. and Quaytor Productions, LLC
All Rights Administered by WC Music Corp.
All Rights Reserved, Used by Permission
Reprinted by Permission of Hal Leonard LLC

"Pretty Little Picture"
from *A Funny Thing Happened on the Way to the Forum*
Music and Lyrics by Stephen Sondheim
© 1962 (Renewed) Rilting Music, Inc.
All Rights Administered by WC Music Corp.
All Rights Reserved, Used by Permission
Reprinted by Permission of Hal Leonard LLC

"The Blob"
from *Merrily We Roll Along*
Words and Music by Stephen Sondheim
© 1981 Rilting Music, Inc.
All Rights Administered by WC Music Corp.
All Rights Reserved, Used by Permission

Reprinted by Permission of Hal Leonard LLC

"Anyone Can Whistle"
from *Anyone Can Whistle*
Words and Music by Stephen Sondheim
© 1964 (Renewed) Rilting Music, Inc.
All Rights Administered by WC Music Corp.
All Rights Reserved, Used by Permission
Reprinted by Permission of Hal Leonard LLC

"We're Gonna Be All Right"
from *Do I Hear a Waltz?*
Music by Richard Rodgers
Lyrics by Stephen Sondheim
Copyright © 1965 by Richard Rodgers and Stephen Sondheim
Copyright Renewed
Williamson Music and Rilting Music, owner of publication and allied rights throughout the world
International Copyright Secured All Rights Reserved
Reprinted by Permission of Hal Leonard LLC

"Send in the Clowns"
from *A Little Night Music*
Words and Music by Stephen Sondheim
© 1973 (Renewed) Rilting Music, Inc.
All Rights Administered by WC Music Corp.
All Rights Reserved, Used by Permission
Reprinted by Permission of Hal Leonard LLC

"Opening Doors"
from *Merrily We Roll Along*
Words and Music by Stephen Sondheim
© 1981 Rilting Music, Inc.
All Rights Administered by WC Music Corp.
All Rights Reserved, Used by Permission
Reprinted by Permission of Hal Leonard LLC

"It's Only a Play"
from *The Frogs*

Words and Music by Stephen Sondheim
© 1974 (Renewed) Rilting Music, Inc.
All Rights Administered by WC Music Corp.
All Rights Reserved, Used by Permission
Reprinted by Permission of Hal Leonard LLC

"Finishing the Hat"
from *Sunday in the Park with George*
Words and Music by Stephen Sondheim
© 1984 Rilting Music, Inc.
All Rights Administered by WC Music Corp.
All Rights Reserved, Used by Permission
Reprinted by Permission of Hal Leonard LLC

"Into the Woods"
from *Into the Woods*
Words and Music by Stephen Sondheim
© 1988 Rilting Music, Inc.
All Rights Administered by WC Music Corp.
All Rights Reserved, Used by Permission
Reprinted by Permission of Hal Leonard LLC

"Buddy's Blues (The God-Why-Don't-You-Love-Me Blues)"
from *Follies*
Music and Lyrics by Stephen Sondheim
Copyright © 1971, 1983 by Range Road Music Inc., Jerry Leiber Music, Mike Stoller Music, Rilting Music, Inc. and
Burthen Music Co., Inc.
Copyright Renewed
All Rights Administered by Herald Square Music, Inc.
International Copyright Secured All Rights Reserved
Used by Permission
Reprinted by Permission of Hal Leonard LLC

"Agony"
from *Into the Woods*
Words and Music by Stephen Sondheim
© 1988 Rilting Music, Inc.
All Rights Administered by WC Music Corp.

All Rights Reserved, Used by Permission
Reprinted by Permission of Hal Leonard LLC

"The Road You Didn't Take"
from *Follies*
Music and Lyrics by Stephen Sondheim
Copyright © 1971 by Range Road Music Inc., Jerry Leiber Music, Mike Stoller Music, Rilting Music, Inc. and Burthen Music Co., Inc.
Copyright Renewed
All Rights Administered by Herald Square Music, Inc.
International Copyright Secured All Rights Reserved
Used by Permission
Reprinted by Permission of Hal Leonard LLC

"Barber and His Wife"
from *Sweeney Todd*
Words and Music by Stephen Sondheim
© 2007 Rilting Music, Inc.
All Rights Administered by WC Music Corp.
All Rights Reserved, Used by Permission
Reprinted by Permission of Hal Leonard LLC

"No One Is Alone—Parts I & II"
from *Into the Woods*
Words and Music by Stephen Sondheim
© 1986 Rilting Music, Inc.
All Rights Administered by WC Music Corp.
All Rights Reserved, Used by Permission
Reprinted by Permission of Hal Leonard LLC

"What More Do I Need?"
from *Saturday Night*
Music and Lyrics by Stephen Sondheim
© 1984 Burthen Music Company, Inc.
All Rights Administered by Chappell & Co., Inc.
All Rights Reserved
Used by Permission of Alfred Music

ACKNOWLEDGMENTS

THIS BOOK WAS COMMISSIONED for the Jewish Lives series by Ileene Smith. Ileene, and her associates at Yale University Press—especially Heather Gold, Chelsea Connelly, Phillip King, and Elizabeth Sylvia—deserve my thanks.

So does a long list of others—for instance, Meryle Secrest, whom I have never met or spoken to. As I suggested in the Prologue, Secrest's fifty hours of interviews with Sondheim, conducted in 1994 and 1995, and her accompanying interviews with many others no longer living, are uncut gems. Anyone writing about Sondheim has to be indebted to Secrest for the scholarly generosity she displayed when she delivered her interview tapes to the Beinecke Library and placed no restrictions on access, or on any writer's freedom to make use of her material.

In 2022, I reviewed Mary Rodgers's memoir, *Shy*, for the *New York Times Book Review;* the author ID mentioned that I was writing a book about Sondheim, and within days I heard from a number of people who were curious about the project. One of these was

Barry Joseph, a Sondhead who was in the midst of writing *Matching Minds with Sondheim: The Puzzles and Games of the Broadway Legend* (Applause Books, 2025). Barry was encouraging from the start and has been helpful all along the way. He also made two absolutely critical introductions: he told me about the Secrest tapes, and he introduced me to Michael Mitnick.

Though hardly an intimate, Michael (himself a writer for stage and film) knew Sondheim personally, has studied him endlessly, and owns a priceless collection of material related to Sondheim, including hundreds of hours of audio and video recordings of interviews going back to the early 1960s. His archive also includes the scripts of *Climb High* and other unproduced Sondheim efforts, as well as a partial manuscript of a novel, *Bequest,* that Sondheim abandoned. From Foxy's library, he has one of the L. Frank Baum *Oz* books, with the very young Sondheim's name scrawled in clumsy pencil. Michael owns—and uses—the daybed Sondheim would recline on while writing.

But more than all that, his knowledge of and insight into Sondheim have been invaluable to me—deeply informed, highly perceptive, and freely offered. He read every word in this book (some of them several painstaking times), corrected more than a handful of errors, and filled in some new and surprising details. Without Barry, Michael, and the Secrest tapes, this book would be much the poorer.

Many others helped me. Mostly live, sometimes over the telephone, in two or three instances by email, I interviewed (in addition to Barry and Michael) Etai Benson, Jamie Bernstein, Jason Robert Brown, Susan Burden, Tommy Cecil, Ted Chapin, Kate Clark, John Doyle, Rabbi Samantha Frank, Richard Frankel, Peter Gethers, Ricky Ian Gordon, John Guare, Wendall Harrington, Mark Eden Horowitz, Bob Hurwitz, Jane Klain, Corby Kummer, John Lahr, Patricia Marx, Bill Mays, Michael Mitnick, Adam Moss, Cynthia O'Neal, Trey Parker, Daisy Prince, Frank Rich, Victoria Roberts, Donna and Ben Rosen, Susan Rothchild, Alex Rybeck, Jonathan Marc Sherman, Meryl Streep, Anthony Tommasini, Jack Viertel, John Weidman, Rob Weinert-Kendt, Laurie Winer, Brenda Withers, Jerry Zaks, and the late Harry Joe Brown Jr.

Sondheim's widower, Jeff Romley, cordially told me that when he moved in with Sondheim, he made a vow to himself never to talk about him with journalists or other writers. Jeff could have thrown up roadblocks, but instead chose to let me proceed with his implicit sanction, even if without his personal input or approval. I also gratefully acknowledge the Stephen Sondheim Estate for permission to use the photograph on the book's cover.

Mark Harris, Alexandra Jacobs, Adam Moss, and Laurie Winer shared unpublished notes from their interviews with Sondheim for their books about, respectively, Mike Nichols, Elaine Stritch, "the work of art," and Oscar Hammerstein II. Bill Goldstein led me to Sondheim's correspondence with Larry Kramer, and John Lahr made available his highly charged exchange with Sondheim at the time of *Sweeney Todd.* Stephen Leibow, M.D., provided one of the previously unknown papers by psychiatrist Milton Horowitz that I've cited and quoted.

I'm very grateful to the archivists who preside over these collections of letters and other documents: at the Library of Congress, the papers of Leonard Bernstein, Hal Prince, Jules Feiffer, Jonathan Larson, Alan Jay Lerner, Arthur Laurents, and Mary Rodgers; at the New York Public Library for the Performing Arts, George Furth, more Hal Prince, and Jerome Robbins; at the Harry Ransom Center at the University of Texas, Mel Gussow and Lillian Hellman (researcher Rick Watson deserves special mention here); at Boston University's Mugar Library, John Lahr, Herb Ross, and Hugh Wheeler; at the University of Wisconsin, early papers of Stephen Sondheim; and at Columbia University's matchless Oral History collection, the *Reminiscences of Stephen Sondheim,* recorded and transcribed in 1982 but not available for quotation until 2022. Natalie Jasso, proprietor of the Instagram site sondheimletters, kindly led me to fruitful correspondence with some of Sondheim's own correspondents: Robert Burnett, George Dalzell, Michael Granoff, Ryan Mekenian, and Thomas Parisi. I'm grateful to all of them—as I am, especially, to Gail Leondar-Wright, who found Sondheim's response to his mother's letter in the Mary Rodgers Papers just before this book went to press.

Further aid, comfort, and research ideas came from Jenny Allen, Jim Byk, Sarah Crichton, Jim Cronin, Greg Curtis, Elena Delbanco, David Denby, Laura Frader, Michael Gross, Thomas Holderness, Fabio Kon, Gail Levenstein, Steve Lipsitz, Megan Marshall, Honor Moore, Shawn Mulligan, Rick Pappas, Dick Pollak, John Rothman, the late Bob Scanlan, Roxanne Smith, Katherine Spencer, Amanda Vaill, Dany Weil, Brynn White, and Larry Wright. I apologize if I've missed anyone; I talked incessantly about this book for nearly three years, and wouldn't be surprised if I got useful insight from someone sitting next to me on the subway.

To one degree or another, I'm indebted to all the books mentioned in the bibliography, but especially (in addition to Meryle Secrest's) to those by Mark Eden Horowitz of the Library of Congress; musicologist Steve Swayne; and Sondheim's first biographer, the late Craig Zadan.

Tony Tommasini, whom I interviewed about his friendship with Sondheim, also took me on a three-hour analytical tour—from his piano bench—of Sondheim's music; he's as talented a pianist as he is a writer. Composer Scott Wheeler, who teaches at Emerson College, also provided astute analyses of Sondheim's compositional techniques; he's as talented at pedagogy as he is at composition. My friends Sean Gallagher and Greg Pliska also pitched in with their own valuable musical insight.

Then there are the Seven, the Eight, and the Three.

Four of The Seven were strangers who responded to a blind item I posted online at the outset of my research. I was looking for Sondheim aficionados to serve as a kind of focus group because I wanted to know why his work meant so much to his most passionate fans. To this quartet I added one old friend (Kathleen Moloney), another I've known since she was an infant (Kate Nocera), and a third whom I knew but had never realized was a Sondhead (Michael Bierut). Together, along with Christine Chen, the late Mark Fetting, Hedy Gutfreund, and Darikka Scollard, we shared a memorable winter evening talking . . . and talking . . . and talking about Sondheim. I was especially lucky to meet Darikka, who went on to conduct some very valuable research on my behalf.

The Eight are people I've known forever who are simultaneously Sondheim devotees and talented editors. Suzie Bolotin, Betsy Carter, Liz Darhansoff, Peter Gethers, Lisa Grunwald, Kathy Hourigan, Corby Kummer, and Kathleen Moloney read various versions of the manuscript and offered wise and helpful counsel. Nick Delbanco is in a category of his own. Nick wasn't an enthusiast at the beginning of the many, many months he had to listen to me talk about Sondheim on our weekly walks. I hope he is now.

Then there are The Three: Becky, John, and Lydia Okrent. The reader could double everything I've ever said about them in the acknowledgments of my previous books, and you will still not know how much they mean to me. John's and Lydia's mates, Xela Herridge-Meyer and Luke Baker, are pretty lovable, too. From the next generation, Oola Okrent and Cosmo Okrent—well, I don't even know how to begin . . .

—D.O.
New York, March 2025

INDEX

Page numbers in italics refer to photographs

Jewish Lives is a prizewinning series of interpretive biography designed to explore the many facets of Jewish identity. Individual volumes illuminate the imprint of Jewish figures upon literature, religion, philosophy, politics, cultural and economic life, and the arts and sciences. Subjects are paired with authors to elicit lively, deeply informed books that explore the range and depth of the Jewish experience from antiquity to the present.

Jewish Lives is a partnership of Yale University Press and the Leon D. Black Foundation. Ileene Smith is editorial director. Anita Shapira and Steven J. Zipperstein are series editors.

PUBLISHED TITLES INCLUDE:

Abraham: The First Jew, by Anthony Julius
Rabbi Akiva: Sage of the Talmud, by Barry W. Holtz
Ben-Gurion: Father of Modern Israel, by Anita Shapira
Judah Benjamin: Counselor to the Confederacy, by James Traub
Walter Benjamin: The Pearl Diver, by Peter E. Gordon
Bernard Berenson: A Life in the Picture Trade, by Rachel Cohen
Irving Berlin: New York Genius, by James Kaplan
Sarah: The Life of Sarah Bernhardt, by Robert Gottlieb
Leonard Bernstein: An American Musician, by Allen Shawn
Hayim Nahman Bialik: Poet of Hebrew, by Avner Holtzman
Léon Blum: Prime Minister, Socialist, Zionist, by Pierre Birnbaum
Franz Boas: In Praise of Open Minds, by Noga Arikha
Louis D. Brandeis: American Prophet, by Jeffrey Rosen
Mel Brooks: Disobedient Jew, by Jeremy Dauber
Martin Buber: A Life of Faith and Dissent, by Paul Mendes-Flohr
David: The Divided Heart, by David Wolpe
Moshe Dayan: Israel's Controversial Hero, by Mordechai Bar-On
Disraeli: The Novel Politician, by David Cesarani
Alfred Dreyfus: The Man at the Center of the Affair, by Maurice Samuels
Einstein: His Space and Times, by Steven Gimbel
Becoming Elijah: Prophet of Transformation, by Daniel Matt
The Many Lives of Anne Frank, by Ruth Franklin
Becoming Freud: The Making of a Psychoanalyst, by Adam Phillips

Betty Friedan: Magnificent Disrupter, by Rachel Shteir
Emma Goldman: Revolution as a Way of Life, by Vivian Gornick
Hank Greenberg: The Hero Who Didn't Want to Be One, by Mark Kurlansky
Peggy Guggenheim: The Shock of the Modern, by Francine Prose
Ben Hecht: Fighting Words, Moving Pictures, by Adina Hoffman
Heinrich Heine: Writing the Revolution, by George Prochnik
Lillian Hellman: An Imperious Life, by Dorothy Gallagher
Herod the Great: Jewish King in a Roman World, by Martin Goodman
Theodor Herzl: The Charismatic Leader, by Derek Penslar
Abraham Joshua Heschel: A Life of Radical Amazement, by Julian Zelizer
Houdini: The Elusive American, by Adam Begley
Jabotinsky: A Life, by Hillel Halkin
Jacob: Unexpected Patriarch, by Yair Zakovitch
Franz Kafka: The Poet of Shame and Guilt, by Saul Friedländer
Carole King: She Made the Earth Move, by Jane Eisner
Rav Kook: Mystic in a Time of Revolution, by Yehudah Mirsky
Stanley Kubrick: American Filmmaker, by David Mikics
Stan Lee: A Life in Comics, by Liel Leibovitz
Primo Levi: The Matter of a Life, by Berel Lang
Maimonides: Faith in Reason, by Alberto Manguel
Groucho Marx: The Comedy of Existence, by Lee Siegel
Karl Marx: Philosophy and Revolution, by Shlomo Avineri
Louis B. Mayer and Irving Thalberg: The Whole Equation, by Kenneth Turan
Golda Meir: Israel's Matriarch, by Deborah E. Lipstadt
Menasseh ben Israel: Rabbi of Amsterdam, by Steven Nadler
Moses Mendelssohn: Sage of Modernity, by Shmuel Feiner
Harvey Milk: His Lives and Death, by Lillian Faderman

Arthur Miller: American Witness, by John Lahr
Moses: A Human Life, by Avivah Gottlieb Zornberg
Amos Oz: Writer, Activist, Icon, by Robert Alter
Proust: The Search, by Benjamin Taylor
Yitzhak Rabin: Soldier, Leader, Statesman, by Itamar Rabinovich
Ayn Rand: Writing a Gospel of Success, by Alexandra Popoff
Walther Rathenau: Weimar's Fallen Statesman,
by Shulamit Volkov
Man Ray: The Artist and His Shadows, by Arthur Lubow
Sidney Reilly: Master Spy, by Benny Morris
Admiral Hyman Rickover: Engineer of Power, by Marc Wortman
Jerome Robbins: A Life in Dance, by Wendy Lesser
Julius Rosenwald: Repairing the World, by Hasia R. Diner
Philip Roth: Stung by Life, by Steven J. Zipperstein
Mark Rothko: Toward the Light in the Chapel,
by Annie Cohen-Solal
Ruth: A Migrant's Tale, by Ilana Pardes
Menachem Mendel Schneerson: Becoming the Messiah,
by Ezra Glinter
Gershom Scholem: Master of the Kabbalah, by David Biale
Bugsy Siegel: The Dark Side of the American Dream,
by Michael Shnayerson
Solomon: The Lure of Wisdom, by Steven Weitzman
Steven Spielberg: A Life in Films, by Molly Haskell
Spinoza: Freedom's Messiah, by Ian Buruma
Alfred Stieglitz: Taking Pictures, Making Painters, by Phyllis Rose
Barbra Streisand: Redefining Beauty, Femininity, and Power,
by Neal Gabler
Henrietta Szold: Hadassah and the Zionist Dream,
by Francine Klagsbrun
Leon Trotsky: A Revolutionary's Life, by Joshua Rubenstein

Warner Bros: The Making of an American Movie Studio, by David Thomson
Elie Wiesel: Confronting the Silence, by Joseph Berger
Ludwig Wittgenstein: Philosophy in the Age of Airplanes, by Anthony Gottlieb

FORTHCOMING TITLES INCLUDE:

Hannah Arendt, by Masha Gessen
The Ba'al Shem Tov, by Ariel Mayse
Bob Dylan, by Sasha Frere-Jones
George Gershwin, by Gary Giddins
Ruth Bader Ginsburg, by Jeffrey Rosen
Jesus, by Jack Miles
Louis Kahn, by Gini Alhadeff
Mordecai Kaplan, by Jenna Weissman Joselit
Henry Kissinger, by Dennis Ross
Fiorello La Guardia, by Brenda Wineapple
Mahler, by Leon Botstein
Norman Mailer, by David Bromwich
Robert Oppenheimer, by David Rieff
Rebecca, by Judith Shulevitz
Edmond de Rothschild, by James McAuley
Jonas Salk, by David Margolick
Susan Sontag, by Benjamin Taylor
Gertrude Stein, by Lauren Elkin
Sabbatai Tsevi, by Pawel Maciejko
Billy Wilder, by Noah Isenberg